Robert Pichler (Ed.)

Legacy and Change

Studies on South East Europe

edited by
Prof. Dr. Karl Kaser
(Graz)

vol. 15

LIT

LEGACY AND CHANGE

Albanian transformation
from multidisciplinary perspectives

edited by

Robert Pichler

LIT

Printed with the support of the university of Graz

KARL-FRANZENS-UNIVERSITÄT GRAZ
UNIVERSITY OF GRAZ

This book is printed on acid-free paper.

Bibliographic information published by the Deutsche Nationalbibliothek
The Deutsche Nationalbibliothek lists this publication in the Deutsche
Nationalbibliografie; detailed bibliographic data are available in the Internet at
http://dnb.d-nb.de.

ISBN 978-3-643-90566-6

A catalogue record for this book is available from the British Library

©LIT VERLAG GmbH & Co. KG Wien,
Zweigniederlassung Zürich 2014
Klosbachstr. 107
CH-8032 Zürich
Tel. +41 (0) 44-251 75 05
Fax +41 (0) 44-251 75 06
E-Mail: zuerich@lit-verlag.ch
http://www.lit-verlag.ch

LIT VERLAG Dr. W. Hopf
Berlin 2014
Fresnostr. 2
D-48159 Münster
Tel. +49 (0) 2 51-62 03 20
Fax +49 (0) 2 51-23 19 72
E-Mail: lit@lit-verlag.de
http://www.lit-verlag.de

Distribution:
In the UK: Global Book Marketing, e-mail: mo@centralbooks.com
In North America: International Specialized Book Services, e-mail: orders@isbs.com
In Germany: LIT Verlag Fresnostr. 2, D-48159 Münster
Tel. +49 (0) 2 51-620 32 22, Fax +49 (0) 2 51-922 60 99, E-Mail: vertrieb@lit-verlag.de

In Austria: Medienlogistik Pichler-ÖBZ, e-mail: mlo@medien-logistik.at
e-books are available at www.litwebshop.de

CONTENTS

ACKNOWLEDGMENTS   1

INTRODUCTION by Robert Pichler   3

PART ONE: IDENTIFYING THE EFFECTS OF TRANSITION IN ALBANIA: THE POLITICAL AND THE LEGAL DIMENSION

1. Michael Schmidt-Neke
   A Burden of Legacies – The transformation of Albania's political system   13

2. Odeta Barbullushi
   EU norms and local practices: The 'Logic of Practicality' in post-communist public administration   31

PART TWO: IDENTIFYING EFFECTS OF MIGRATION IN POST-COMMUNIST ALBANIA

3. Julie Vullnetari
   Internal migration in Albania: a critical overview   47

4. Daniel Göler, Dhimitër Doka
   "Should I stay or should I go?" Out-migration, return migration and development in Albania – The migration-development-nexus at a dangerous crossroads   69

5. Vassilis Nitsiakos
   Albanian migrants to Epirus (Greece) after 1990: Transnational migration deconstructed   81

PART THREE: THE TRANSFORMATION OF THE FAMILY IN THE POST-COMMUNIST 'ALBANIAN SPACE'

6. Karl Kaser
   Family and kinship in Albania: Continuities and discontinuities in turbulent times   97

7. Ermira Danaj
    Family in Albania as a primary solidarity network   117

8. Carolin Leutloff-Grandits
    *The "social glue" of wedding festivals in Kosovo's South: Linking
    the village to migration and reshaping gender and social relations*   135

PART FOUR: WOMEN'S MOVEMENT AND THE IMPLEMENTATION OF GENDER QUOTAS IN TRANSITION

9. Delina Fico
    Is there a women's movement in Albania?   165

10. Eglantina Gjermeni
    Gender quota and its implementation in Albania   175

ACKNOWLEDGMENTS

This volume is the final product of an international workshop entitled "Back to the future? Understanding the Turbulences of Albanian Transition from contemporary and historical Perspectives." The workshop was financed by the Friedrich Ebert Foundation (FES) and took place at the Chair for Southeast-European History of Humboldt-University in Berlin in September 2011 (within the project "Ambiguous nation-building in Southeastern Europe" funded by the Volkswagen Foundation and the Austrian Science Fund (FWF) : International Programme I71).

I'm particularly grateful to Michael Weichert, the former director of FES in Albania, who was the driving force behind this event. His constant interest and curiosity to better understand the turbulent processes of transition in the country where he was in charge of pushing forward an agenda that aimed at bringing Albania closer to the EU were decisive for the realization of this project. I'm also indebted to Hannes Grandits, Professor for Southeast European History at Humboldt University, who hosted the workshop and participated actively in planning the event, as well as to the co-organizers of the workshop in Berlin MA Delina Binaj and PhD Carolin Leutloff-Grandits.

    I'm grateful to BA Duncan Bare who did the language editing and to the Center for the Study of Balkan Societies and Cultures (CSBSC) for financially supporting this process. Particular thanks also go to Brigitte Knaus who worked on the formatting of the final manuscript.

ROBERT PICHLER

INTRODUCTION

Albania's transition from communism to democracy was all but smooth or seamless. The system change shook the country and was all-embracing leaving no Albanian unaffected. The demise of communism began later and turned out to be more disorderly than in other central and eastern European countries. Seen from a broader angle, the country revealed a number of extreme phenomena. System change was accompanied by an almost total collapse of the economy, the decay of the monopoly of power and the break-up of the most rigid border regime. Almost immediately, Albanians were exposed to the forces of globalisation and market economy. Regardless of existing social, cultural, and institutional conditions, market-based shock-therapy was seen as a panacea for the salvation of the destitute country. The disintegration of the centralised economy was accompanied by high unemployment and uncertainty. At the same time people were full of hope and expectations that their country would swiftly catch up to the west. But Albania had no experience with private entrepreneurship and her citizens thus had to swiftly adapt to the new, often chaotic economic conditions. This situation could be partially mitigated by a quickly growing informal sector and by remittances sent from relatives abroad. As a result of the radical changes of the post-communist economy, weak state structures, and a widespread legal vacuum, informality became a way of life for a large part of the population. The formal labour market offered hardly any reliable alternative and provided neither a steady income nor social insurance. It is all the more astonishing that society did not completely collapse. Within a rather short period of time, Albanians managed to develop strategies to cope with these internal hardships and to create ways to make a living with the meagre means at their disposal. Flexibility and creativity were certainly distinguished qualities that helped to overcome the most severe period of the transition crisis. Additionally, the fact that Albania had and still has a comparatively young population played a positive role in this process. This young generation channelled much of their energy in vivid productivity. In their future-oriented activism they tried to escape the darkness of the past as quickly as possible.

However, informality also has limits. The transition to market economy went hand in hand with the appearance of dubious companies offering high returns on investments. The rudimentary formal financial system which was unable to satisfy the rising private demand for credit also played an important role in this development. In this vein, an informal credit market based on family ties and remittances grew in the country. Many of these companies turned into or indeed were from their outset pyramid schemes which spread across the country. With support from senior government officials the companies enticed more and more Albanians to invest their savings owing to the promise of high returns. At their heyday (in 1996) nearly two-thirds of the population had invested in these corporations, many having gone so far as selling their apartments and private plots to maximise their monthly pay-outs. When the pyramid schemes eventually collapsed later that year, the country descended into anarchy, only narrowly averting civil war. Nonetheless, around 2,000 people lost their lives in the ensuing turmoil.

The consequences of the pyramid schemes' uncovering and their collapse were manifold. Apart from the temporary breakdown of the economy, civil disorder and the accompanying loss of confidence in the government's ability to handle the transition were major causes for concern. It was not so much the government budget that was adversely affected as it was the property of the ordinary people who often lost all savings. This had profound social effects leaving many, after a period where it had been widely believed that the economy was rapidly growing, in a desperate and impoverished state. The crisis of 1997 again spurred accelerated emigration towards Italy and Greece and it took time and enormous efforts with strong international support to restore order in the country. But what was even more fatal, was the considerable loss of trust in the political establishment due to a widespread conviction of having been conceived and betrayed by the new political leadership. Frustration and mistrust towards these institutions had been boiling ever since. Instead, family and kinship networks became even more important as the most reliable and effective means in coming to terms with the crisis.[1]

All the creative efforts and initiatives from the side of the people to master the transition period cannot hide the fact that Albania is still far from a consolidated democracy and possessing a functioning market economy. The lack of a democratic tradition, the legacy of an authoritarian political culture and the weak civil society are reflected in a chronic political instability. The new political elite consisted mostly of converted members of the old regime who were inexperienced in decision-making processes based on compromise and rational discussion. Ever since the country morphed into a multiparty democracy, the political culture has been characterised by a relentless power struggle between two extremely antagonistic camps.

Another dimension of the difficult transition to democracy is related to the decade's long isolation from the outside world. Also within the country mobility was subject to strict regulation. From the early 1960s onwards the Albanian authorities pursued a policy of rural retention and minimal urbanisation with the aim of equalizing living standards between the urban and rural areas (Sjöberg 1994). This policy of curbing mobility intended to create a very stable and manageable society. Society was designed by its elites as a well-functioning social apparatus with all its parts fulfilling their particular purposes for the sake of the whole nation. Historical processes were interpreted in a teleological manner governed by dialectical rules which enabled the linking of the past with the present and the future in a well-designed and generally intelligible framework. Enver Hoxha's anti-revisionist Marxism-Leninism was loaded with strong nationalism. His aspiration for a genuine Albanian socialism was guided by the idea that everything pertaining to the life of the Albanian people had to be home-grown and not imported from abroad. As Hoxha put it, Albanian culture "[…] cannot be truly so if it is not part of the blood and the flesh of the people who create it

---

[1] Frustration with the political class was strikingly expressed in a survey on the political culture in the country. In the survey conducted with 145 adult Albanians of both sexes the question was posed what makes the interviewees proud of their country. 78.16% of the respondents referred to the physical beauty, 52.8% to the peaceful and tolerant relations between the religious communities and only 1.41% expressed their proud of the political institutions and the government (Bedini 2010, 23).

and use it, if it is not conceived in their history, life, struggle, and interest." (Hoxha 1985, 104 quoted in Vickers and Pettifer 1997, 118-119) The notion of (national) culture was based on a primordial understanding of the nation as being rooted with a certain territory. The underlying concept was that every people had to be aware of its origin, they had to come from somewhere, to own their genuine place and to know their clearly defined history. This theory of culture related the social identity of a community to its territory, its morality, its laws and customs and its folk art within the framework of a socialist development. Cultural development in socialist terms meant the eradication of all the differences in class, status, and religious belonging for the sake of a uniform and homogenous identity. The resurrection of the nation as the main framework for the moulding of a very identity was not an Albanian particularity within the Eastern Bloc (Brunnbauer 2004). What made the Albanian case so special, however, were its renunciation from the socialist brother countries and its seclusion from the outside world. With the regime change in 1991 this seemingly well-structured 'organism' faded away. The strict order was replaced by anarchy, rage and destruction. Within a short period of time the majority of the people were left on their own, devoid of any routines, regulations and security mechanisms that had guided their lives over the previous decades. The change of the system came as a rupture, as a sudden end where state prescribed values lost their long held meaning and social norms and orientations dissipated.

The system change also ended the rigid policy of isolation and internal mobility control that had dominated previously. Within a rather short period of time hundreds of thousands of people left their impoverished homes and moved away in search of better living conditions. Some of them tried to reach Italy by boat, many more escaped to Greece. At the same time a constant flow from the mountains to the plains, from the East to the West und from the periphery to the towns and urban centres set in that led to a lasting transformation of the country's demographic structure with the capital Tirana, as the most affected city, increasing tremendously in size while whole areas in the southeast and in the upper north largely depopulated. No other country in the region experienced such tremendous migratory movements, both within the country and abroad. The 'migration explosion' (Barjaba and King 2005, 3-4) had a lasting effect across all segments of society. Most of the migrants who left the country maintained strong ties with their family back home and established a plethora of trans-border networks. These networks appeared to be of enormous importance in terms of economic assistance, social security and cultural transfer. The recent economic crisis in both the primary destination countries (Greece and Italy) has strong repercussions for the viability of these trans-local networks. Tens of thousands of returnees are oversaturating the dysfunctional labour market thus cutting the lifeline for many of those who made a living primarily from remittances earned abroad. However, the medium-term consequences of these return flows for the country's economy and social relations are unforeseeable at present.

These are but a few, albeit important, phenomena that characterize Albania's peculiar transition from authoritarian rule to democracy. The articles collected in this volume will shed light on different aspects of the turbulent process of transition. The emphasis has been placed on the social dimension of the transition process, although political and economic aspects have also been considered. The scholars invited to contribute hail from different scientific fields, ranging from anthropology to sociology, history, political sciences, geography, and gender studies. This multidisciplinary approach enables a broader understanding of the complex social developments in the country. Since political developments, structural reforms of the economy, the administration and the legal system have already gained more attention in literature dealing with the transition, there is not much research tackling the people's responses to the uncertainties of this period. These everyday realities and practices of the actors, which are often ignored or simply seen as expressions of macro-structures, are highlighted in some of the contributions. In a similar vein, topics on gender relations gain special attention.

Beyond that, the interest of this volume is guided by questions that relate to long-term historical structures and processes. Though system-change was hardly anywhere else as dramatic as in Albania, it was obvious that continuities were still at work on different levels. When it comes to matters of change, historical factors cannot be ignored since they do have varied and sometimes persistent influence on transition trajectories. One can argue that the imperatives of the transition met with the legacies of the past and created a multifaceted post-communist heterogeneity. The for decades prevailing concept of socialist modernization, which suggested that cultural transformation proceeded to a logic of linear progression encountered the multidirectional and contradictory disorder of market liberalisation and globalisation. From a phenomenological perspective the country has transformed in almost all aspects, indeed it looks like as if no stone was left unturned, but if one focuses on underlying long-term structures, past legacies are discernible as well. Though it is, strictly speaking, not easy to determine the dividing line between continuity with and change from the past, some of the contributions offer a historical approach that enables a better understanding of processes and continuities that reach beyond the regime change of the early 1990s. The legacy debate has a long tradition in the social sciences and humanities; however, it is not the aim of this volume to engage in it on a broader and comparative level. The purpose of this work is more modest. First, not all the articles apply the historical approach, and second, those which do, refrain from the localisation of past legacies. Moreover, one has to be cautious where it concerns historical explanations for the many political, social, and economic failures that appear in the transition period. This pertains particularly to the communist legacy which often serves as a self-explanatory devise and a depository for the deficiencies of democratisation. On the other hand, one cannot ignore the communist legacy when it comes to the implication of isolationism, ideological indoctrination, surveillance, mobility control, education, etc., simply due to the fact that the entire populace which experienced the system change has been socialised within communism. However, from a deeper historical perspective, communism can also be seen only as a short episode and its separate Albanian path as resting on preceding structural givens which are, e.g., the particularly geographically fragmented nature of the country, its social, legal, and religious diversity and its backward economy that was far from being integrative. Enver Hoxha's particular intransigent route to socialist modernity thus could be interpreted as an attempt to radically integrate this culturally loose society and to forge a unified national community. Its harshness and militant character which, at its climax, aimed at eradicating the multiplex religious heritage can be seen as a response to the lack of an immersive national consciousness and social cohesion. Historical approaches are therefore essential to provide insight into deeper relationships in order to gain a better understanding of the recent developments.

STRUCTURE OF THE BOOK

The volume is structured along four thematic parts.

Part one
Identifying the effects of transition in Albania: The political and the legal dimension, contains two contributions, each with a unique focus. **Michael Schmidt-Neke** tackles the question as to why Albania's system transformation is so difficult and fraught with set-backs. His answers derive from an evaluation of the country's particular historical development from the very beginning of its state-formation in the early 20th century. From a regional comparative perspective he identifies key-features of Albania's political history with long-term effects for post-socialist democratic consolidation. The lack of a genuine dissident movement, the particular party leadership culture ('strong men'), and the weakness of civil society can be counted, according to Schmidt-Neke, among the reasons for the country's historical development. Schmidt-Neke refers to the socialist policy of homogenisation which aimed at minimizing social disparities for the sake of society as a whole, where all became equally dependent on the goodwill of the political elites. This concept of 'the people' which was primarily based on loyalty finds its repercussions in the post-socialist political space where political affiliation is hardly related to political interests and content, but to networks of membership and belonging. This leads to a complex system of political patronage where state resources are used to reward individuals (and companies) for their electoral support.
Odeta Barbullushi takes a thorough look at the discrepancies that exist between EU-integration discourse and the administrative reality on the ground. She aims to explain the difficulties of implementing EU-norms and standards into the Albanian administrative structure by exploring the perceptions and expectations of practitioners, civil servants and experts of public administration. Her agency approach, which focuses on the interface of discourse and practice, enables an understanding of the 'logic of practicality' that governs the political routines within their situational context. It becomes obvious that transmissions of standards, norms, and regulations from the side of the EU are always polysemic processes of translation and domestication. Concepts therefore, never mean what they meant either in the source or the target context.

Part Two
Identifying the effects of migration in post-communist Albania contains three contributions which tackle aspects of Albanian migration that have been underexposed in the otherwise rich Albanian migration studies. **Julie Vullnetari** provides a brief history of internal migration in Albania with a special focus on the communist period. A thorough look at the communist policy of movement and development is decisive to understand the reasons for the enormous migration flow that set in with the collapse of the communist regime. A detailed analysis of figures and migratory patterns illustrates

the dimension and the consequences of internal migration for the transformation of the country's demographic structure. The study strikingly shows how intimately internal migration is linked to emigration and how those who moved abroad triggered movements of those who stayed behind and vice versa. Vullnetari finally sheds light on the manifold social consequences of rapid urban growth which are particularly obvious in the Tirana-Durrës agglomeration. Urban planning and the development of social and material infrastructure are weak and cannot hold pace with the speed of immigration and the power of the widespread informal and illegal construction industry. **Daniel Göler** and **Dhimitër Doka** examine the nexus of migration, development and entrepreneurial activity and the reasons and effects of remigration for the country. The analysis of remigration patterns and processes elucidate that return migrants exert crucial influence on social, economic, and cultural transformations. However, the Albanian case also shows how fragile the viability of an economic system is when a large share of its national economy depends on the remittances from abroad. With regard to the transfer of capital, knowledge and entrepreneurial spirit the authors point at an interesting counter-effect to the previous collectivism, namely a widespread aversion to all forms of collective activity and a strong tendency to engage only in intra-family business. **Vassilis Nitsiakos** provides an ethnographic account of various informal practices and arrangements that exist between Albanian migrants, Greek officials, and locals along the Greek side of the border in the Konitsa region. Nitsiakos speaks of 'silent arrangements' with migrants who regularly cross the border to work in different branches of the local economy. This informality is confined to the immediate border area where relations between people on both sides have been reanimated following the collapse of the communist regime. Nitsiakos further points to the political economy in the border area which created very uneven conditions for Albanians and Greeks. He further argues that the concept of transnationalism is not very useful in understanding the migration situation in the border area; instead he favours the notion of 'transborder mobility' which in turn, enables a better analytical understanding within the given context.

Part three
The transformation of the family in the post-communist 'Albanian space' highlights the importance of family and kinship in post-communist Albania and Kosovo. **Karl Kaser** pursues a long-term approach in his analysis on family and kinship structures in Albania. His starting point is the census of 1918 which provides ample evidence of the prevalence of patriarchal family relations in most parts of the country. The communist period was characterised by massive state intervention into family life and forced dissolution of complex households. The post-communist era, however, brought about a re-emergence of family and kinship cohesion as a consequence of weak-and unreliable state structures. But the family is now, given the turbulent conditions of post-communism, faced with different challenges. On the basis of the data evaluated, Kaser points to the enormous significance of family and kinship as social networks which are, however, accompanied by a protracted influence of patriarchal values and norms. **Ermira Danaj** takes the collapse of the state's social security system in 1991 as the starting point for her analysis of the role of the family as a primary security network. Danaj argues that without the tightly woven family and kinship networks as well as the remittances transferred from abroad, the country would have descended into chaos

and anarchy. However, familial networks are crucial but their capacities are limited and their sustainability does not rest on terra firma. Beyond that, Danaj emphasizes that the weakness of a formal social security system amplifies social inequalities in the country. **Carolin Leutloff-Grandits** ethnographic study on wedding festivals in southern Kosova is the only contribution concerning a topic outside of Albania. However, this does not detract from the relevance of her topic for Albania and other areas which are strongly affected by trans-local migration. Leutloff-Grandits explores the multifaceted meaning of wedding festivals and the social roles, status, and expectations which it entails and signifies. She highlights the importance of such rituals for people who live scattered throughout Europe but return home during summer. The rituals not only bring them together but mainly make them aware of their membership and the basic values and commitments their community rests upon.

Part four
Women's movement and the implementation of gender quotas in transition tackle questions of the woman's role in politics and civil society during the transition period. Given the fact that gender policy in socialist Albania was very ambivalent, providing opportunities for education and labour, but maintaining very conservative female role models, the question arises as to which options and constraints do exist in the post-socialist environment and how women activists fight for their rights in a pervasive patriarchal social climate. **Delina Fico** raises the question as to whether there does exist a women's movement in Albania and how women organised in NGOs articulate their voices for the advancement of gender equality. Fico looks at the development of women's activism over the last twenty years and thoroughly investigates different movements and expressions. Fico further places the development in Albania in a broader regional and historical context that enables a better understanding of the constraints and difficulties women's activism faces and must contend with in Albania. Finally, she tackles the question as to whether this women's activism is endued with feminism or not. **Eglantina Gjermeni** explores the implementation of gender-quotas in Albania in the aftermath of communism. She explains women's marginalization in decision making processes as the by-product of a deeply rooted historical heritage of a male dominated culture. Within the last 20 years the legal framework for women's rights has improved considerably, but there remains, still, a huge gap between the de-jure and the de-facto situation of women in the country. Gjermeni refers to far reaching mental barriers that prevail in Albanian society and constrain the opportunities of women to freely develop their careers.

REFERENCES

Barjaba, Kosta and King, Russel. 2005. "Introducing and theorising Albanian migration," in *The New Albanian Migration* edited by Russel King, Nicola Mai and Stephanie Schwandner-Sievers (Brighton, Portland: Sussex Academic Press), 1-28.

Bedini, Belina. 2010. "Albanian political culture in transition: Helping or stumbling the democracy's consolidation?" *International Journal of Arts and Sciences* 3(8), 20-28.

Brunnbauer, Ulf (ed.). 2004. *(Re)Writing History. Historiography in Southeast Europe after Socialism* (= Studies on Southeast Europe 4). Münster: Lit.

Sjöberg, Orjan. 1994. "Rural retension in Albania: Administrative restrictions on urban-bound migration," *East European Quarterly* Vol. 28 (2), 205-233.

Vickers, Miranda and Pettifer, James. 1997. *Albania: From Anarchy to a Balkan Identity.* London: Hurst.

PART ONE

IDENTIFYING THE EFFECTS OF TRANSITION IN ALBANIA: THE POLITICAL AND THE LEGAL DIMENSION

MICHAEL SCHMIDT-NEKE

BURDEN OF LEGACIES – THE TRANSFORMATION OF ALBANIA'S POLITICAL SYSTEM

ALBANIA – BETWEEN MAINSTREAM AND MAVERICK

The phase of transition from communism to a viable democracy in Albania has, until now, lasted for 22 years. This represents nearly half the lifetime of the regime of the Party of Labor of Albania (PPSH), and is longer than the troublesome period between the reestablishment of Albania's statehood by the Lushnja Congress in January 1920 and her loss of independence following the Italian invasion in April 1939. In other words, it is by no means premature to judge this transition as being anything but smooth and successful.

Albania aims to be a full-fledged member of the European Union as soon as possible. It took the country until autumn 2013 for the first encouraging signs to be received from Brussels. The annual report of the European Commission on prospective member states which had been released on 16 October 2013 recommended granting Albania candidate status. However, the question still remains why Albania's system-wide transformation is so difficult and full of set-backs?

It would be simplistic to blame the Communists and only the Communists for Albania's backwardness. When they took over the country in November 1944, Albania was Europe's least developed country, and when they handed over to their elected successors in 1991/92, it was still an underdeveloped country on the brink of collapse. Nonetheless, Albania had profoundly changed, for better and for worse.

What are Albania's common and her distinct features vis-à-vis the other nations in South Eastern Europe (or at least their majority)? To start with commonalities the following features can be singled out:

(1) Albania was part of the Ottoman Empire for centuries;
(2) Albania went through a series of authoritarian or dictatorial regimes;
(3) Albania was ruled by a communist regime after World War II;
(4) Albania had a state socialist economy;
(5) Albanian communism fell from power in the early 1990s.

However, the fate of Albania is shaped by several (more or less) individual features:

(1) Albania won independence very late in 1912, meaning Ottoman influence lasted longer than in other Balkan countries; additionally Albania lost her independence twice (from 1914-20 and 1939-44);
(2) Albania failed to develop any stable tradition of political pluralism, party system or democracy;

(3) Albania's communist regime was not imposed by Soviet occupation, but came to power via a resistance war which morphed into a civil war (like in Yugoslavia);
(4) Many people in Albania never regarded their state as a legitimate representative of their interests, but as a threatening, repressive apparatus, so they saw (and still see) their extended families and regional networks as the basic and most reliable societal structures;
(5) Albania did not remain a member of the Soviet bloc, but aligned herself first to Yugoslavia, the Soviet Union and finally to China, ending up embracing isolationism in the late 1970s;
(6) Albania's brand of communism was more radical than the East European regimes, banishing religion and any form of private economic activity, as well as holding fast to Stalinist mechanisms of repression.

ALBANIAN NATIONALISM

Albania is a belated nation. The mentality of the vast majority of Albanians remained rooted in pre-nationalist categories, such as family, region or religious affiliation. The unpreparedness of the peasants and highlanders for a modern nation state served as an argument against Albanian statehood before and even after the proclamation of independence on 28 November 1912 in Vlora. All regimes, King Zog, Enver Hoxha and the post-communist republic, have attempted to propagate a teleological Albanian national consciousness which presented Albanian history as a continuous path through the millennia, beginning with the Illyrians as the supposed ancestors of today's Albanians, culminating in Skanderbeg's heroic fight against the Ottoman invaders, reemerging only in the nationalist movement of the 19th and early 20th century, appropriately titled the movement for Albanian National Rebirth (*Rilindja Kombëtare Shqiptare*), and finally realizing the efforts of previous centuries in the present Albanian state. Enver Hoxha's ubiquitous catchphrase: "The Albanian people have paved their way through history with a sword in their hand" summarized the idea of a small, unique people with a successfully fulfilled historical mission.

After 1991, this concept of history was not abandoned, but rather modified. The communist regime had bankrupted the country and was by no means seen any longer as the fulfillment of the Albanians' aspirations. As opposed to being the encircled beacon of Marxist-Leninist orthodoxy, now the idea of being a European core nation which had once defended Western and Central Europe against the Turks and now claimed its 'birthright' to be integrated in the European and Western family gained traction.

How vital historical myths remain among Albania's academic community, politicians and public, showed in the aftermath of a controversy begun following the publication of an academic biography of Skanderbeg by Oliver Jens Schmitt (Schmitt 2009), an expert on Albanian history at Vienna University. He was savagely attacked because his image of Scanderbeg contradicted the traditional concept of Albania's national hero (Schmidt-Neke 2010).

Post-isolationist Albania has an identity crisis. Many people still cling to the self-concept of being part of a proud and virtuous nation which has been a victim of history and to which the West is indebted. At the same time, many Albanians possess an inferiority complex vis-à-vis the West, uncritically adapting everything 'Western' and trying their utmost to leave their country for good. This had a considerable demographic impact, especially with a brain drain effect as skilled Albanians were more liable to permanent emigration than unskilled.

The Albanians had to change their allegiance to a higher authority very quickly, switching within a few years from the cult of 'Uncle Enver' (*xhaxhi Enver*) to the idolization of 'Uncle Sam' (Ditchev 1998). After the collapse of the self-image as the 'shining beacon of socialism on the shores of the Mediterranean', Albania—this means the public as well as the politicians—has not settled the issue of her own national identity (Schwandner and Fischer 2002) which has been object of a public debate led by expatriate author Ismail Kadare and Kosovar author and politician Rexhep Qosja (Ceka 2006). Kadare sees his nation as one of the most ancient European peoples; neither 500 years of Ottoman rule nor the islamization of the majority of Albanians could change that, so her place should be nowhere else than in Europe as a family of nations. Qosja argues that any national identity was formed by minor local, regional, dialectal and religious sub-identities; thus, an Albanian émigré to the USA would still be an Albanian and at the same time an American, while not being a European. The Ottoman epoch, too, was part of the historical heritage of the Albanians; Qosja berates Kadare for excluding Muslims from being 'true Albanians'.

It is interesting that the Muslim-born Kadare holds to the patterns of nationalist historiography as it was defined under communism and ever since (composed more or less by the same scholars). What this means, in essence, is that the Ottoman rule was seen only as a 'yoke' period (a topic prevailing in other Balkan national historiographies as well). Few were the voices like that of the Kosovar orientalist Hasan Kaleshi who argued that the islamization of the majority of the Albanians saved them from assimilation into Greeks and Slavs (Kaleshi 1975).

In this context, Albania has not undergone the 'revaluation of all values'. Whereas the vast majority of Albanians submit to this dichotomic understanding of history (Ottomans = evil, Skanderbeg and anti-Ottoman forces = good) in reality, relationships with Turkey are rather good, while those with Serbia are traditionally very bad owing to Kosova.

Until now, Albania has not settled the very urgent issue of her political orientation between Europe and the USA. After many decades of vitriolic propaganda against the imperialist superpower, the reestablishment of US presence in the country resulted in uncritical adoration which was strengthened by the leading role of the US in the Kosova War. Huge crowds cheered US Foreign Secretary James Baker in June 1991 and President George W. Bush 16 years later; even the then Socialist-led city administration of Tirana renamed one of the major roads of Tirana after this very controversial leader. Albania took part in the occupation of Afghanistan and Iraq, while the Iraq War created a rift within NATO between the interventionists (USA, UK) and non-interventionists (France, Germany) demonstrating that the strategic interests within the Western alliance system are no longer identical.

Albanian nationalism is not intrinsically linked with a specific religion or denomination. There is a critical debate about a topos developed during the Rilindja when

Pashko Vasa wrote the verse: "the faith of the Albanians is Albanianism (*Feja e shqyptarit asht shqyptaria*)". But whether Catholic and Orthodox Christianity and Sunni and Alevi Islam were deeply rooted among the population or whether the Albanians were always ready to switch between the religions according to political opportunity, there is no national faith or church, comparable to the constitutive role e.g. of Catholicism for Polish or Croat nationalism or of Orthodoxy for Greek, Serb or Bulgarian national identity. Thus, the reemerging religious communities after 23 years of illegality had to face a young and secularized society which was ready to adopt any faith which ensured them a better future–ranging from evangelical movements to fundamentalist Islamic teachings.

BELATED PLURALISM

Until 1990, there was no room for dissidents, neither individual nor in organizations such as churches which played a decisive role in other East European countries. Thus, the demise of communism could not be a Zero Hour in which the social elite in power was completely substituted by a new one. Only once in her history, Albania had witnessed such a Zero Hour: in 1944, when the old elites (land owners, merchants) were toppled, and killed, imprisoned or exiled.

The Albanian leadership reacted harshly to the first signs of open unrest, but refrained from waging Beijing-style open warfare against the people. Even when in February 1991, Enver Hoxha's statue on Tirana's Skanderbeg square was toppled by a large crowd, police and armed secret police (*sigurimi*) forces did not open fire. The Romanian civil war and the death of the Ceaușescu couple had sent a lesson to Tirana: losing power might well mean losing life. Ramiz Alia, then head of state and party, coordinated a strategy of controlled pluralism. He could not prevent the forming of the Democratic Party (PD), which was followed by other parties. However, the fact remains that many leading personalities of these new forces had been members of the PPSH and Alia's role remains highly disputed.

The emergence of a party system (Schmidt-Neke 2011) had no roots in any historical parties, as neither in the interwar era nor after World War II did political pluralism exist. The so-called parties in the short-lived elite democracy of the early 1920s were hardly more than unstable factions of deputies or local voters' associations. The dictator Zog (1924-1939) did not even bother to form a regime party. The Italian occupiers did albeit with no real success. And when the Albanian Communists won their two-front war against the occupiers as well as against their adversaries, they skipped the popular front phase which in most Eastern European countries allowed some short years of tolerated pluralism. Whoever dared to set up non-communist political organizations paid dearly for this, evidenced by Musine Kokalari, a young woman who formed a social democratic party (Kokalari 2000).

During the collapse of communism, Albania skipped past the stage of Citizens' Movements against the communist regime and entered immediately into that of establishing political parties. Other than in Kosovo and Macedonia, the establishment of a party system from scratch followed the typical West European pattern along a right-left schism. Between the PD and the Socialist Party (PS), there exists a polarity and a tendency toward a two-party-system strengthened by incessant changes in the electoral legislation. The chances for most minor parties depend on their ability and willingness to form pre-electoral alliances which ensure their representation in the parliament.

The basic differences between the parties are not related to programs, as with very few exceptions these goals are one in the same, namely establishing a working Western-type parliamentary democracy and a thriving market economy without corruption, embedded in all Western supranational structures (OSCE and NATO, both of which were realized) and the European Union (not even candidate status in sight), are by no means controversial. Both the PD and PS are members of the international party associations, the PD as an observer in the European People's Party, the PS as a full-fledged member of the Socialist International and as an associated member of the Social Democratic Party of Europe. However, both sides hold each other responsible for the failure in realizing these goals, and not even mediation attempts by the European structures have been able to mitigate the highly aggressive and poisoned political culture, which may well be seen as an heirloom of the authoritarian tradition of thinking which prevailed until 1990.

Some observers even deny that the Albanian parties represent any real political ideas, but are only parts of networks representing the interests of businessmen fighting for resources (Schmitt 2012, 178). This notwithstanding, it should not be disregarded that it is rather normal along Western European standards for the mainstream parties to not be divided by ideological controversies, but by different approaches to current problems. Competing political parties are—for better or for worse—integral parts of civil society, responsible for organizing an estimated 200.000 Albanian citizens; their commitment should not be disregarded.

Albania has a long, rich and versatile constitutional history (Schmidt-Neke 2009), over the course of which most political systems have been authoritarian regimes. Until 1991, Albania's parliaments had only rarely been pluralistic representative organs which could decide on the formation of the government, on law-making and on budgets, but usually acclamatory assemblies with the sole duty to legitimize the will of the president, king or party leadership on whom they had no influence. Before they were put forward as draft-laws and voted by the deputies, all political decisions had been met in other formal or informal bodies, such as the Political Bureau and the Secretariat of the PPSH Central Committee or in King Zog's ruling camarilla.

Strangely enough, all communist regimes until now have stuck to elected representative organs on a national, regional and local level, so Albania too had her National Assembly (*Kuvendi Kombëtar*) which was elected to a four-year term. But the system of power under communism was top-down: the leading party echelons concluded the decisions which were sanctioned by the representative bodies and realized by the administration; thus, the Council of Ministers was less a government than a supreme administrative board. The real influence of the Prime Minister or any other member of the council depended on his position within the party leadership.

That meant that after 1990 the interdependence between the state institutions had to be rearranged according to the principle of checks and balances. While the 1976 constitution candidly defined the Party of Labor of Albania as the nation's primary political institution, from now on the political parties were reduced to NGOs whose aspirations to lead the country depended on their support in the ballot box and their ability to form a government.

Contrary to this, the role of parliament and government had to be upgraded. Parliamentary elections which until 1990 had been ritualized plebiscites with absurd results equating to 100% turnout and 100% approval of all candidates proposed by the Democratic Front (an umbrella organization led by the PPSH)[2] now rested on the guidelines of Albania's policy—insomuch as these guidelines were set by domestic politicians and were not linked to the international obligations of a nation which struggled first for support, and later for integration within Western structures such as NATO and the European Community.

The 1990s were more or less a lost decade for the consolidation of Albanian democracy as the country and its leaders did not really decide on a course to follow: a mainstream West European style parliamentary democracy with two poles of power the parliament and the government—or the French 'presidentialist' model with three poles—the parliament, the government and the president.

Sali Berisha who in 1992 led his Democratic Party to a landslide victory and was afterwards elected Albania's first non-communist president since 1928[3] clearly preferred the presidentialist option but failed to garner enough public support for his draft constitution in an improvised referendum in 1994. The 1998 constitution approved by the Socialist dominated parliament and sanctioned by a referendum reduced the power of the president but not to a degree that he became a mere representative figure like the German Federal President.

On many occasions, the presidential powers as defined in the 1998 constitution have provided ample fuel for conflicts between government and president, especially when the latter refused to sign laws voted by the parliament or to dismiss or appoint a high ranking civil servant. Until now, all presidents after 1997 (Socialist Rexhep Meidani, Independent Alfred Moisiu and Democrat Bamir Topi) firmly resisted all pressure exerted by the prime ministers, even if they belonged to their own political party. In Spring 2012, Prime Minister Berisha refused to support Topi's eventual bid for reelection, who in turn reacted by founding a new center-right party which he may come to lead after the end of his term.

In any case, Albania's political landscape has always been and is still dominated by strong leaders – 'strong' not meaning the ability govern well, but the ability to cling to positions. Albeit all speculation that Albania's most renowned writer Ismail Kadare might accept a leading role comparable to that of Václav Havel or Göncz Árpád was mistaken, namely inasmuch as these men were always politicians, never representatives of their respective culture. Their grip on their parties was very firm and stable. Sali Berisha was the actual leader of the PD since its inception[4], the same applies to Skënder Gjinushi of the Social Democrats (PSD). Edi Rama was the second chairman of the PS, Fatmir Mediu the second chairman of the Republican Party (PR). This strong position of these leaders does not prevent dissident opinions and the development of party wings, but more typically dissidence results in breakaway parties (e.g. the Democratic Alliance Party (PAD) and the New Democratic Party (PDR) from the

---

2 These results were published after the 1970 and 1974 elections; on other occasions at least one or two invalid ballots were allowed; for results see Schmidt-Neke 1993, 200.
3 In that year dictator Ahmet Bej Zogu changed the form of his regime from a presidential republic to a kingdom becoming King Zog I.
4 During its terms in power (1992-1997) the PD was led successively by Eduard Selami and Tritan Shehu who acted as caretaker chairmen for Berisha.

PD, the Socialist Movement for Integration (LSI) from the PS). Owing to the strong position of the leaders of the respective parties, political clashes took the form of personal infighting and vendettas between strongmen; during the 1990s and after, domestic politics were overshadowed by a rivalry between Berisha and Nano, after Berisha's comeback and Nano's resignation as PS leader, a highly personalized conflict between Berisha and the new PS leader Edi Rama has broken out, whereas Nano has become a tactical ally of Berisha against Rama.

Decentralization and depoliticization (meaning the end of subservience to the party's grip) of course had to be applied across all branches of state administration, the armed forces, the judicial system as well as local administration. This was rendered difficult by the lack of tradition in local self-government or independent courts. In Albania, between 1966 and 1990 lawyers did not even exist. So, when establishing new structures, there was a dire choice between working with judges, state attorneys etc. who had been educated under communism and had been faithful servants of that regime or to sack them while substituting them with persons whose lack of formal qualification had to be mended by short courses. The government chose to do both, thus opening a doorway to arbitrariness and corruption which remains the crucial problem of Albania's judiciary and administration.

Albania has no spoils system which formally entitles the winner of an election to substitute all holders of important public offices with his own supporters and party members. In fact, every new government has found its ways to remove unsympathetic officials, usually by charging them with sleaze and corruption.

Furthermore, the weakness of the post-communist state, which in 1997 culminated in a breakdown of state authority, brought back a phenomenon which was thought to have been eradicated long before: remnants of the customary law (*kanun*) in the Northern Highlands. In spite of all attempts to deny news of reemerging blood feuds amongst the foreign media, living life shut-in, in towers (*kullë*) became the only way for many youngsters to evade assaults by hostile families. Neither the state nor NGOs or religious communities have been able until now to reestablish the rule of law. The customary law is no longer applied as it had been before 1944 firmly protecting women and juveniles (Voell 2004), but is used as a camouflage for criminal violence.

HOMEGROWN COMMUNISM

If there was any European country which was not ripe for a communist system it was Albania which had inherited feudal structures dominating not only the economy but also the political system. Industrialization had just begun (Fishta and Karaco 1996). The social structure was dominated by poor and landless peasantry while the working class—destined to be the ruling class in socialism—was still in its infancy. Thus, Albania had not only failed to bring forth a modern bourgeois political party system but was a rather barren ground for any kind of workers' movement, be it social democratic, communist or trade unionist. Not more than small circles of young urban male members of the social elites and anti-Zogist émigrés existed, and the forging of some of these local groups into a Communist Party of Albania (PKSH) on 8 November 1941, was possible only after Germany's attack on the Soviet Union which in the eyes of the communists changed the character of World War II from a clash between imperialist blocs to the Great Patriotic War of the Soviet Union, to be supported by the world proletariat whose fatherland was the Soviet Union (Frashëri 2006).

It was a remarkable development that this party was within only three years able to organize an extremely strong and efficient partisan army which waged war against the Italian, later the German occupying forces and their Albanian collaborators. Additionally from 1943-44 they also engaged rivaling resistance movements which aimed to restore Zog's rule (the so-called *Legaliteti* movement) or to make Albania a Western style democracy with or without deep social reforms (the *Balli Kombëtar*). Although the victory of the communist-led partisans would not have been possible without the victory of the Allies over the Axis powers, the Soviet Army did not set foot on Albanian soil. Undoubtedly, there was a strong influence exerted by Tito's emissaries (Miladin Popović and Dušan Mugoša), and communist Albania indeed was a 'sub-satellite' of Moscow's satellite Yugoslavia which faced the very real danger of being gobbled up, supposing that Stalin's alleged recommendation had been followed (Danylow 1982). But by ostracizing Tito, Stalin saved Albania's independence and remained a patron saint of the PPSH regime until 1990.

So, contrary to most communist-ruled nations of Eastern Europe, there was no way for the post-communist society to denounce communism as an alien system which had been imposed by an occupier. But the Yugoslav impact was exaggerated to justify terms like 'Slav communists' (*sllavo-komunistë*) and to charge the communists and Enver Hoxha personally with treason against the nation as they allegedly handed over Kosovo once more to the Yugoslavs even sending partisan units to crush the resistance of Albanian nationalists. These critics failed to answer how the Albanian leaders might have managed to keep Kosovo a part of Albania in 1944.

Regardless, contending with the communist heritage is more complicated than in other parts of Eastern Europe. Like in most European formerly communist states, the PPSH not only the ruling, but the sole existing party, as no bloc parties existed— reinvented itself under the label of the Socialist Party of Albania (PS), expelling the senior members of the PPSH leadership. During the ensuing years, the former members of the Politbureau and of the Secretariat of the Central Committee retired completely from politics, as many of them had to defend themselves against charges of homicide, crimes against humanity and embezzlement of public funds. A series of trials in the early 1990s resulted in draconic verdicts, including several death sentences which were not carried out. Several high-ranking politicians (like Ramiz Alia and Nexhmije Hoxha) had to serve time in prison. (Only Muho Asllani, on behalf of his low level of education albeit one of the most derided Politbureau members, was an active member of one of the tiny communist parties whose history is fragmented and of little substance save for a handful of nostalgic and protest voters.)

From 1990-1992, there was no opportunity for a change in the elites, as there was no alternative elite at hand. The ruthless grip of the repressive state organs prevented any kind of dissidence, that is, outside of prisons and internment camps. So, the new leaders of the country inevitably were by-products of the toppled elite. Sali Berisha, the leader of the first non-communist party, the Democratic Party, had been a successful founder of the Republican Party, had won much acclaim as an author of historical novels; Skënder Gjinushi, who is still the founding leader of the Social Democrats, had been Minister of Education; Fatos Nano, a young reformer and the last communist Prime Minister, became the first chairman of the PS.

The last 22 years have seen a vitriolic exchange of accusations and counter-accusations about the involvement and collaboration of the respective political adversaries with the communist dictatorship, especially the secret police Sigurimi. So, neither a transparent and viable law on public access to the Sigurimi files nor a law on the ousting of former Sigurimi informers has been passed (Arapi 2005).

STATE VERSUS FAMILY

Albania's social and political culture is overshadowed by the supremacy of the family which in a Balkan context means extended family networks. This applies to all social strata and all Albanian-inhabited regions of the Balkans and even the 'Diaspora', the stronghold, however, being the Northern Highlands.

It was not unusual that powerful landowning families split their political affiliations and loyalties thus creating mutual insurances in the event of clashes. So, we find members of the feudal dynasties Vrioni and Vlora among the supporters of an abortive rebellion in 1935. Eleven of 53 participants who received death sentences were executed—all of them gendarmes; the lives of others were spared (Schmidt-Neke 1987, 248-49).

This scheme did not work during the partisan war. With very few exceptions, the members of old elite families either accepted collaboration with the Italian and German occupiers or set up socially conservative resistance movements. A last attempt to unite all resistance forces at a conference in the village of Mukje (north of Tirana) in August 1943 was seemingly successful, but soon turned out that both delegations—especially that of the Communist led partisan movement—had by far exceeded their competences. The Communist Party could not risk losing Tito's support, thus could not agree with the Greater Albania strategy of the nationalist Balli Kombëtar (Lewin 2007, Neuwirth 2008). After that éclat, the Liberation War simultaneously became a civil war which the Communist-led National Liberation Front (FNÇ) won.

Thus, the take-over by Enver Hoxha's Communist Party far more represented a Zero Hour than the proclamation of independence in 1912 or Ahmet Bej Zogu's victory over Fan Noli's revolutionary regime in 1924 had. By nationalizing land, natural resources and enterprises with the assistance of persecution, the old elites were destroyed.

Hoxha was neither able nor willing to spare even the life of Bahri Omari, the husband of one of his sisters who had served for a brief term as foreign minister in a collaboration government under German aegis and was subsequently sentenced to death and shot; the only consolation was that Omari's family was not persecuted like those of nearly all other condemned (Fevziu 2011, 136-140).

Particularly in the 1960s and 70s, the Albanian leadership struggled to destroy traditions which they regarded as retrograde and reactionary. This did not exclusively include the religions, but also at the remnants of customary law in the North and at patriarchalism, e.g. early betrothal and marriage by arrangement, exclusion of women from paid jobs and public functions etc.

The communists however, failed at the removal of the core problem: the role of the family networks. On the contrary, they had adapted this system for themselves. In the founding years of communist Albania, Hoxha understood that this familiarism was alien to any Marxist or Leninist theory of socialist leadership and tried to prevent the evolution of family networks within the leadership (Kadare and Shehu 1994, 51), but Albanian tradition proved stronger than theory.

In order to understand the internal structure of the communist regime, especially the very many bloody purges which lasted until 1982-83, it is indispensable to analyze which leader had which links with which other leader (Kadare and Shehu 1994, 50-51). That way, a little known fact like the marriage of Hoxha's elder son Ilir with a niece of Alia in the 1970s (Fejziu 2011, 294) is a decisive factor for the latter's rise to the top position.

This network was not exclusively Southern-based, even though it was dominated by Tosks. A map from the 1970s showing the origins of major party and state figures (Byron 1976, 74-75) shows seven leaders hailing from the regions north and 20 from those south of Shkumbini river. Four of the seven northerners and nine of the 20 southerners fell victim to purges.

Prime Minister Mehmet Shehu stayed clear of these marital links (*krushqi*), and it was precisely this mismatch in his son's engagement which was used as a pretext for his downfall.

The family network within the communist leadership was by no means insurance against misstep. Kadri Hazbiu, a long-serving member of the Politbureau and interior minister, was linked by a rather distant brother-in-law (*krushqi*) with Ramiz Alia which was not enough to save even his life in the last bloody wave of purges after Shehu's death (Kadare and Shehu 1994, 51).

Intrinsically linked with this network system is a phenomenon which communist Albania shared with most dictatorships but applied to a much higher degree than elsewhere: the social cleavage between 'good' and 'bad' families. Good families were those linked with the partisan war and the communist party, bad families were those of the old elites (landlords, officials of the Zog era), of collaborationists, but also of anti-communist fighters of monarchist, republican or tribalist background.

Being a member of a 'bad family' was an inherited fate; it would exclude even grandchildren from university education and from climbing the career ladder. There were rare chances to climb, if family members had affiliations with both sides.

'Good families', conversely, could never be too sure about their future as the constant purges might affect them at any time. The path from a villa in the *bllok* (the nomenclature ghetto in the centre of Tirana) to a shack in an isolated internment village could be very short (Lubonja 2009).

Another important issue is the role of women which without doubt was profoundly changed by the communist system. Not only the rather formal right to vote was granted to women in 1945; the mere existence of female partisans was propagated as the beginning of a new era of full participation in every social field, primarily education and paid work. Literacy, compulsory schooling and finally access to the labor 'market' defined a new role for Albanian women, in society as well as in the family—at the price of a double burden, as they were hardly relieved from any of their traditional burdens in the household and relating to the upbringing of the children.

When the economic structures collapsed within a very short time and unemployment hit Albanian society, the women were the first victims. Economically marginalized, they were now more dependent than ever on their husbands and families; domestic violence (until then officially denied) became a social problem. Family and state failed to protect girls and young women who were now vulnerable targets for criminals, and the trafficking of Albanian women who were forced or even sold into prostitution abroad marked a widespread violation of human rights.

Politically, too, women were on the losing side. Under communism they had won access to political offices. In 1974 more than one third of the 250 deputies of the People's Assembly (*Kuvend Popullor*) were female; later this percentage declined slightly. The higher the actual power of the leading bodies was, the lower the percentage of female members was; in the Party Central Committee between 11 and 20%, half their share of the Party membership (40%). In the Politbureau and the Central Committee Secretariat we find one female member in the 1950s (Liri Belishova) and in the 1980s (Lenka Çuko)—certainly not a worse record than in other communist countries, like the USSR or GDR.[5] From the mid-1970s until 1990 between one and three members of the Council of Ministers were women. Not to be forgotten were women who as wives of prominent leaders obtained powerful positions for themselves (comparable to Elena Ceaușescu and Margot Honecker). Primary amongst these was Enver Hoxha's wife, Nexhmije, who as director of the Institute for Marxist-Leninist Studies, was charged with writing and re-writing the history of the party and for editing her husband's works; she held on to much of her influence even after Enver's death in 1985.

After the downfall of communism, female representation dropped dramatically: the female share among the members of the first two pluralist parliaments was 3.6% and 2.1% (today risen to ca. 14%), in the standing boards of the parties less than 10% (Schmidt-Neke 1993, 238). Today, five of 18 (28%) members of the PS Standing Board (*Kryesia*) and 8 of 27 (30%) PD Standing Board members are women.[6] The first post-communist female minister was appointed in 1996.

Political power in post-communist Albania is intrinsically linked with economic power. Albanian business is still dominated by men. Therefore, the chances for women to gain political influence are much smaller than those of men. Sometimes couples or family members share influence according to a pattern that the husband (or brother) is a businessman and his wife (or sister) is a politician.

Communist rule in Albania has transformed the nation greatly, creating social and educational facilities which enabled people from peasant or workers' families to climb up the social ladder and to gain access to qualified vocational and social positions which had never been accessible to them before. The price to pay was conformism and loyalty; this price had to be paid not only individually, but by the entire family. Failing to do so by a single member of the family (e.g. by trying to escape from Albania or by being in any kind of disloyalty) would have dramatic consequences for the kin of that family who would lose good jobs, good housing, the right to study and even their liberty. Improved access to health care and nutrition had the effect that people lived

---

5 In the pre-Gorbachev era, Ekaterina Furceva was the only female member of the CPSU Politbureau and CC Secretariat. In the GDR, no woman ever was elected as a full member of the Politbureau of the SED, Ingeburg Lange being a candidate Politbureau member and a full member of the CC Secretariat.
6 Data according to the websites of the two main parties, accessed May 9, 2012, www.ps.al and www.pd.al.

much longer and that infant mortality, while still very high within a European context, was drastically reduced (Gjonca 2001). Under communism, the population had tripled and was the youngest within Europe.

The deliberate pro-natality politics had negative consequences for Albania's society as the active percentage of the population steadily declined whereas the combined shares of minors and pensioners rose. Even the centralized labour market could not cope with ever-rising numbers of school and university graduates who could hardly secure formal employment.

Before 1991, the right (and duty) to work were enshrined within the constitution (Art. 44). As the state (including the agricultural cooperatives) was the only employer, there was formal full-employment which camouflaged a surplus labor force. Low wages (especially in the cooperatives where food and housing was free but payment nearly nonexistent) and an ever-declining level of consumption during the 1980s were the price.

The sudden collapse of the economic structures hurled large parts of the active population into unemployment without access to public benefits. The family networks once again were the structure to rely upon.

The strategies of many Albanians, especially of young men, were migration from the rural and mountainous districts to the cities where unregulated suburbs mushroomed, from Albania to Western Europe and North America and included the setting up of shadow economies in Albania and abroad, with disastrous results for the external image of their people.

FROM ISOLATIONISM TO INTEGRATION

The politics of isolationism aimed at good, working diplomatic and economic relations with most Western European countries, as long as they did not result in any kind of foreign interference in internal affairs or dependency. As economic considerations were paramount, it was possible for Albania to have solid economic relations with West Germany before diplomatic relations were established in 1987 as until then Albania had insisted on reparations for killings and damages during the German occupation of Albania (1943-44) which West Germany refused. Any form of relations with the USA or with the USSR was out of question as both were regarded as 'imperialist superpowers' and as such an imminent threat for peace and sovereignty of other countries.

The collapse of the 'Shining Beacon' had not only a deep impact on the Albanians' national consciousness and self-image. No other European country had to reinvent its foreign and security policy within such a short time. The communist leadership had tried to find economic relief in reactivating old connections with China and Soviet bloc nations (not the USSR itself) which was welcomed by the more intransigent East European rulers who tried in vain to forge an anti-Perestroika alliance.

In 1991, the foreign policy of Albania's constantly changing governments was guided by two motives: garnering as much economic emergency aid as possible and protection against an eventual spill-over of the Yugoslav conflicts. As reintegration into the Soviet bloc had become obsolete, integration into 'the West' became the political mantra.

As the bulk of Albanian émigrés poured across the borders to Italy and Greece, these two neighboring countries became the preferred regional partners. Other than with Germany, World War II issues had been settled between Albania and Italy in the 1947 Peace Treaty between Italy and her former enemies. Both countries had rather good relations, especially in the foreign trade sector.

Greek-Albanian relations had been rather uneasy; Greece officially considered Albania as one of the four occupiers during the war together with Italy, Germany and Bulgaria, while Albania condemned the mass expulsion of Muslim Albanians (çamë) in retribution for their alleged collaboration. There were substantial steps towards normalization: diplomatic relations were established in 1971, e.g. under the military regime, and right after Hoxha's death in 1985 an excerpt volume from his diaries on Greek-Albanian relations was published under the title "Two friendly peoples". Greece (herself not known as a defender of minority rights) saw the Albanian ban of any religion as an attempt to destroy the cultural identity of the Greek minority; on the other hand, the country did not openly defend the harsh Albanian frontier regime but felt rather insulated from an unwelcome influx of Albanian labor forces.

The desperate uncoordinated attempts of thousands of Albanians to leave their country at any price and the brutal and disappointing countermeasures of their destination countries became a burden for the image of the Albanians and for Albania's foreign relations. Particularly crisis-ridden Greece is a hotbed of albanophobic bias.[7]

Albania had to revise her blunt refusal of relations with the USA und the USSR, termed 'imperialist superpowers' by the Party. With the USSR being on the brink of dissolution, Albania naturally looked towards the USA as the preferred 'partner', which meant supporter and protector. The US presence in Tirana began with the reestablishment of diplomatic relations in 1991, followed by a spectacular visit from Secretary of State James Baker. From the beginning of the post-communist era, US ambassadors have played (and still play) a role which by far exceeds that of a diplomat, directly interfering in domestic politics.

Only a small fraction of the Albanian emigration made their way to Germany,[8] but as the chief donator of economic aid, this country plays a greater role in Albania than could be expected.

In the 1990s, the Berisha administration was not picky vis-à-vis potential partners. The controversial membership in the Organization for Islamic Cooperation opened Albania not only for investors from Islamic countries, but also for all sorts of Muslim proselytizing activities and for Islamists of the most radical brand. For several years, Albania was a safe haven for them, until (after Berisha's ousting in 1997) the USA became aware of the inherent danger and used their influence to stop the mushrooming of NGOs and foundations with obvious links to Near Eastern terrorism.

Under Communist rule it would have been sacrilege to even consider such an option, but Albania applied for NATO membership as early as 1992, joining the Alliance

---

[7] The fascist party „Golden Dawn" (Chrisi Avyi) which won 7% in the May 2012 general election is notorious for riots and attacks against Albanian émigrés.
[8] In 2011 only 10.293 holders of an Albanian passport lived in Germany, compared to 136.937 Kosovars (most, but not all, ethnic Albanians) and 67,147 Macedonian citizens (many of them Albanians), (Statistisches Bundesamt 2012).

only in April 2009. Meanwhile it has been prepared for membership within the Partnership for Peace; as Albania was (naturally) an ardent supporter of the NATO airstrikes on Yugoslavia in 1999, NATO protected Albania's territory against any Serbian counterattack. This Western integration was unanimously approved, even by former communist elites like Enver Hoxha's widow Nexhmije (Flottau 2004).

Only a few weeks after joining NATO, Prime Minister Berisha submitted an application for EU membership. EU representatives had warned him against such a premature act, as Albania is very far from fulfilling the Copenhagen criteria for membership (Bogdani and Loughlin 2007). The humiliation that Albania's application has since then regularly gleaned is all the greater as Serbia was awarded candidate status in March, 2012.

Public support for EU membership is still overwhelming, but has sensibly decreased from 98% in 2002 to 93.4% in 2010 and 80.7% in 2011 (Albanian Institute for International Studies 2012). As citizens of Albania can travel to the Schengen area without the need for a visa from 15 December 2010, one of the main motives for EU membership—free movement within Europe—is obsolete, and the EU crisis which has hit Albania's neighbor Greece with most severe social consequences has claimed its toll.

OVERCOMING THE LEGACY

Albania's political and social system is deeply marred by her historical legacy. This legacy persists well beyond the communist regime which was in power for less than half a century. This legacy consists of economic backwardness in a European as well as a regional context, family-focused social structures and a lack of pluralist traditions. The communist system struggled, but ultimately failed to subdue the nation's backwardness and patriarchalism; instead it expanded the authoritarian structures to their extremes.

The political elites of today are closely linked, especially by kinship, to those of the communist era. Due to the profound social change under communism, especially the creation of working education and health systems, the elites are much better established today than until 1944, so they must fight for political influence which is synonymous with access to economic resources.

Albania's political system is often described as a defective democracy, with low standards of civil rights and freedom of press. Her problem is not the legal system which is meticulously coordinated along EU legislation; it is a feuding political class which is still unable to give priority to the interests of their country over those of their own.

REFERENCES

Albanian Institute for International Studies (AIIS), accessed January 20, 2012, http://www.aiis-albania.org/Exec_Sum_Percep_2011.pdf.

Arapi, Lindita. 2005. "Albanien. Schlussstrich oder Offenlegung der Geheimdienst-Akten," *Deutsche Welle*, February 17, 2005, accessed June 9, 2012, http://www.dw.de/dw/article/0,,1492774,00.html.

Bogdani, Mirela and Loughlin, John. 2007. *Albania and the European Union. The Tumultuous Journey towards Integration and Accession*. London, New York: I.B. Tauris.

Byron, Janet L. 1976. *Selection among Alternates in Language Standardization: The Case of Albanian*. Den Haag, Paris: Walter de Gruyter.

Ceka, Egin. 2006. "Dokumentation: Die Debatte zwischen Ismail Kadare und Rexhep Qosja um die nationale Identität der Albaner," *Südosteuropa*. 54/3: 450-460.

Danylow, Peter. 1982. *Die außenpolitischen Beziehungen Albaniens zu Jugoslawien und zur UdSSR 1944-1961*. München, Wien: Oldenbourg.

Ditchev, Ivaylo. 1998. "D'Oncle Enver à Uncle Sam: les ruines de l'utopie," in *Albanie utopie. Huis clos dans les Balkans,* edited by Sonia Combe, Ivaylo Ditchev (Paris: Edition Autrement), 28-39.

Fevziu, Blendi. 2011. *Enver Hoxha*. Tirana: Shtëpia Botuese UET PRESS.

Fishta, Iljaz and Kareco, Theodor. 1996. *Prona private në Shqipëri 1924-1944 (përmes burimeve arkivore e bibliografike)* [Private property in Albania 1924-1944]. Tirana: Dituria.

Flottau, Renate. 2004. "Wir töteten nie ohne Grund," *Der Spiegel*, April 5, 2004, accessed June 3, 2012, http://www.spiegel.de/spiegel/print/d-30414363.html.

Frashëri, Kristo. 2006. *Historia e lëvizjes së majtë në Shqipëri dhe e themelimit të PKSH-së 1878-1941 (Vështrim historik me një shtojcë dokumentare)* [History of the movement of the Left in Albania and of the foundation of the Communist Party of Albania 1878-1941]. Tirana: Ilar.

Freedom House. 2012. "Nations in Transition. Albania," accessed June 9, 2012, http://www.freedomhouse.org/report/nations-transit/2012/albania.

Gjonça, Arjan. 2001. *Communism, Health and Lifestyle. The Paradox of Mortality Transition in Albania, 1950-1990*. (= Studies in Population and Urban Demography 8), Westport (Conn.), London: Greenwood Publishing Group.

Kadare, Ismail and Shehu, Bashkim. 1994. *Vjeshta e ankthit. Esse.* Tirana: Albinform.

Kaleshi, Hasan. 1975. "Das türkische Vordringen auf dem Balkan und die Islamisierung – Faktoren für die Erhaltung der ethnischen und nationalen Existenz des albanischen Volkes," in *Südosteuropa unter dem Halbmond. Untersuchungen über Geschichte und Kultur der südosteuropäischen Völker während der Türkenzeit,* edited by Peter Bartl, Horst Glassl (München:Trofenik), 125-138.

Kokalari, Musine. 2000. "Si lindi Partia Social-Demokrate [How the Social Democratic Party was founded]," in *Artikuj, shkrime, esse dhe kujtime*, edited by Novruz Xh. Shehu (Tirana).

Lewin, Erwin. 2007. *Antifaschistischer Widerstand in Albanien (1942-1943/44).* Neue Quellen zu Akteuren und Zielen. (= Diskurs. Streitschriften zur Geschichte und Politik des Sozialismus 24) Leipzig: Rosa Luxemburg-Stiftung Sachsen.

Lubonja, Fatos. 2009. *Second Sentence. Inside the Albanian Gulag.* London, New York: I.B. Tauris.

Neuwirth, Hubert. 2008. *Widerstand und Kollaboration in Albanien 1939-1944.* (= Albanische Forschungen 27) Wiesbaden: Harrassowitz.

Schmidt-Neke, Michael. 1987. *Entstehung und Ausbau der Königsdiktatur in Albanien 1912-1939* (= Südosteuropäische Arbeiten 84), München: Oldenbourg.

Schmidt-Neke, Michael. 1993. "Politisches System," in *Albanien, Südosteuropa-Handbuch* Bd. VII, edited by Klaus-Detlev Grothusen, Göttingen: Vandenhoeck & Ruprecht, 169-242.

Schmidt-Neke, Michael. 2009. *Die Verfassungen Albaniens. Mit einem Anhang: Die Verfassung der Republik Kosova von 1990* (= Albanische Forschungen 28) Wiesbaden: Harrassowitz.

Schmidt-Neke, Michael. 2010. "Skanderbegs Gefangene: Zur Debatte um den albanischen Nationalhelden," *Südosteuropa* 58/2: 273-302.

Schmidt-Neke, Michael. 2011. "The Development of Albania's Party System," *Südosteuropa-Mitteilungen* 51/1: 80-86.

Schmitt, Oliver Jens. 2009. *Skanderbeg. Der neue Alexander auf dem Balkan.* Regensburg: Pustet.

Schmitt, Oliver Jens. 2012. *Die Albaner. Eine Geschichte zwischen Orient und Okzident.* München: C.H. Beck.

Schwandner-Sievers, Stephanie and Fischer, Bernd J. (eds.). 2002. *Albanian Identities. Myth and History.* London: Hurst.

Statistisches Bundersamt (ed.). 2012. "Bevölkerung und Erwerbstätigkeit. Ausländische Bevölkerung. Ergebnisse des Ausländerzentralregisters," accessed June 3, 2012, https://www.destatis.de/DE/Publikationen/Thematisch/Bevoelkerung/MigrationIntegration/AuslaendBevoelkerung2010200117004.pdf?__blob=publicationFile.

Voell, Stéphane. 2004. *Das nordalbanische Gewohnheitsrecht und seine mündliche Dimension.* Marburg: Philipps Universität.

ODETA BARBULLUSHI

EU NORMS AND LOCAL PRACTICES: THE 'LOGIC OF PRACTICALITY' IN POST-COMMUNIST PUBLIC ADMINISTRATION

INTRODUCTION

Albania's path to democratic consolidation has been one of the most difficult ones, even when compared to those of the Western Balkan countries. As in other Southeast European and the Western Balkan states, the process of EU integration has run parallel to democratization and the adaptation to democratic norms and rules. Thus, EU conditionality has served as a strong impetus for democratic change in post-communist Albania. This has been the case particularly, in the period following 2005 when the Albanian leadership tackled some of the most intransigent problems of Albanian democratic transition, such as corruption and organized crime, thus leading to Albania signing the Accession and Stabilization Agreement in 2006. Yet, despite progress, convergence with the EU norms has remained largely elusive and Albania's integration model has been coined as 'Janus-faced' (O'Brennan and Gassie 2009, 62). This means that on the one hand Albanian legislators have accepted EU recommendations and sought to transpose and implement policy measures on the ground. On the other hand, policy implementation has been deficient and partial at best.

This chapter critically investigates the current literature on Albania's democratization and European integration. It specifically questions two possible 'stories' which explain the shortcomings and deficiencies related to implementation of EU norms and legislation. The first story is an elite-centered narrative which blames the Albanian 'political class' and the political elites for not complying to EU conditionality; even when they do comply, they are paying lip-service to Brussels, the story goes. The second, less dominant story refers to the cultural aspects of Albanian society at large, and the organizational culture of public administration, in particular which might be detrimental to the importation and application of European models and rules which emanate from very different social and cultural contexts.

This chapter offers an alternative explanation which is grounded on this latter story while making some significant modifications to it: First, it seeks to ground the concept of 'culture' or 'local opinion' or 'tradition' in specific social contexts, such as public administration. Public administration is chosen as the site of exploration for its reform and Europeanization has become the pinnacle of state Europeanization and modernization: in this connection, debates about transparency and efficiency of the Albanian public administration replicate debates about the transformation of former communist bureaucracies into Weberian style efficient bureaucracies which serve the public and not private entities, and moreover are not hijacked by political interests. Second, the chapter proposes to examine the shortcomings of administrative reform not through the eyes of universal categories and the theoretical lens of transition studies[9] but through the interpretations of 'good governance' and 'democracy' of the actors who are involved in the daily practices of public administration. Under such a context, this chapter explores how actors position themselves in relation to what is perceived as 'deviation' from European normality or from the 'democratic norm'. In this sense, instead of imposing a bounded concept of 'culture', I will look at the actors' practices of making sense of reform and Europeanization or lack thereof. Third, through the first previous interventions, the chapter criticizes the concept of 'culture' or authenticity in favor of the 'logic of practicality' concept.

This chapter has two main objectives: First, to examine the mismatch between EU norms and the political and social realities of their implementation through the eyes of actors involved in constructing these realities, i.e. civil servants. Thereafter, this chapter seeks to explore how actors position themselves in relation to this mismatch or these 'contradictions' of Albanian transition. At the methodological level, the chapter uses new unpublished materials, which are MA theses on the reform of public administration. The authors of these theses are MA students as well as civil servants or experts in public administration. MA theses were chosen owing to their interstitial character which rests between formal documents and informal narratives.

THE LOGIC OF CONSEQUENTIALITY AND 'FAKE EUROPEANIZATION'

A quick perusal of the EU annual reports and the Commission's Opinions to the European Council and European Parliament regarding Albania's integration reveals the EU's concern with the partial implementation and formal adaptation of EU norms (European Commission 2011). As the latest Opinion Paper of the European Commission to the European Parliament and Council demonstrates, "Despite constitutional regulations, there is a lack of effective parliamentary control over the executive and the Parliament is not an independent institution [...] The strong partisan culture polarizes the political positions in the parliament and this makes it impossible for the parliamentary commissions to be efficient" (European Commission 2011, 13). Similar problems are cited in relation to the functioning of various administrative units, particularly concerning the politicization and lack of transparency in recruitment procedures (European Commission 2011, 9). The reasons for these deficiencies are found in the lack of inherent state capacity, political polarization and a distinct lack of political will.

There is also a consensus in the integration literature relating to the Western Balkans regarding the 'fake character' of democratization and compliance with EU conditions in the region (Elbasani 2012; Bogdani and Loughlin 2007; Noutcheva 2007). According to scholars of Europeanization and European integration of Albania, the logic of 'consequentiality' rules over the logic of 'appropriateness' (Borzel and Risse 2000). Accordingly, elites push for change—however limited—for instrumental reasons and with an eye on the perceived losses and gains. They do not wish to 'do things

---

9 For a comprehensive analysis of the 'transition culture' and its ramifications see Kennedy 2002.

otherwise because it should be thus done, but because it is required and needed'. As such, ideational and identity change only occurs at the rhetorical level, but nothing or little of these changes permeate beyond that point.

However, these analyses emphasize the importance of political elites and, more broadly, of 'politics' for impeding Albania's progress regarding democratization and EU integration. What is lacking from the picture is *how* in practice the EU norms and policies are resisted or 'faked', to use Noutcheva's term (Noutcheva 2007, 2), all the way down to the practitioners and public administration functionaries, specialists and experts who are responsible for the implementation and compliance with the EU norms and practices. Furthermore, it does not explore how 'political intervention' occurs in such a way as to affect implementation or how it perpetuates certain 'deviant' or 'non-democratic' behavior.

The second criticism to be levied pertains to the dualism between the strategic action of Albanian figures, on the one hand, and the normative model which the EU offers, on the other. Social actions of the Albanian national elite and more broadly, of social figures are widely understood within a narrow model of the strategic/rational actor. In fact, numerous examples stemming from public administration or political parties and other public institutions demonstrate that many actions of the social agents are not purely rational. In most cases, actions follow some 'common way' of doing things and need to be compatible with the actors' stories of themselves. Strategic thinking and calculation cannot solely explain enduring patterns. In the following section, I examine the alternative explanation, which is best summarized as 'Albanian culture'.

Cultural difference as explanatory variable

How can we then, account for this incompatibility between the imported EU model and practices at the ground, which undermine the process of integration? The problem of incompatibility between EU norms and local or 'traditional' models has been increasingly tackled by a number of social scientists. The Albanian social theorist Artan Fuga claims that the local/Albanian 'public opinion' is rarely in step with the laws which are being imported: "If we are at the receiving end of laws, legal norms and administrative regulations which build on a Western-European spirit, and which arrive at us through the recommendations of the European Union, does this mean that they must be in full compliance with the social Albanian opinion?" (Fuga 2006, 26). As a case in point of the incompatibility between the European norm and the local opinion, Fuga mentions reform in the sector of public administration. According to Fuga, there are norms which would by any definition fall under the category of 'fair procedures', such as 'calls for applications', 'open competitions' etc.; however, "the prevailing procedures of employment in the sector of public administration attest to the dominance of political 'favors' or 'rewards' vis-à-vis fair competition" (Fuga 2006, 27). Fuga implies that these prevailing procedures have already become such common practice that they have replaced collective expectations for how business is done. Although not fully elaborated, Fuga's concept of 'local[10] opinion' replaces the category

---

10 A contextual reading of the text suggests that 'local' refers here to 'national' or 'Albanian' as opposed

of national 'common-sense' and it serves to highlight the incompatibility of what happens in practice on the one hand, and what is formally and normatively expected of Albania, on the other. From a legal-anthropological perspective, Nebi Bardhoshi suggests that the transition from customary law to the European-inspired models and legal systems has not been a smooth process. Indeed, he suggests that many aspects and characteristics of the previous customary law co-habit with and, at times clash with the EU legal model and practices. Bardhoshi points at the transformations Albanian legislation has undergone over the past two decades in an attempt to import and adapt to EU legal models. These transformations take the form of 'transplantation' of one 'model' into an existing legal tradition (Bardhoshi 2009). However, the authors suggest that these 'other' Western models are born out of other cultural contexts, which differ considerably from the cultural context of the Albanian traditional laws. Both scholars suggest that there must be some 'traditional' culture and 'local opinion' which does not accept the 'transplantation' of foreign norms and models. Their analysis direct attention to the specificities of each local setting as well as to 'softer' factors such as identity, ideas and representations. However, these arguments resonate broadly with popular distinctions between 'Western' and 'local' and do not aspire to build a conceptual framework of the distinction between these two categories. Thus, I suggest two further specifications to this distinction between the foreign and the 'traditional', or 'local opinion'. The first specification is concerned with the category of the 'local' or the 'traditional'. The category of the traditional or the local is not fixed, but also in constant change and reformulation by members of the community. Furthermore, it does not stand in opposition to the European norms and models. Instead, the juxtaposition between 'European' and 'traditional' is in itself discursively constructed and as such, it is not politically or culturally neutral. What is 'ours' or 'Albanian' on the one hand, and what is 'European' and the 'norm', on the other hand are constantly negotiated in various discursive terrains. Secondly, cultural manifestations change constantly and these changes cannot be viewed only at the macro-structural level of the Albanian 'political system' but also by a thorough study of the specific narratives and discursive practices which spring in a specific context at a certain time.[11]

In this sense, instead of speaking about local tradition or local opinion, one could investigate how a discourse of culture and 'Albanianness' or 'authentic tradition' constructs various subject positions within a discourse of democratic governance and statehood. Therefore, the juxtaposition of 'traditional' versus 'European' or foreign can only serve analytical or political purposes, for in 'practice' it does not quite hold. By shifting the attention away from tradition or 'local opinion' to discourse and practices of mid-level experts and civil servants—instead of national elites and the EU—I aim to give a more contextual picture of the implementation of EU norms on a daily basis at specific administrative sites.

---

to 'European' or 'foreign'.
11 For a contextualized study on the transformation of the institution of diplomacy in Norway in the 1990s, see Neum

TOWARDS A 'LOGIC OF PRACTICALITY' OF EUROPEANIZATION

Despite the attempts of the EU--among other actors of the International Community, such as the World Bank etc.—to measure the scale and extent of non-implementation of the legal instruments and the Inter-Sector Strategy for the Reform of Public Administration, little effort has been given with regards to the perceptions and expectations of practitioners, civil servants and experts of public administration on the 'transition' from one administrative model to another. Literature concerning Europeanization and the reform of public administration in Albania focuses on various steps of implementation and the measurable indicators of progress but much less so on the *process* of 'deviation' from the prescribed democratic model or on the actors' positioning towards these deviations.

The exploration of the process of implementation on a daily basis and in specific contexts is crucial to the better understanding of the shortcomings of reform. Furthermore, social actors—civil servants, experts, officials alike—need to interpret their institutional context in order to act. Hence, the actors' interpretation of the context in which they act and of their actions, too, is paramount to the understanding of the stability of certain behavior patterns.

However, focusing solely on actors' narratives offers a fractured view: Actors' interpretations follow from and reinforce their daily practices.[12] There is a constant interplay between the discursive element and the practical element at work: For example, a set of practices of offering and promising bribery and reward to the right person at the right time and in a commensurate way with respect to the favor which is asked, are embroiled in a broader discourse of living under stateless conditions.[13] Indeed, corruptive practices not only do follow stories about corruption and of what corruption means, and play themselves out in a specific discursive field opened by social agents, but also reinforce a certain discourse of corruption and stabilize the identities of those engaged in corruptive practices.

Discourse and practice are herein understood not as opposite, but rather as co-constitute: Whereas discourse may be understood as a system for the formation of statements (Bartelson 1995), practices are "socially recognized forms of activity, performed on the basis of what members learn from others" (Barnes quoted in Neumann 2002, 631). For example, a certain discourse of the stateless society consists of a multiplicity of social identities, such as the 'strong one' (*i forti*)-a category type of the early nineties which referred to the one who solved puzzles and overrode obstacles through the use of physical force or the blunt use of money--or the 'practical/swift one' (*i zoti* or *i shkathëti*) which refers to the one who solves problems though negotiations and by subverting the formal institutions and formal norms.[14] At the same time, these identities or categories are not neutral and prescriptive—describing what must be done in order to survive economically or to cut short the unnecessary hurdles and entanglements of institutions—but also normative, for they allow for and constitute the 'common sense' of a society or a social group. The discursive terrain and so-

---

[12] For insight into the relationship between discourse and practice, see Neumann 2002, 627.
[13] For an analysis of corruptive practices in post-communist societies, see Misztal 2000.
[14] For a media analysis of the predominance of this social category in post-communist Albania, see Godole 2004.

cial practices which inhabit it form a common ground for action, which is commonly known 'culture'. In the formulation of Theodore Schatzki: "[...] Discourses are the precarious fixities that precipitate from human practice and from which further practice arises. In this sense, every institution might have a constitutive story about itself, and this story is reproduced and reiterated through daily routine practices of individuals" (quoted in Neumann 2002, 631).

This chapter postulated that there is a 'logic of practicality' at work which pushes forward processes of political change and forms the basis of social action on a daily basis. With the 'logic of practicality', I refer to the daily and persistent practices of agents at their daily work sites and in those contexts. Although agents do normally act as rational actors—which means attaining their maximal objectives at minimal costs—their actions are embroiled in broader discourses and must match certain 'common ways of doing things'. The 'logic of practicality' is herein understood as different by any intrinsic and objective 'reason' which can be attested via validity claims or other premises of positivism. Nor is it a substitute for discourse in the sense that it might provide the reasons and pre-conditions for action. Instead, it is herein understood as the dynamic interplay of both discourse and the practice of social actors. We could use the term 'culture'—as Iver Neumann does in his study of the transformation of the institution of 'diplomacy' (Neumann 2002). Yet, the term 'logics' embraces both subjective and inter-related factors, as well as direct our attention to one specific moment of daily policy-making and life inside state institutions: problem-solving. Thus, the 'logic of practicality' plays itself out in response to 'problems' and paradoxes: it makes itself seen in the way social actors interpret problems or problematic situations or act upon these interpretations. As Anne Lynch argues in a different theoretical context: "By beginning with social problems, we are able to observe local (perhaps competing) strategies of political action and the resources employed to pursue them. Placing this dynamic at the centre of research recognizes people in post-communist societies as active creators and interpreters of the various aspects of collective life" (quoted in Kennedy 2013, 389). This conceptualization has broader implications for the understanding of 'Albanian culture' too: it criticizes the concept of culture as a national and unitary phenomenon tied strictly to a population and national territory. Instead it conceptualizes culture as a dynamic interplay of actors' narratives of their political surrounding and of their own (moral, power) position in it, as well as their practices which reinforce and stem from those narratives (Ledeneva 2008). The use of 'logic' adds a more agency-based dimension to the concept of culture, for it pays attention to the capacity of social actors to recognize—if not to change—situations of tension and paradoxes between what is required by the EU norm-setting discourse and the reality, where they are situated.

In order to do this, I suggest that we direct our attention to the middle ground of daily politics, which are the experts and civil servants of public administration. It is these actors who translate political discourse on the EU and Albania's democratization into practice. At the same time, these actors are in constant contact and interact on daily basis with sections of society, such as citizens in need of their services or businesses, interest groups etc. As such, public administration practitioners are situated at the intersection of state-society relations, or between the public and private sphere: on the one hand they obtain information about what needs to be done in terms of compliance with *acquis communitaire* as well as with EU conditionality. On the other hand, their daily practices are embedded in a broader political culture: in order to serve the public, public administration servants need to understand the specific needs—and language in which these needs are coated—of the broader public.

Questions I raise here are: how do they approach EU conditionality, particularly with regards to their immediate institutional setting? Also, how do they frame 'problems' of non-implementation, delays and informality? The materials I use to address these questions are the MA theses of students at the European University of Tirana. These students work in the field of public administration[15] and at the same time write theses on the reform of public administration in Albanian, corruption in public administration and EU conditionality, with a particular focus on the public service. Some of these theses do not comply with strict academic writing rules; hence the authors do not shy from expressing their own views and judgments on how things are and how they should be. The authors position themselves as both students of and practitioners of European integration and Albanian politics.

BUREAUCRACY, PUBLIC ADMINISTRATION AND EUROPEAN INTEGRATION

State bureaucracy and administration are key pillars of EU governance in the aspiring and candidate countries. Public administration obtains a new significance and an enhanced role in the context of Albania's EU integration, for its reform is part of political conditionality. Indeed, reform of public administration was framed by the EU as a process of modernization of former communist states (Elbasani 2009). In a way, its reform has become the final test for the transformation of the former communist state, where the political party controlled every segment of the state machinery, into the post-communist state where public interest is insulated from political parties.

The prioritization of reform of public administration followed the gradual institutionalization of relations between Albania and the EU, with the latter using the instrument of conditionality, strengthening its presence in Albania after 1997 (Elbasani 2008) In its SIGMA paper on *Preparing Public Administrations for the European Administrative Space*, the EU commission has asked that candidate countries adopt a civil service law guaranteeing civil servants political independence and professionalism; establish a career system; institute pay reform and facilitate training (Elbasani 2008, 18) Yet, the Albanian case remains the most difficult one, even compared to the other Western Balkan states, with regard to reform and to public administration. Politicization, which verges on militant attitudes combined with legal loopholes and a broader political culture which does not distinguish between the 'state' and the 'government' of the day (Elbasani 2008, 125-126) are some of the enduring patterns of post-communist public administration in Albania.

As for the role of the EU in changing enduring patterns of administrative behavior, Erolda Elbasani suggest that despite introducing new legal frameworks and creating

---

15 Some of these students previously worked in public administration while writing their theses however their current job positions are hard to trace. In one case, a student states in the introduction of the thesis his wish to become a part of the public administration in the future, see Beshiku 2010, 6.

small communities of experts on EU affairs, change has been superficial and has not weakened the impact of politics over administration (Elbasani 2008, 124). One reason for this may be the fact that the Union lacked institutional models and the common rules needed to regulate the sphere of public administration, except for the general principles of accountability, transparency and effectiveness (Radaelli quoted in Elbasani 2008, 122) These principles are also outlined in the Inter-Sector Strategy of the Albanian Council of Ministers for the reform of public administration 2009-2013. The strategy states very clearly that it aims to transform the Albanian administration into:

> "A professional and sustainable administration which is renewed only through honest and open competition and which creates career opportunities. A good administration which is thus organized as to accomplish tasks within the system of a small but effective state, which is grounded on (the principles of) decentralization and de-concentration. An administration which is based on transparent inclusive and responsible decision-making processes vis-à-vis the public." (Departamenti i Administratës Publike/Department of Public Administration 2009, 16)

In the following section, I look at how these general principles are approached individually by civil servants and which the practices constitute in their eyes deviations from European norms and conditions. Furthermore, I am interested in investigating how the historical legacy of the Albanian state and public administration is reconstructed through these texts.

The 'European model' and historic legacies

In various theses, it is acknowledged that a 'democratic, fair and transparent public administration' is paramount to the general progress of Albania in the European integration process. The second general presupposition is that there exists a strong legal basis for the implementation and adaptation of EU conditions; yet, implementation is problematic owing to political interference. The analysed theses, like the relevant literature on the reform of public administration and more broadly, democratization in Albania, acknowledge that there are some specific features of the Albanian case which do not allow for the adequate implementation of the EU conditions. At the same time, the reasons for non-compliance are the usual illnesses of post-communism: favoritism or nepotism, corruption and political interference.

> "The Constitution of 1998 defines very clearly the division between political institutions and public institutions. […] This would imply that like in USA, Germany, Britain and elsewhere, the change of government would only be followed by a change of political staffs. At the same time, the processes of recruitment, monitoring and promotions would be separate from the political process and would be only based upon professional and apolitical merit […] In Albania, there have been attempts to implement this constitutional principle, though there is still much to be done. Here, there is a model, wherein not only political rotations, but even political reshuffling or the change of ministers from the same governing party leads to changes at the level of public administration." (Xhajaj-Asllani 2011, 71)

There are several conclusions we might draw from the passage: first, there is an acute sense of incompatibility between the Constitution and the Western model on the one hand, and the reality 'on the ground', on the other. Secondly, the passage unintentionally draws the symbolic geography of 'normal democracies', where public interest is clearly separate from politics: American, British and German democracies are knowingly very different from Albanian realities, but they constitute the 'norm' or, at the very least, the ideal that Albania should strive for.

In the conclusions, the author points to the uniqueness of Albanian administrative culture which makes the Albanian case a particularly difficult test for the EU model of democratic transformation:

> "The current administrative culture in Albania is a combination of various influences, particularly of the family culture and the broader societal culture which perceives the state as the 'invader', of rules inherited from the communist regime, of two difficult decades of transition as well as of attempts to harmonize these realities with the standards of the European Union. This combination of cultures and rules has impacted the present profile of public administration and has impeded its reform." (Xhajaj-Asllani 2011, 82)

As the passage suggests, the Albanian administrative cultures consist of various and, at times, conflicting layers of influences and practices, of which the EU model is the latest. This, according to the theses from which the quote is taken, can be traced back to the history of state-formation of the country: "In general, Albania lacked the rich and continuous tradition of local government, in which programmes and implementation of reform of local autonomy can be grounded, in compliance with the experience of Western democratic countries" (Xhajaj-Asllani 2011, 33).

The temporal reconstruction of history is interwoven into the spatial reconstruction of identity (Hansen 2006, 78-81). Symbolic geo-politics is constantly referenced in the analyzed texts, as the authors compare Albania to other countries but also reflect upon the discrepancy between where it should ideally be, which is Europe, and where it is in practice, which is the undefined zone between 'transitional' and 'developing'. As one thesis states: "Albania of 2010 can be considered to be a developing country which has already passed the phase of being what the press and mass media commonly refer to as a 'transitional country'" (Zeqaj 2011, 34). Yet, as the author insinuates, the inefficiencies of Albanian public administration do not suggest much progress.

It is also interesting to note that despite the frequent references to the EU documents or EU-inspired governmental documents, there are also examples taken from 'advanced democracies' such as the USA or Canada. They serve as reference points of that 'universe of normality' from which Albania seems to be excluded, while at the same time aspiring to belong.

Recruitment, procurements and corruption

Most of the MA theses I have analyzed for the purposes of this chapter are concerned with the stability of public administration staff and procedures of recruitment. Rules of recruitment and the rights of public administration are outlined in the government's strategy on the reform of public administration.[16] However, the analyzed texts highlight the permanent sense of uncertainty among civil servants. This is owing to the fact that the enforcement of legal procedures is either absent or not fully implemented. In one thesis, the recruitment practices from 2001 to 2009 are scrutinized in order to identify methods of circumventing the legal procedures:

> "According to the Bulletin of Public Service Commission, application procedures have been all in order, but participation (in the competition) has been fictitious in many cases, and some of the evidenced problems are as follows: 1. A minimal number of candidates have entered the competition, something which can be common in competition for posts in all public institutions at a time when the job market offers numerous opportunities (but is this the case?). This is the consequence of the fact that at the time of publication of the call for applications, the advertised vacancies are already filled with civil servants who are hired on contracts. This is the reason why many people interested in the vacancy consider applying for the post futile, for it is simply a procedure to legitimize the employment of the person who has already filled the vacancy on a contract." (Beshiku 2010, 42)

Another thesis suggests that although the first formal steps of the job application process for staff members are generally fair and in congruence with legal procedures, the last step of selection is often left in the hands of the first line director of the sector which is hiring (Xhajaj-Asllani 2011, 77). On the other hand, there is another strategy for circumventing the legal procedures: temporary contracts. Although the only legal procedure of recruitment is 'open to applications' and the law requires that the call for applications begins one year in advance, an exception can be applied in cases when a ministry needs an employee before the one year application deadline and hence hires someone on a 'temporary contract' (Ibid).

The MA theses suggest that hierarchy is constantly circumvented through shortcuts. In one of them, the author claims that circumvention occurs for two main reasons: the first is the indecisiveness and lack of professionalism of high ranking managers; the second is the inclination of the highest official to address problems which are far below his rank and duties. Another similar problem is the large number of 'actual' subordinates reporting to the highest officials, though this hierarchical relationship is not reflected officially:

> "Members of staff prefer to report directly to the highest responsible official and this is a wide spread tendency [...] One of the main reason for delays and confusion amid public administration is that the highest superiors are allowed to claim direct responsibility over many subordinates simultaneously. This often occurs with the ministerial structures, where ministers have the tendency to regard all directories and sectors as directly subordinated to them." (Xhajaj-Asllani 2011, 63)

Thus, there exist two systems of hierarchy: the one which is on paper or which corresponds to the formal structures of the institutions and the second which better reflects

---

16 In November 1999, the Albanian parliament passed Law No. 8549 on 'The Status of the Civil Servant'. This law strengthened the position of DAP (Department of Public Administration) which remains the institution responsible for the management of staff of public administration, for the enhancement of human resources in Public Administration and for leading reform in this sector.

reality. This duality of hierarchical structures combined with an overlap of institutional structures leads to different ranges of salaries for the same jobs and administrative positions.[17] At the same time, there seem to be no clear and unified strategy for promotion, awards and demotion. Under these conditions, there is space for political interference or for the circumvention of formal hierarchy in rewarding and punishing civil servants.

The political factor

Legal loopholes and the overlap of instruments aside, the main reason why 'things do not work' seems to be political in nature: Normality is interrupted by politics, experts need to become partisan in order to hold their jobs and planning is impossible owing to 'political intervention'. In fact, every time there is a general election, it is widely accepted that the public administration staff—of all levels, high, mid, and low—are reshuffled. Both horizontal and vertical changes, which at the level of minister/vice minister/director etc. and the level of directories and sectors and their respective staffs, follow the political turnover and even the occasional change of ministers (Xhajaj-Asllani 2011, 72) Another MA thesis which focuses on the processes of public procurements, suggests:

> "The main problem of public administration is its politicization and the lack of respect for legislative measures which guarantee the status of the public servant. It is regrettable to see how the most capable specialists of Albanian administration do not survive longer than eight years in the same position [...] There are very few technical experts who can weather the appetite of politicians and (and their attempts) to reward their party loyalists or their family members with administrative posts. As a consequence, a strategy which is-initiated or drafted by one expert is disrupted and must be continued by another newly nominated expert. Thus, projects and professional strategies are interrupted, badly administered and changed along the way, without much certainty upon their final destination." (Zeqaj 2011, 29)

The problem is articulated in terms of security: there are no guarantees, either for the staff or for the implementation of strategies. As the above text illustrates, the 'public interest' is interwoven with individual security. However, political interference is not easy to point out, as it is easily enmeshed in nepotism and corruption:

> "The loss of professional independence means that the official does not think independently i.e. consider the matter based on its own merits. Bribes, pressure, uninhibited political ambition and the desire for promotion are the most common reasons contributing to the loss of independence. Bribes lead to the loss of independence because of illegal profit. Pressure leads to the loss of independence owing to fear. Political ambition or professional greed makes the officials blind in relation to praise and forces them to blindly obey the desires of their superiors, and hence silence and curtail their own judgements." (Beshiku 2010, 37)

---

17 For an insight into how these overlaps affect the system of salaries in public administration, see Bajraktari 2011.

As we see, the passage refers vaguely to 'pressure' but it is not clear *who* exerts this pressure. However, it indicates that this pressure is exerted not through direct control but through various possibilities for corruption, bribery and nepotism.

CONCLUSIONS

In this chapter I have sought to illuminate the shortcomings and limitations of the implementation of the European model of public administration in post-communist Albania through the eyes of those working as civil servants or specialists in public administration. I chose to do this through the use of an unusual type of text, namely the academic theses of specialists and civil servants. This choice was made owing to the contextual specificities of texts of the academic genre in Albania, which is a combination of detailed description and subjective judgment. As such, these texts help us to understand not only the obstacles of implementation of the legal instruments and strategies which aim at bringing Albanian public administration in line with the Western Weberian model of bureaucracy, but also how these obstacles are created on a daily basis, and interpreted by the actors. Furthermore, through the perceptions of students/civil servants, the paper aimed at exploring how these civil servants position themselves vis-à-vis nepotism, political pressure and corruption which they denounce in their MA theses.

One finding of these texts is that political interference and political pressure are understood as the key reason for the other deviations such as inefficiency, irresponsibility, lack of transparency etc. Furthermore, this pressure is seen to be exerted both, directly, through the centralization of competences and dual hierarchy, and indirectly through the overlap of various legal instruments and strategies.

The other important insight is that the daily practices of work create expectations and form obstacles in the process of the reform of public administration. These daily practices contradict openly the rationale of unbiased public institutions and public interest. Yet naming them as corrupt would be inadequate. On the other hand, the category of the 'informal' would also be erroneous, for these practices are broadly accepted and have become part of the 'commonsense' of a particular institutional setting. It is only by jumping into another setting—namely academia—that the civil servants can question and take a normative distance from what takes place in their daily work environment. This chapter is an attempt to open the way for more in-depth and contextual analysis into administrative practices in various institutional sites.

REFERENCES

Bajraktari, Drinalda. 2011. "C'farë kushtesh administrative kërkon BE-ja nga vendet kandidate për anëtaresim" [EU conditionality in relation to administration in candidate countries], (MA thesis, Faculty of Social Sciences, European University of Tirana).

Bardhoshi, Nebi. 2009. "Njeriu Kanunit në post-socializem ['Man of Kanun' in post-socialism]," *European University of Tirana, Revista* 8: 114-132.

Bartelson, Jens. 1995. "A genealogy of Sovereignty," in A genealogy of sovereignty edited by Jens Bartelson (Cambridge: Cambridge University Press), 1-43.

Beshiku, A. 2010. "Ecuria e Reformave të Shërbimit Civil në Periudhën post-komuniste në Shqipëri [Progress of Reforms in the sector of Civil Service in the post-communist period in Albania. Its problems in Public Administration]," (MA thesis, Profile: Economy and Sustainable Development. Faculty of Economics, European University of Tirana).

Bogdani, Mirela and Loughlin, John. 2007. Albania and the European Union: The Tumultuous Journey Towards Integration and Accession. London: I.B Tauris.

Borzel, Tanja and Risse, Thomas. 2000. "When Europe hits Home: Europeanization and Domestic Change," European Integration online Papers (EIoP) Vol. 4/15.

O'Brennan, John and Gassie, Esmeralda. 2009. "From Stabilization to Consolidation: Albanian State Capacity and Adaptation to European Union Rules," Journal of Balkan and Near Eastern Studies 11/1.

Departamenti i Administratës Publike (DAP). 2009. *Strategjia Inter-sektoriale e Reformës në Administratën Publike, në Kuadrin e Strategjise Kombëtare të Zhvillimit dhe Integrimit* [Department of Public Administration, *Inter-Sector Strategy of Reform in Public Administration in the context of National Strategy for Development and Integration* 2009-2013], Chapter 2, accessed June 14, 2012, http://www.pad.gov.al/APreforma.pdf.

Elbasani, Arolda. 2008. "EU Enlargement and State Institutions after Communism – Reforming Public Administration in Albania," *L'Europe en Formation* 349-350, 3/4 (2008): 119-134, accessed July 25, 2012, http://www.cairn.info/revue-l-europe-en-formation-2008-3-page-119.htm.

Elbasani, Arolda. 2009. "EU Administrative Conditionality and Domestic Downloading: The Limits of Europeanization in Challenging Contexts," (KFG Working Paper No. 2): 1-22.

European Commission. 2011. *Albania 2011 Progress Report* (Brussels 20.10.2011), accessed July 27, 2012,
http://ec.europa.eu/enlargement/pdf/key_documents/2011/package/al_rapport_2011_e n.pdf.

Fuga, Artan. 2006. "Norma Evropiane dhe Opinioni Lokal: Mangësitë e Përqasjes Institucionaliste [The European Norm and Local Opinion: The shortcomings of the institutional approach]," *Polis* 2: 25-30.

Godole, Jonila. 2004. "Apologji për të shkathëtin [An apology for the swift/practical one]," *Shekulli*, November 14, 1 & 15.

Hansen, Lene. 2006. Security as Practice. The Bosnian War and the Western Responses. Routledge: London and New York.

Kennedy, Michael M. 2002. Cultural Formations of Post-communism. Emancipation, Transition, Nation and War. Minneapolis and London: University of Minnesota Press.

Kennedy, Michael D. 2013. "Mobilizing justice across hegemonies in place: critical post-communist vernaculars," in Post-communism from within: Social justice, mobilization, and hegemony, edited by Jan Kubik and Amy Lynch. New York and London: New York University Press.

Ledeneva, Alena. 2008. "Blat and Guanxi: Informal Practices in Russia and China," Comparative Studies in Society and History, 50: 118-144.

Misztal, Barbara A. 2000. Informality: Social Theory and Contemporary Practice. London: Routledge.

Neumann, Iver. 2002. "Returning practice to the Linguistic turn: The case of Diplomacy," Millennium: Journal of International Studies 31/3: 627-651.

Noutcheva, Gergana. 2007. "Fake, Partial and Imposed Compliance: The Limits of the EU's Normative Power in the Western Balkans," *CEPS Working Document No. 274.*

Xhajaj-Asllani, Ana. 2011. "Menaxhimi i burimeve njerëzore dhe performancë e administratës publike [Management of Human Resources and Performance of Public Administration]," (MA Thesis, Faculty of Social Sciences. European University of Tirana).

Zeqaj, Merita. 2011. "Politika në sistemin e prokurimit publik shqiptar 1990-2010 [Politics in the system of Albanian public procurement, 1990-2010]", (MA Thesis, Faculty of Social Sciences, European University of Tirana).

PART TWO

IDENTIFYING EFFECTS OF MIGRATION IN POST-
COMMUNIST ALBANIA

JULIE VULLNETARI

INTERNAL MIGRATION IN ALBANIA: A CRITICAL OVERVIEW

INTRODUCTION

The third post-communist decade is upon us and Albania sits high on the horse of transition venturing down the road to Europe. Yet there is also good news. At the dawn of this new decade (December 2010) it was announced that Albanian citizens— or at least most of those still left in the country after massive emigration—could finally travel to Western Europe (the Schengen area) without requiring a visa. This was followed a year later with another milestone: for the first time in its short history as an independent state Albania was/is no longer a rurally centered society. Or so the 2011 preliminary census results would want us to believe. According to these more than half the population (53.7%) now resides in urban areas (INSTAT 2011, 16). However, it is necessary here to briefly reflect on the meaning of urbanization in Albania, as it represents a very complex process with certain specificities. There is no dispute that there is an increase in the population inhabiting urban areas, the result of primarily rural-urban migration. Yet, how 'urban' are these migrants' lifestyles and their living conditions? A closer examination of the economy and infrastructure of a number of urban—especially peri-urban—areas reveals that the distinction between rural and urban in the classical sense is rather blurred. Three aspects can be singled out at this point: first, in many urban areas inhabitants sustain themselves through a mixture of rural and urban income-generation, combining, for example, wage work for young men in construction with pasturing the family cows as several older women do. Second, and related to the first, rural income generating activities are not only performed locally but also in rural areas of origin as migrants are in fact trans-local migrants who live between their village of origin where they produce from their agricultural plot, and the city of destination where they then trade this produce (Vullnetari 2012). Finally, the physical infrastructure in many peri-urban areas and even peripheral zones within more established cities is sometimes worse than in villages with streets pockmarked with potholes, clogged by cars, exposed sewage pipes and limited access to potable water. Indeed, some sociologists speak of 'urban ruralization' rather than of a clear urbanization process (Dervishi 2001). Nevertheless these transformations are considered by many optimists in Albania as products of the country's 'modernization' paving the way for EU accession. As numerous events took place to celebrate the 100th anniversary of independence from the Ottoman Empire (November 2012), there was excitement amongst politicians and ordinary citizens regarding an anticipated bestowal of EU candidate status, ironically signaling a loss of independence as some powers will increasingly be handed over to Brussels.

Migration has been a key component of these two tempestuous decades of post-communist transformations. There now exists a burgeoning catalogue of literature documenting and analyzing international migration and its associated features and effects. In contrast, internal movements have received very limited attention in academic writings and policy-making thus far. On the one hand this contrast reflects the intensity and specific characteristics of Albanian international migration, quite unique in a way (King, Uruçi and Vullnetari 2011). On the other hand, it also mirrors the priorities of those funding research. International migration is important to host country governments—by far the largest funders of such research—who need the cheap labor migration provides but are concerned about 'problems' of integration. This emigration is also important to the Albanian government acting as it does like a 'pressure valve' to release unemployed citizens, while funneling much-needed foreign currency—through remittances—into the country to cover the trade deficit. Yet this neglect of internal migration has been noted in migration and development discourses worldwide, prompting calls to turn attention once more to these 'forgotten migrants' (Laczko 2008). This chapter thus marks a contribution to address this imbalance, by providing a critical overview of the key debates and issues linked to internal migration in Albania over the last 20 or so years.

The chapter is organized as follows: after this introduction, I provide a brief history of Albania's internal migration followed by an analysis of the key factors that triggered and sustained this movement. Next comes an outline of figures and migratory patterns. A discussion then follows, regarding the key impacts this migration has had on the country and migrants themselves. The final section offers a conclusion.

A BRIEF HISTORY OF INTERNAL MIGRATION IN ALBANIA

As the theme of this volume emphasizes, contemporary events in Albanian society are best understood against the historical background which shaped them. The same holds true for migration—whether domestic or international. Scholarly literature suggests that Albanians were relatively mobile within and outside of the Ottoman Empire. While the boundaries between internal and external migration during this time were rather blurred, the emergence of the new Albanian state put an end to such ambiguity. Internal migration was now a movement within the territory of Albania only. The limited literature we have relating to this time suggests that these movements continued with little or no administrative restrictions, nonetheless, including in the direction of expanding towns (Tirta 1999).

Yet, with the communists' ascendance to power after the Second World War came a planned economy and a system that regulated practically all aspects of life. Internal movements too became part of this practice, the consequences of which would be felt beyond the communist years. While international migration was banned and considered treason against the fatherland, internal—especially rural to urban—movements were subject to strict controls and regulations. Thus, two phases of internal relocation can be distinguished. The first, corresponding roughly to 1945–1965, was characterized by large-scale internal movements, albeit centrally regulated, and incorporating a high degree of urbanization. The vast majority of these movements were designed to supply much-needed labor to industrialization projects around the country. While many of these projects took place in existing towns, others triggered the construction of new urban centers. Thus, during the years 1945–1989, some 43 new towns were built around the country, half of which were related to metal extraction and energy resources (Bërxholi 2000; Rugg 1994, 63). These towns such as Bulqizë, Laç,

Kurbnesh and Ballsh absorbed a large proportion of rural-urban migration until 1989; but they became important expulsion centers after 1990, when the industries they were built around, closed.

Unlike the early post-war years, a policy of rural retention and minimal urbanization was pursued from the early 1960s onwards. This was largely achieved through the application of a set of administrative restrictions, forming what Sjöberg (1994) calls an 'anti-migratory system'. Many of these restrictions meant nothing more than a 'legal prohibition on migration' and included, among others: permission to change domicile (to leave one's domicile), or *leje e shpërnguljes* and dwelling permission or *pasaportizim*.[18] They were aimed primarily at rural-urban migration, and were especially prohibitive of settlements in the capital Tirana. Nevertheless, some migration outside the prescribed parameters did take place. For example, some migrants moved to the adjoining rural areas of the 'forbidden' cities, while marriage with urban dwellers was used in other cases to circumvent the rules (Sjöberg 1992).[19]

Tirana, more than any other city, was the focus of internal movement; it was the most desirable destination for a considerable number of Albanians, especially young people, yet out of reach for the majority of them. As a major industrial, politico-administrative, educational and cultural centre, its periphery attracted what Sjöberg (1992) calls 'diverted migration'. In other words, migratory flows heading for Tirana experienced a deflection to the rural periphery adjoining it. Since most would-be migrants were not able to obtain permission to move their residence to Tirana proper, they managed to migrate to one of the rural cooperatives or state agricultural enterprises close to the city. These 'diverted in-migrants' in turn contributed to the formation of densely populated 'extra-urban settlements' (Sjöberg 1992, 13), a prelude to post-communist patterns as we shall see shortly. Following this restrictive policy for settlement in the capital, Tirana's share of the country's population actually *declined* after the 1960s. A few years before the communist regime collapsed, the spectacular growth of the city that was to follow was almost unimaginable, even for attentive scholars such as Carter. He wrote: "[T]he idea of a Tirana-Durrësi urban agglomeration emerging in the near or more distant future seems remote" (Carter 1986, 281). By 2005 precisely this area housed nearly a third of Albania's total population (Doka 2005, 100) and by 2012 this share had risen to represent half of the population of Albania.

The ideology which reinforced policy-making concerning internal migration during this period was also reflected in the terminology that was employed in the official and academic discourse on such matters. The term 'mechanical movement' or '*lëvizje mekanike*' was used to present this migration as the opposite of a natural process, and therefore, something that needed to be controlled (e.g. see Misja and Vejsiu 1990).

Migration was effectively legalized as a human right soon after the collapse of the totalitarian regime. Article 22 of the Law on Amendments to the Constitutional Provisions in 1993 enshrined the right of every Albanian citizen to choose their place of

---

18 *Pasaportizim* derives its name from the use of domestic passport/ identity cards or *letërnjoftim* as the main pillar in the process of internal movement. All citizens were required to have these passports with them at all times. For more details see Sjöberg 1994.

19 A popular rhyme in the Albanian parlance of the south at the time was: *burrin sa një këndes/ shtëpinë sa një qymes/ vetëm në qytet të vdes* (Small like a cockerel my husband may be / small like a henhouse my house may be / as long as I can live and die in the city).

residence and move freely within the state's territory, and emigrate abroad. However, by that date large-scale spontaneous emigration and internal migration had already started.

POST-COMMUNIST INTERNAL MOVEMENTS

Key influencing factors and timing

The large-scale internal migration and the chaotic urbanization process that Albania experienced in the post-communist years is shaped by a number of direct factors, the most important of which were as follows. First, the abysmal state of living conditions in villages by the end of the 1980s provided an undeniable push factor for people seeking to flee from the villages and look for better opportunities elsewhere, whether internally or abroad. Given that most of the country's population lived in rural areas, there was larger-scale migration from here towards the cities, especially as those from the cities more often emigrated abroad. Second, urban life has traditionally been considered in Albania as being superior to that in the villages not only because of its better socio-economic opportunities, but also because of the urban lifestyle which offers more time and opportunity for leisure and pleasure, and less conservatism and gendered oppression. Throughout the communist years, Tirana stood out as the pinnacle of urbanity within Albania, its urban life often featuring as a model of 'socialist modernity' in movies made for public consumption and broadcast by the state-controlled TV. Third, after four decades of controlled mobility, Albanians were finally free to move and decide for themselves where to work and make a living. They certainly wanted to take advantage of this freedom in spectacular ways. Fourth, once it was clear that the regime was on the brink of collapse, a widespread disregard for law and order ensued, as the pent-up frustration of decades of close surveillance and for many—oppression—exploded on a massive scale. At the same time, and my fifth point, it soon became obvious that the state's ability to enforce the law and restore order was also rapidly dissolving. Finally, the privatization in 1992 of what had been until then public property was the final nail in the coffin of socialism harkening a turning point in Albanian society.

The privatization of agricultural land marked the end of the cooperatives, a sure sign in rural areas that the regime had practically come to an end. This apprehension was reflected in the way that everything public, such as irrigation systems, orchards, vineyards, warehouses and even harvest in the field—until then all belonging to the cooperative and hence considered common property—was stolen or brutally destroyed. The resulting chaos meant that the privatization needed to be sped up so as to distribute amongst the population that which could be saved. Nonetheless, destruction of what continued to remain public continued. The parallel privatization process in urban areas provided urban dwellers with a chance to own their own dwelling by purchasing it at a symbolic price. Until then, these flats—often built using the unpaid 'volunteer' labor during the after-work hours of their future dwellers—had been rented from the state for a nominal sum. More ambiguous was the question of land that was administered through agricultural state enterprises (*ndërmarrje bujqësore*) and which did not officially belong to its members but to the state. This land was distributed on a usufruct basis for a 15 year period or longer (Felstehausen 1999). To complicate matters further, initially the privatization process dealt with the distribution of land and other immovable property by excluding the claims of former owners, who had been disposed without due compensation by the communist regime following the latter's post-war ascendance to power.[20]

Most of the 1990s were thus characterized by large-scale internal movements, land grabbing in urban and peri-urban areas followed by squatter settlements, especially in the Tirana-Durrës conurbation, and a frightening contraction of common spaces, as the 'private' mercilessly exacted its revenge on the public. This is how Felstehausen (1999, 13) describes the process of a typical squatter settlement claim in peri-urban Tirana: "The head of a family locates an unoccupied piece of land (men were the only ones observed to engage in land claims). The interested party asks existing neighbors if they have any objection to having a new family mark out a house plot. If there are no objections or serious warnings about conflicts, the new claimant 'places the stones', a ceremony marking the four lot corners, usually with white rocks. This ritual is conducted in the presence of witnesses. By placing the stones, the new claimant has established a personal and familial right to a homestead—a place to live. Customary rules give some protection to new citizens of the community. [...] Hundreds of unauthorized claims like these are created every month. It is unclear how they will be ultimately resolved" (see also World Bank 2007a; also Bardhoshi 2011, who confirms that engaging in land claims is a male specificity).

Census and Albanian Standards Living Measurement Survey (ALSMS) data also confirm the immediate post-communist restructuring years of 1991–1993 as one of the two peaks of intensity for internal movements, along with the years following the financial pyramids' collapse of 1997 (Carletto et al. 2004, 7). During and following this, internal movements continued, but at a steadier pace, although population registers records for the Kamëz municipality (2008) tell a different story. The impressive growth of this area in the 1990s (precisely between 1992 and 1999) is as follows: from 6,000 in 1989; to 9,600 in 1992; to 48,000 in 1995; to 60,000 by 1999.[21] The national statistics office suggests that the start of the second post-communist decade (2000–2001) signaled a decrease of internal migration overall, including towards coastal areas (INSTAT 2004). According to ALSMS data, this decline began as early as 1999 and was rather sharp, although not uniform as Tirana continued to gain in-migrants, especially after this turning point (World Bank 2007b, 39).

---

20 However, most land distribution in the north of the country was carried out along lines of ownership preceding the land confiscation and collectivization. Yet, this did not prevent disputes which at times led to honor killings and blood-feuds, triggering some internal and mostly international forced migration.
21 The discrepancy may be due to the different data sources and collection methodologies, as I discuss later.

Motives to move

Extant literature on internal migration reveals a combination of economic, social and cultural reasons for such moves. Thus, according to Carletto et al. (2004, 7), in almost three-quarters of the post-1990 internal moves, the migration of households was attributed to factors such as starting a new job, looking for a better job, or having insufficient land. Yet, more detailed ethnographic research has revealed the equally strong family character of this migration, which is often of a permanent nature (Cila 2006, 14; Çaro 2011; Vullnetari 2012). This is also reflected in the gendering of these migration streams, which according to the census figures are biased in favor of women. A higher share of women does not necessarily mean family migration, as patterns in countries such as the Philippines or Ukraine show, where women are in the majority independent migrants. In the Albanian context we note two key trends: on the one hand female migration as part of the family whereby men move first although women are involved in all stages of the migration process and are often its initiators. This is particularly the case for migration from northern Albania as Çaro (2011) discovered in her research amongst such migrants living in Tirana's peri-urban area of Bathore. For other migration streams to Tirana, such as those from the south, young women often migrate on their own, first as students and then to work in the various expanding service industries of the capital. Parents and other siblings may follow later, but this is not always the case. My own research amongst rural migrants from the south-east revealed that young migrant women chose to move to Tirana because of its liberal/emancipator potential, in contrast to the conservative and oppressive village life (Vullnetari 2012). In such cases gendered social factors rather than economics were at the heart of the decision-making process.

Access to better education and healthcare have been key factors from the early 1990s and continue to motivate more recent migrants as well, as rural areas and small urban peripheries continue to suffer from dilapidated social and physical infrastructure (Çaro 2011; Tomini and Hagen-Zanker 2009). The capital, which hosts the vast majority of the country's educational and health institutions cannot be disputed as the most attractive destination within the country for migration. The situation is perpetuated further as rural areas are depleted through the flight of the skilled, who seek better work and life opportunities in cities instead. Tirana also acts as a magnet for businesses who re-locate there to take advantage of the population concentration, as well as the various structural facilities often not available in other areas (Tirana Regional Council 2005). Its population serves not only as a crucial pool of skilled and readily available labor, but also as a much-needed mass of consumers (Doka 2005). Such re-location is affected by return migration as migrants who return with capital from abroad often end up investing in Tirana and other bigger cities, away from their areas of origin (Kilic 2007; Vullnetari 2012).

Internal migration in figures

Data on internal migration in Albania is derived from three main sources: population censuses carried out by the national statistics office INSTAT; population registers held at the local commune or municipality (now within the institutional framework of the

Ministry of Interior); and the set of Albanian Living Standards Measurement Surveys (ALSMS) conducted by INSTAT with the support of the World Bank. Before analyzing the data available, a few words should be said concerning these sources of information. First, the census data: The two most relevant censuses for our discussion here were those of 1989 and 2001, which recorded population *present* at the time of enumeration by usual place of residence (Lerch and Wanner 2008). However, as with all censuses, they offer only a glimpse into the demographic situation at a particular point in time. Furthermore, censuses have a tendency to under-record certain groups, for example mobile populations such as the Roma, irregular immigrants, those not officially registered as internal movers, or internal movers who have emigrated abroad (see also Agorastakis and Sidiropoulos 2007).

The second source, the population registers, records *resident* population at the commune and municipality level, by place of *legal* residence (Lerch and Wanner 2008). These data are reported monthly to INSTAT. However, their accuracy and reliability have been questioned by various analysts. First, the systems have been, until very recently, largely manual and thus very slow to respond to rapid population changes due to migration. However, the pace of population change has also been extremely rapid. In a report of the Korçë Regional Council (2005, 15), for instance, the authors emphasize that: "[D]ue to its high rate of internal and foreign migrations, it has been difficult to keep accurate official data on the present-day population in the communes and municipalities." A similar evaluation is provided by Tirana's regional authorities: "[T]he city of Tirana […] is growing and changing by the day. It is a real challenge to keep up with Tirana's pace of economic and social changes and it is even more difficult to capture this transformation in the form of coherent and reliable data" (Tirana Regional Council 2005, 32). Moreover, it is in the individual commune or municipality's interest not to quantify the extent of the population loss, for fear of losing resources such as fiscal transfers and being downgraded in importance (Arrehag, Sjöberg and Sjöblom 2005; World Bank 2007a, 9). Thus, in contrast to the census, this method's tendency is to inflate numbers. This can be seen, for instance, when comparing INSTAT's (2011) reported figure of 4.2 million residents in the country for 2010 according to population registers, with the 2.8 million recorded by the 2011 census. Another example refers to the Tirana district, which had 750,000 inhabitants according to the 2003 population registers, but only 520,000 in the 2001 census (Tirana Regional Council 2005, 19). Thus, INSTAT-produced data must be cautiously used and critically assessed (for more on this, see World Bank 2007a, 9–10; also Agorastakis and Sidiropoulos 2007).

The third source of data has been the set of ALSMS from 2002, 2005 and 2008 and the follow-up wave panels of 2003 and 2004. Using a sophisticated (but very long) module on migration, these results have generated a number of studies, some of which are discussed in this chapter.

The significance of internal movements is apparent from several angles, not least numbers. However, as discussed earlier, figures differ according to sources used, units measured, and the time-period they cover. Table 1 is composed from census, ALSMS and population registers data for *migrant stocks*, broadly covering the first post-communist decade. As the table shows, the closer we zoom in on a geographical or administrative unit, the higher the figure is.

Table 1: Estimates of Albanian internal migrants according to various sources, 1989–2005

Year/period	Number	Type	Source	% total
1989–2001	182,639	Inter-regional[22]	Census	5.7
1989–2001	252,735	Inter-prefecture	Census	
1989–2001	295,870	Inter-district	Census*	
1989–2001	355,230	Inter-district	Census	
1992–2001	1,356,750	Inter-commune/municipality	Population registers	
1990–2005	450,000	Non-specific	2002 & 2005 ALSMS	20

Source: 1989 and 2001 censuses in INSTAT (2004, 12–13), Carletto et al. (2004,Table 8); population registers in Bërxholi, Doka and Asche (2003, 68); 2002 and 2005 ALSMS in World Bank (2007b, 33)
* According to data computation by Agorastakis and Siridopoulos (2007, 474).

Analyzing ALSMS data for 2002 and 2005, a World Bank team reported that nearly 20% of Albania's population had moved internally between 1990 and 2005, and if movers since birth were included, this figure would rise to a third. The peak of moves (1997–1998) following the collapse of the pyramid investment schemes saw a *flow* of nearly 40,000 migrants per year, but these then decreased by about half to an average of 20,000 per year (World Bank 2007b, 33–34).

The vast majority of these internal migrants have relocated to Tirana, which together with Durrës has experienced what is considered explosive population growth. Estimates of those living in the Tirana-Durrës metropolitan area[23] vary between 850,000 and 1 million inhabitants—or 75% of the country's urban population—by the mid-2000s (World Bank 2007a, 5). Within this area, Tirana is by far the most important since, according to ALSMS data, a third of all internal migrants between 1990 and 2005 moved there. Between 2002 and 2004 four out of every 10 migrants were moving to the capital (World Bank 2007b, 34). Official (census) records for the population of the Tirana district suggest a population increase from 368,000 in 1989 to 520,000 in 2001 (INSTAT 2002). However, unofficial sources estimated that the district contained 800,000 people already by 2002 (De Soto et al. 2002, 113), and had approached the 1 million mark by 2005 (Lulo 2005). The confusion over the extent of the increase is owing to many recent in-migrants who are not registered, making their precise numbers unknown. Examining on a smaller scale, the municipality of Tirana only, the 2001 census figures show just how dramatic the population increase was—of more than 40%—from 238,057 residents in 1989 to 343,078 in 2001 (World Bank 2007a, 5). This seems to have decreased in the last decade or so, if we assume that the 2011 preliminary census figures are correct: the growth is now around 20%, or half of

---

22 INSTAT defines three regions: central/west (Prefectures of Tirana, Durrës, Lezhë, Fier and Elbasan); north-east (Prefectures of Shkodër, Kukës and Dibër); south-east (Prefectures of Berat, Gjirokastër, Korçë and Vlorë). This is different from the ALSMS division.
23 Consisting of the four districts of Tiranë, Durrës, Kavajë and Krujë.

where it was, meaning that the total population of the municipality is now 421,286 residents (INSTAT 2011, 20).[24]

MIGRATORY PATTERNS

Patterns of internal migration over the last two decades display a complex typology, which nevertheless has many similar features with moves in earlier decades, although those were rather restricted. The most noted of these features is the direction of internal movements: from rural to urban areas, from the highlands to the valleys, and from the north and south towards the coastal west. The intensity of such moves, however, as well as accompanying challenges, remain very unique to the post-communist decades. Similarly unique in contemporary patterns is also the link between internal and international migration, considering that international migration was almost non-existent during the communist years.

Facing the sea: spatial and geo-administrative directions

Let us examine some of these patterns in more detail, starting with the direction of internal movements. First of all, there is a clear population shift from the north (especially the north-east), the south-central and south-east towards the western lowlands. More than 90% of all internal migrants moved in this direction between 1989 and 2001. The north contributed the most to this central-westward flow with 60% of its migrants moving in this direction (INSTAT 2004, 12). Top senders were the districts of Kukës, Tropojë, Dibër, and Pukë which by 2001 had lost approximately a third of their 1989 population due to internal migration (Carletto et al. 2004, 8; INSTAT 2004, 19). These are all geographically landlocked mountain areas, with some of the highest unemployment and poverty rates per capita in the country and very few opportunities to sustain livelihood locally (Lundström and Ronnås 2006, 24–25).

Second, within the coastal area of in-migration, the majority of migrants relocated to the Tirana-Durrës conurbation. The census records show that more than two thirds (72%) of inter-censual internal migrants moved to this area (INSTAT 2004, 13). The Tirana Prefecture alone hosted more than half of all internal migrants. At the district level, Tirana recorded a population increase of 36% due to in-migration; Durrës came second with 23% (Carletto et al. 2004, 9; INSTAT 2004, 19; Zezza, Carletto and Davis 2005, 189). Besides these, the other districts with the highest population increase in absolute numbers were Lushnjë, Fier and Vlorë—in that order, but gains were also recorded for Lezhë. This pattern is in fact a continuation of what had been taking place during the communist years, although at that time migration was almost always 'diverted' to rural areas (Borchert 1975; Sjöberg 1992).

Third, while most migrants settled in the coastal areas, the 'pairing of sending and host locations can be observed in some cases. For example, 70% of inter-prefecture

---

[24] For key readings on Tirana's development and growth as Albania's capital, see Aliaj et al. (2003), Carter (1986) and Pojani (2010a).

migrants from Kukës and Dibër moved to Tirana, where they constitute nearly half (47%) of all in-migrants. The vast majority of them have settled in the peri-urban area of Bathore, as we shall see later. Similarly, 30% of migrants from Shkodër (most likely from rural areas) moved to neighboring Lezhë (INSTAT 2004, 25). This pattern suggests chain migration as a strong influencing factor in increasing migrant communities. Indeed, ethnographic data confirm that often entire neighborhoods are reconstituted in host areas along blood-lines and kin relations, at times resembling exactly the patterns in their villages of origin (see, e.g. Bardhoshi 2001; also Çaro 2011; Tomini and Hagen-Zanker 2011).

Fourth, besides these country-wide trends, more local and regional shifts are also taking place. They continue to be directed from the remote mountainous hinterland towards the urban and peri-urban areas of their respective region, thus moving over shorter geographical distances. For example, the city of Shkodër has become a major destination for in-migration from its rural hinterland; according to census data more than half of in-migrants in this city came from the district of Malësia e Madhe (INSTAT 2004, 17). A similar pattern can be observed in Gjirokastër in the south, where the majority of the city's population increase is due to in-migration from the adjacent mountainous rural areas and from adjoining rural districts such as Tepelenë and Përmet (Kosta 2005). Similarly, the region of Korçë in the south-east displays such patterns of internal regional and local movements (Doka 2005).

These local movements are worthy of note as they help present a more complex picture, otherwise brushed over by the broad country-wide trends. They reveal that even within districts that are regarded as sources of out-migration from a country perspective, there are small pockets of in-migration, usually centered on the municipality of the district. For example, the Sarandë district is a major sender of migrants, yet the Sarandë municipality (town) is clearly a receiving zone (Zezza, Carletto and Davis 2005, 188).

Directions according to settlement types

Looking at settlement type, we can distinguish the following predominant directions:

Rural-urban
Post-communist internal migration has clearly increased Albania's urbanization, with regards to the total population living in urban areas. In the first inter-censual decade, nearly 60% of all in-migrants migrated to urban areas (INSTAT 2004). ALSMS data suggest that between 1990 and 2005, rural areas contributed 65% of internal migrants country-wide (World Bank 2007b, 34). Census data show that in the 1989–2001–2011 period the country's urban population increased from 35 to 42 to 54% of the total (respectively), primarily due to migration (INSTAT 2002; 2011). In contrast, rural areas have experienced severe population loses, especially in the northern and southern highlands.

Urban-urban
Although less systematically researched, these flows are not negligible. For instance, in 2001, two thirds of in-migrants to the city of Tirana came from other urban centers

(Heller et al. 2005, 70). ALSMS data suggest that between 1990 and 2005 nearly a third of internal migrants originated in urban areas, a share of which moved to other urban areas and Tirana (World Bank 2007b, 34). Important senders of these flows were the new towns—such as Bulqizë and Laç—created during the communist years to exploit mineral and energy sources, but which became pools of unemployment when these industries shuttered in the early 1990s (UNDP-Albania 2000). Since most of them were located in the mountainous north of the country, they are part of the much larger regional movement from that area towards the coast (Rugg 1994; Tirta 1999).

Rural-rural
According to INSTAT (2004, 15), around 40% of internal migrants who moved from one prefecture to another in the inter-censual period settled in rural areas. Almost half of these rural in-migrants relocated to the rural area of the Tirana prefecture, mostly in the informal peri-urban settlements. High levels of such migration are also noted for Durrës and Fier in terms of absolute numbers. With the exception of Durrës, Elbasan, Gjirokastër and Vlorë, in all other prefectures the share of rural in-migrants is higher than that of urban in-migrants. The trend and share were confirmed by ALSMS data as continuing well into 2005 (World Bank 2007b, 34).

Analyzing data from the 2002 and 2005 ALSMS, the World Bank team report an interesting change not only in the yearly fluctuation of internal flows, as noted in the previous section, but also in the direction of these flows. The critical turning point seems to be the year 1999, which witnessed a number of changes, the most important of which is the rise of Tirana as the most preferred destination. Before that, most rural migrants re-located either to rural areas or to other urban areas, not Tirana. Half of all internal migrants by 1999 preferred to settle in other urban areas. After this year, both rural-rural and rural-urban migration more generally experienced a sharp decrease to only about 2,000 migrants per year, leaving Tirana as the absolute dominant destination, where a third of internal migrants settle (World Bank 2007, 34). This interesting dynamic is almost certainly closely linked to the economic situation as well as to the various political shocks and social instabilities that the country went through during the majority of the 1990s, of which the collapse of the pyramid schemes and the near civil war that followed are probably the most significant. It is arguably also closely affected by international migration, which I discuss next.

Internal and international migration linkages

While the focus of this chapter is internal migration, the analysis would be incomplete without considering emigration as well. This is particularly crucial in the Albanian context, where both migration types are closely linked and used as parts of complex livelihood strategies by many individuals and families (King 2005; Vullnetari 2012). Emigration affects internal migration in a number of ways. First, remittances from abroad have been crucial in financing the internal movements of the residual family in Albania (Çaro 2011; King, Mai and Dalipaj 2003; Vullnetari 2012). For many youth in rural areas, especially in the North, it can be said that the road to Tirana has for a long time passed through Athens' Omonia Square,[25] or by boat across the Adriatic Sea (King, Mai and Dalipaj 2003; King and Vullnetari 2003). Second, an internal host location is often used as a stepping stone towards an international move. Such a sequence may see first an internal move away from the remoteness of village life in northern or southern Albania to a place in coastal/central Albania, which then acts as a platform both for a better life for the family as a whole, and for the emigration of some of its younger members abroad (King, Mai and Dalipaj 2003; Hagen-Zanker and Azzarri 2010). Third, an internal host location—often an urban area—becomes the place of settlement for international migrants upon their return from abroad. Forth, internal and international migration combines in complex ways to affect development in areas of origin and destination within Albania. I will turn to this aspect shortly. Finally, individual trajectories may overlap with family and household paths: at the same time as their individual family member(s) are moving abroad, many Albanian families from the rural north and south pursue a parallel, internal migratory strategy to secure their long-term future in Albania (King, Mai and Dalipaj 2003; Vullnetari 2012). At other times, several members of the same family will pursue parallel migration paths abroad in different countries.

In terms of sequences of internal migration, the existing literature provides several examples pointing to a complex set of moves. Besides the direct moves from rural areas to the cities, there is also a process of step-wise migration to be observed. Particularly interesting in this pattern are smaller towns that act as stepping stones to the final destinations. Becker (2005, 83–87), for instance, shows how the town of Bajram Curri in the north has become an important transit point for many villagers from its surrounding hinterland, who aim to ultimately settle in the Tirana-Durrës area. This may not be the final destination, as settling in this conurbation may open up opportunities for another move, this time abroad. Analyzing data from the 1989 and 2001 censuses, Agorastakis and Sidiropoulos (2007, 480) argue that internal mobility appears to have become more apparent towards the time (the late 1990s) when large-scale international migration flows started to decline. Linked to this will have been the financial capital that international migrants sent from abroad, which was in turn used to enable an internal move, as noted earlier.

Characteristics of internal migrants

Census data[26] reveal three key characteristics of internal migration, at least for the first post-communist decade. To begin, migrants are young—almost 46% of inter-prefecture migrants being younger than 30 years by 2001. Second, there is an internal 'brain drain' as migrants are more highly educated than the population they leave behind, and some strands equally if not more educated than non-migrant populations in their host locations. Third, there is a feminisation of internal migration in terms of numbers, as more than half (54%) of migrants are women. The same three trends are also confirmed to have been relevant until 2005 according to ALSMS data (World Bank 2007b, 39).

---

25 This square in Athens was used as an informal labour market where Albanian migrants waited to be picked up by Greek employers for—often casual and manual—jobs.
26 This section is based on INSTAT (2004) unless otherwise referenced.

Although the above findings are hold on a country-wide scale, there are some differences to note for migrant groups originating in various parts of the country. For example, those younger migrants are more pronounced amongst those moving from the north, reflected also in the figures of the population registers in areas with a high concentration of such migrants as Kamëz. Here, more than a third of the population was under 15 years old by 2007 while the average age was 27 (Kamëz Municipality 2008, 15). In these migrant streams from the north, there is also a gender balance in shares of men and women, which together with a large share of children suggests a typical family migration. This family character of migration is confirmed by ethnographic research amongst northern migrants living in peri-urban Tirana (Cila 2006; Çaro 2011), as well as quantitative data (2005 ALSMS; see Hagen-Zanker and Azzarri 2010). In slight contrast, those moving from the south and the south-east are slightly older than this first group (although younger than the populations they leave behind). Women, by far, outnumber men thereby suggesting a tendency towards independent female migration, alongside family movements. Indeed, as shown earlier, my own research on internal migration from the rural south-east to Tirana and Korçë emphasised the significance and importance of such independent migration of young women, particularly to Tirana (Vullnetari 2012). Higher shares of women compared to men for southern migrants may also be the result of greater numbers of men from the south having emigrated abroad, while their residual families move internally.

Furthermore, we note the higher levels of education amongst all internal migrants compared to the populations they leave behind in their respective areas of origin. Comparing the two groups of migrants suggests that those from the south and south-east have higher levels of education than those originating in the north and north-east. This would be expected not only given the respective age difference, as noted earlier, but also the difference in socio-economic conditions of the two regions as is widely known. On a country-wide level, this data suggests a flight of the higher educated and skilled from rural to urban areas, from the periphery to the coastal/centre, with Tirana being the biggest beneficiary of such moves. Ethnographic research amongst internal migrant communities confirms this internal 'brain drain', which negatively impacts— especially rural—areas of origin (Vullnetari 2012).

INTERNAL MIGRATION AND KEY DEVELOPMENT TRENDS

There are a number of issues that are closely linked to how internal migration interacts with processes of social and economic development in Albania, whether on their own or through the mediation of international migration. In this last section of the chapter I focus on two key aspects, selected here because of their perceived prominence in the relevant literature.

Challenges of urbanization and population distribution

One of the key impacts of internal movements in Albania is urbanization. Indeed, as we noted earlier, just over half of the country's population now lives in urban areas, just enough to make it qualify as an urbanized nation. However, a number of remarks are in order at this point. First, urbanization has been increased not only by the obvious rural-urban migration, but also through the more indirect route of rural-rural movements. That is to say that some host rural areas have become 'urbanized' owing to their increased population size and density, as well as their economic structure being dominated by urban activities. The classic example is that of the Kamzë municipality which gained urban status in 1996, reflecting its rapid population growth from around 6,000 inhabitants in 1989 to nearly 50,000 by 1996. As rural (and other) migrants are generally in the young working and reproductive ages, urban population growth is also affected by the higher fertility of the in-coming migrants (see e.g. Hagen-Zanker and Azzarri 2010).

A second remark is that urbanization is clearly a spatially concentrated phenomenon, characterized by a skewed population distribution around the Tirana-Durrës magnet, but also, more generally, along the littoral. By 2001, nearly half (47%) of Albania's urban population lived in the five biggest municipalities (with more than 75,000 people) with 23% of the urban population residing in Tirana alone (World Bank 2007a, 7).

Third and connected to the second is that while the Tirana-Durrës metropolitan area and other coastal zones have, in general, experienced significant *population densities*, several rural areas of origin have been depleted beyond sustainability (see e.g. migrants' stories in Çaro 2011). For example, the preliminary results of the latest census reveal that the Tirana municipality has a population density of nearly 11,000 inhabitants/km², significantly higher than the country's average of around 100 and beyond comparison with the Leskovik municipality (south-east) which has the lowest density at just below 2 inhabitants/km². This affects the provision of social and health care while impacting the cost-effectiveness of other structural investments, perpetuating the cycle of deterioration.

This population concentration has not been accompanied, let alone guided, by forward looking policy action. Most policy documents produced at the national or local level often look like reviews of past trends and current situations, rather than the forward thinking and long-term visionary plans that they ought to be. As a result, social services and public infrastructure have been put under severe strain making residents' life an everyday struggle. Examples abound with regards to the overpopulation of public schools in the city, the lack of schools in peri-urban areas, a great deficit in public health centers outside of key city centers, traffic congestion especially inside the Tirana orbital (which is often grid-locked throughout the day), inadequate public transport services especially for peri-urban areas, the neglect of solid waste management and of public green spaces and very high air and noise pollution (see also Pojani 2011). The problems are compounded in Tirana, but other major urban areas face similar challenges, albeit on a much smaller scale.

Migration, poverty and gendered social change

Shifting our attention now from the macro- and meso-level to the more micro-level, this last segment of the chapter discusses the impact of internal migration on migrants and their families, a much debated issue in the Albanian context. Most literature seems to find positive outcomes, albeit with some qualifying caveats. For example, in her study of rural migrants in Bathore, Cila (2006) found that migrants' livelihoods had, in general, improved after migration. Using a livelihood framework to assess change in well-being and collecting data through her own survey, she found that although incomes were higher than prior to migration, so were living expenses. Furthermore, incomes were more precarious and volatile. Positive outcomes were noted regarding the number of years of education and increased knowledge, albeit with some gender differences that disadvantaged women. More uncertain was the evaluation of migrants' health status, which although reported fine in general, can be scrutinized following the uncovering of problems related to inadequate sanitary conditions, travel distances to hospitals and under-the-table payments. Deda and Tsenkova (2006) were less optimistic as their findings show that despite higher incomes, peri-urban households often still lived in poverty due to increased expenses for public services such as electricity, sewage and garbage disposal. Analysing ALSMS data, Zezza, Carletto and Davis (2005) discuss a re-location of poverty from the rural north to peri-urban Tirana. Similarly pessimistic is the picture presented by Hagen-Zanker and Azzarri (2010) who, analyzing the 2005 ALSMS data, compare migrants in peri-urban Tirana with rural non-migrants. They suggest that although migrants' incomes have increased, this is not necessarily accompanied by an improvement in living conditions, as living expenses are now also higher, while employment is unstable in part-time jobs of the informal economy. Indeed, the Kamëz municipality (2008, 14) reports a 50% unemployment rate in the greater Kamëz area (including Bathore and other peri-urban areas), a rate much higher than the national average and even higher than some rural areas. Women are less likely to be formally employed than their rural counterparts, although it must be acknowledged that almost all employment of rural women is in the agricultural family plot—hardly emancipating work. Time is a crucial factor in increasing well-being, as those who have settled are more likely to have better jobs and living conditions, compared to recent arrivals that are poorer and live in more precarious situations.

Other recent research suggests that migrants address their mercurial job situations and difficult living conditions by relying on their kinship and friends networks, thus receiving much-needed support (Tomini and Hagen-Zanker 2009). However, financial transfers were more important than goods and services, reflecting the increased individualization of post-migratory relationships, as well as the change in the economic structure of the household economy and activities. Migration to urban and peri-urban areas also seems to increase the importance of friends, over more distant kinship relations, although more solid ethnographic research is needed to confirm such trends.

The question then naturally rises: why do migrants keep moving to the cities, despite obvious poverty and unstable jobs? The expectation that things will improve in the future seems to prevail over the crushed hopes and desires that village life has to offer (Todaro 1969). An analysis of macro-data suggests that economic growth and poverty reduction are strongly related to urbanization, making it 'the best hope of escaping poverty' in Albania (Pojani 2010b).

More recent in-depth ethnographic research in the Kamëz peri-urban areas provides a fuller view of how internal migrants themselves perceive their new life and future in their host locations (Çaro 2011). Despite the various challenges and difficulties, they feel empowered by the migration experience, hold that their lives have definitely improved and more importantly, that the future will be even better. Such findings may reflect the earlier argument that time is important in delivering positive change, and Çaro's research has captured migrants' lives nearly between one and two decades after they settled, and certainly several years later than all previous studies. In fact, one of her findings is that the length of residence is crucial for the positive outcome of migration. And things do get better for women especially, Çaro finds, despite the various challenges they face in their patriarchal homes and patriarchal environment where they settle.

CONCLUSION

The last 20 years of post-communist transformations have witnessed tremendous social and economic change for Albania and its people, including internal and international migrations of epic proportions. Both migration types reflect inventive and practical responses of Albanian individuals and families to the emerging geography of opportunities after the collapse of the communist regime. They have contributed to a re-distribution of demographic, economic and social resources country-wide in a contrasting process to the centrally planned economy of the communist years. Internal migration has emerged as a key component of this re-constitution, not least through its role in the country's increased urbanization. Tirana and its peri-urban areas—especially Bathore—are examples *par excellence* of the rapid and wild, yet necessary urbanization that has taken place in almost complete absence of complementary policy country-wide. Understandably, most research has focused on migration to this area, as well as its associated economic, structural, social and cultural impacts. Yet this migration represents only one type of internal movement, given its high homogeneity in terms of areas of migrants' origin (north and north-east). It certainly is *not* representative of *all* internal migration, as diverging results presented in this chapter show. It is thus time to widen the scope of research to other types of internal migrants beyond those living in Kamëz/Bathore. For example, we know very little regarding how their migration and settlement differs (if at all) from those moving to urban areas—e.g. in the dilapidated former industrial complexes—or from those moving to other cities, let alone to rural areas such as in the south.

Moreover, it is important to recognize the role that gender plays in data collection and subsequent analysis. Quantitative surveys—whether those administered through ALSMS teams or by individual researchers—almost always ask the household head for responses concerning the entire household. Generally, and especially in Albania, these are men. For example, 96% of household heads sampled in a 2008 survey in peri-urban Tirana were men (Tomini and Hagen-Zanker 2009). While men's opinions are valid in their own right, they cannot be generalized across the board without some qualification for gender bias, especially when it concerns information on migration motivations or decision-making. The gendered and generational negotiations of power brought by more ethnographic and gender-aware research is all the more valuable in this context (see e.g. Çaro 2011; Vullnetari 2012).

Considering the high rate of international migration and the complex ways in which it has been intertwined with internal moves, as various studies discussed in this chapter have also shown, it is equally imperative that future research brings the analysis of these two migration types together. This is necessary, particularly to help understand the developmental impacts of these linked migration types, including its effects on rural areas of origin and vulnerable groups such as older people left behind on their own (see e.g. Vullnetari and King 2006).

Above all, sound research needs to inform policy—whether at national or local level—in order to deal with the challenges that migrants as well as cities and villages are experiencing as a result of such massive population moves, and to better anticipate and plan for the future. Migration is a normal aspect of social change and transformation, and should be taken into consideration as such in planning and development action. In so doing, it is important to listen to migrants' voices in order to understand their reality, and appreciate that behind numbers and figures, beyond the 'ruralization of urban areas' by '*çeçen*' or '*malok*'[27], are fellow human beings with dreams and desires for a better life.

REFERENCES

Agorastakis, Michalis and Sidiropoulos, Giorgos. 2007. "Population Change due to Geographic Mobility in Albania, 1989–2001, and the Repercussions of Internal Migration for the Enlargement of Tirana," *Population, Space and Place* 13, 471–81.

Aliaj, Besnik, Klejda Lulo and Genci Myftiu. 2003. *Tirana: The Challenge of Urban Development*. Tirana: Cetis.

Arrehag, Lisa, Örjan Sjöberg and Mirja Sjöblom. 2005. "Cross-Border Migration and Remittances in a Post-Communist Society: Return Flows of Money and Goods in Korçë District, Albania," *South-Eastern Europe Journal of Economics* 3, 9–40.

Bardhoshi, Nebi. 2011. "An Ethnography of Land Market in Albania's Post-Socialist Informal Areas," *Urbanities* 1, 11–20.

Becker, Hans. 2005. "Small Towns in Northern Albania as Part of a Chain Migration from Periphery to Centre," *Geographical Studies* 16, 83–87.

Bërxholi, Arqile. 2000. *Regjistrimet e Përgjithshme të Popullsisë në Shqipëri: Vështrim Historik* [*Censuses in Albania: A Historical Perspective*]. Tirana: Academy of Sciences, Geographical Studies Centre.

Bërxholi, Arqile, Dhimitër Doka and Hartmut Asche. 2003. *Demographic Atlas of Albania*. Tirana: Ilar.

---

27 Derogatory words meaning 'uncouth and tribal highlanders' used in Albanian public discourse to refer to in-migrants from rural areas, especially from the north.

Borchert, Johan G. 1975. "Economic Development and Population Distribution in Albania," *Geoforum* 6, 177–86.

Carletto, Gero, Benjamin Davis, Marco Stampini and Alberto Zezza. 2004. "Internal Mobility and International Migration in Albania'. FAO/ESA Working Paper 04–13, Rome.

Carter, Francis W. 1986. "Tirana: City Profile," *Cities* 3, 270–81.

Cila, Jorida. 2006. "Making a livelihood: A study of rural migrants in Bathore, Tirana" (MA theses, University of Rotterdam).

Çaro, Erka. 2011. "From the Village to the City: The Adjustment Process of Internal Migrants in Albania". Amsterdam: Rozenberg Publishers (PhD diss., University of Groningen).

Deda, Luan and Tsenkova, Sasha. 2006. "Poverty and Inequality in Greater Tirana: The Reality of Peri-Urban Areas," in *The Urban Mosaic of Post-Socialist Europe*, edited by Sasha Tsenkova and Zorica Nedovic-Budic (Heidelberg: Physica Verlag), 151–70.

Dervishi, Zyhdi. 2001. "Urbanizimi i jetës së popullsisë fshatare apo ruralizimi i qyteteve? Rasti i Tiranës [Urban life of rural migrants or urban ruralisation? The case of Tirana]," *Politika dhe Shoqëria*, 1(8), 33-42.

Doka, Dhimitër. 2005. "Zhvillime Socio-Ekonomike dhe Rajonale të Shqipërisë pas Vitit 1990 [Albania's Post-1990 Socio-Economic and Regional Developments]," *Geographical Studies* 24. Postdam: Institute of Geography and Geoecology, University of Postdam.

Felstehausen, Herman. 1999. "Urban growth and land-use changes in Tirana, Albania: with cases describing urban land claims" (Land Tenure Center Working Paper 31, University of Wisconsin-Madison).

Hagen-Zanker, Jessica and Carlo Azzarri. 2010. "Are Internal Migrants in Albania Leaving for the Better?" *Eastern European Economics* 48, 57–84.

Heller, Wilfried, Dhimitër Doka and Arqile Bërxholi. 2005. "Tirana, Mbajtësja e Shpresës: Migrimi në Kryeqytetin e Shqipërisë [Tirana, Retaining the Hope: Migration to Albania's Capital]," *Studime Gjeografike* 15, 63–74.

INSTAT. 2011. *Preliminary Results of the Population and Housing Census 2011, Albania*. Tirana: Instituti i Statistikës.

INSTAT. 2004. *Migration in Albania, 2001 REPOBA*. Tirana: Instituti i Statistikës.

INSTAT. 2002. *The Population of Albania in 2001: Main Results of the Population and Housing Census.* Tirana: Instituti i Statistikës.

Kamëz Municipality. 2008. *Development Strategy 2008–2015.* Kamëz Municipality.

King, Russell. 2005. "Albania as a Laboratory for the Study of Migration and Development," *Journal of Southern Europe and the Balkans* 7, 133–56.

King, Russell and Vullnetari, Julie. 2003. "Migration and Development in Albania" (Development Research Centre on Migration, Globalisation and Poverty, Working Paper C5, University of Sussex).

King, Russell and Vullnetari, Julie. 2006. "Orphan Pensioners and Migrating Grandparents: The Impact of Mass Migration on Older People in Rural Albania," *Ageing and Society* 26, 783–816.

King, Russell, Nicola Mai and Mirela Dalipaj. 2003. *Exploding the migration myths: Analysis and recommendations for the European Union, the UK and Albania.* London: The Fabian Society and Oxfam.

King, Russell, Esmeralda Uruçi and Julie Vullnetari. 2011. "Albanian Migration and its Effects in Comparative Perspective," *Balkan and Near Eastern Studies* 13, 269–86.

Korça Regional Council. 2005. *Regional Development Strategy, Millennium Development Goals: Korça Region.* Korça Regional Council.

Kosta, Valentina. 2005. "Ndryshimet Gjeodemografike në Rrethin e Gjirokastrës gjatë Periudhës 1989–2001: Konkluzione dhe Rekomandime [Geo-Demographic Changes in the District of Gjirokastër during 1989–2001: Conclusions and Recommendations]," *Studime Gjeografike* 15: 112–19.

Laczko, Frank. 2008. "Migration and Development: The Forgotten Migrants," in *Migration and Development Within and Across Borders: Research and Policy Perspectives on Internal and International Migration*, edited by Josh DeWind and Jennifer Holdaway (Geneva and New York: IOM and the Social Science Research Council), 7-11.

Lerch, Mathias and Wanner, Philippe. 2008. "Demographic Data in Albania: Results of an Assessment" (Geneva University Working Paper).

Lulo, R. 2005. "Probleme të Urbanizimit në Shqipëri [Problems of Urbanisation in Albania]," *Studime Gjeografike* 15, 95–102.

Lundström, Susanna and Ronnås, Per. 2006. "Migration and Pro-Poor Growth in Albania: An Integrated Economic Analysis" (SIDA Country Economic Report 5, Stockholm).

Misja, Vladimir and Vejsiu, Ylli. 1990. *Shtesa e Popullsisë së Tiranës nga Lëvizjet Mekanike* [The Expansion of Tirana's Population through Mechanical Movements]. Tirana: The Academy of Sciences.

Pojani, Dorina. 2011. "From Carfree to Carfull: The Environmental and Health Impacts of Increasing Private Motorisation in Albania." *Journal of Environmental Planning and Management* 54, 319–35.

Pojani, Dorina. 2010a. "Tirana: City Profile," *Cities* 27, 483–95.

Pojani, Dorina. 2010b. "Urbanization of Post-Communist Albania: Economic, Social, and Environmental Challenges," *Debatte: Journal of Contemporary Central and Eastern Europe* 17, 85–97.

Rugg, Dean S. 1994. "Communist Legacies in the Albanian Landscape," *Geographical Review* 84, 59–73.

Sjöberg, Örjan. 1994. "Rural Retention in Albania: Administrative Restrictions on Urban-Bound Migration," *East European Quarterly* 28, 205–33.

Sjöberg, Örjan. 1992. "Urbanisation and the Zero Urban Growth Hypothesis: Diverted Migration in Albania," *Geografiska Annaler* 74B, 3–19.

Tirana Regional Council. 2005. "Millennium Development Goals: Global Targets, Local Approaches. Tirana Regional Report," Tirana Regional Council.

Tirta, Mark. 1999. "Migrime të Shqiptarëve, të Brendshme dhe Jashtë Atdheut: Vitet '40 të Shek.XIX-Vitet '40 të Shek.XX [Internal and International Migration of Albanians: 1840s–1940s]," *Etnografia Shqiptare* 18.

Todaro, Michael. 1969. "A Model of Labour Migration and Urban Unemployment in Less Developed Countries," *The American Economic Review* 59, 138–48.

Tomini, Florian and Jessica Hagen-Zanker. 2009. "How has Internal Migration in Albania Affected Transfers Amongst Kinship Members?" (Maastricht Graduate School of Governance Working Paper 2009/013, University of Maastricht).

UNDP-Albania. 2000. "Albanian Human Development Report 2000". Tirana: UNDP Albania.

Vullnetari, Julie. 2012. *Albania on the Move: Links between Internal and International Migration*. Amsterdam: Amsterdam University Press.

World Bank. 2007a. "Albania Urban Sector Review," (World Bank Working Paper no. 37277-AL, Washington, DC).

World Bank. 2007b. "Albania Urban Growth, Migration and Poverty Reduction: A Poverty Assessment," (World Bank Working Paper no. 40071-AL, Washington, DC).

Zezza, Alberto, Gero Carletto and Benjamin Davis. 2005. "Moving Away from Poverty: A Spatial Analysis of Poverty and Migration in Albania," *Journal of Southern Europe and the Balkans* 7, 175–93.

DANIEL GÖLER, DHIMITËR DOKA

"SHOULD I STAY OR SHOULD I GO?" OUT-MIGRATION, RETURN MIGRATION AND DEVELOPMENT IN ALBANIA – THE MIGRATION-DEVELOPMENT-NEXUS AT A DANGEROUS CROSSROADS

INTRODUCTION

Migration is a hallmark of Albanian society. Migration—or, more precisely: emigration—forms an established pattern of social resilience that runs like a thread through epochs of Albanian history. The Albanian language even has a special word, *kurbet*, for the experience of journeying from home and sojourning in foreign places. It is only logical, then, that migration was once more seen as an option by huge numbers of people in the immediate aftermath of the opening of the country at the end of the restrictive Communist era. Today, it is estimated that 45.4% of the total population of Albania have experience of migration (data from 2010; World Bank 2011, 54). Remittances in the form of cash and in-kind transfers from migrants have secured the economic survival of numerous families during the two difficult decades this period of transformation has lasted until now, and they have even, not infrequently, provided families with the basis for a reasonably comfortable standard of living. Migrants are, therefore a mainstay of the Albanian economy.

Or is that a truism which has already become dated? Familiar migration patterns and the explanations that have been offered for them appear in a new light against the backdrop of the global economic crisis that has been on-going since 2008. Numerous Albanians in Greece, the main destination for Albanian emigrants, have been hit hard by the crisis that has engulfed their host country, and parallel developments elsewhere have also been observed. Given the dramatically altered circumstances, the question as to the consequences of migration in East and South East Europe, and especially in Albania, must now be evaluated afresh. This is especially relevant for the question of positive and negative interdependencies between migration and development in the sending countries (Castles and Miller 2009, 59-63).

In what follows, an outline of pre-crisis findings on migration, development and entrepreneurial activity in Albania that are documented extensively elsewhere shall first be given (Göler 2007, 2011, 2012; Nikas and King 2005; Labrianidis and Hatziprokopiou 2005; Kilic et al. 2009; Germenji and Milo 2009; King et al. 2011). This will form the departure point for a discussion of the currently foreseeable consequences of recent and current crisis-induced return migration to Albania and its possible effects. While the question "Should I stay or should I go?" is typically not one that has even presented itself to many emigrants from other Eastern European countries (the "stayers" abroad generally dominate; Apsite et al. 2012), a reversal of previous migration patterns seems perceptible in the Albanian context, although a clear pattern has yet to emerge. It thus seems appropriate to follow up on an earlier theses of the present author (Göler 2007, 205) and suggest a differentiated approach to evaluating return migration characterized by success during the period of political and economic stabilization and the economic upswing after 2000 (to which migrants made a substantial contribution!) in contrast to recent crisis-induced remigration. While these 'older' patterns were supported by robust empirical research, insights into more recent developments are based primarily on an analysis of the current discourse on return migration in the Albanian media, in which the topic is strongly represented. This contribution aims less to predict the future course of Albanian development than to show (possible) positive and negative effects of remigration from a spatial and societal perspective.

SHIFTS IN THE FRAMEWORK OF ACTION: FROM OPPORTUNITY-DRIVEN TO CRISIS MIGRATION

Recent global economic problems and the financial crisis in parts of Europe have affected international migration significantly (Findlay et al. 2010). This also holds true for Albania, although the impact of the global crisis on the Albanian economy itself seems to have been relatively weak thus far. That can be attributed to both the country's relative insignificance in economic terms (on a global scale) and its low level of integration into the world economy. In this regard, emigration has had a stabilizing effect up to now and has lent itself to interpretation as a factor boosting development: migration removed pressure from the domestic labor market, and at the same time, remittances and migrants' businesses stimulated the economy directly.

The negative effects of economic problems in the areas that formed the main destinations for emigration in the past two decades of transformation in Albania are now exacting a particular toll through the current wave of return migration. These effects cause Albanian emigration and remigration to appear in a very different light. Not all that long ago, the considerable pool of savings amassed by Albanians abroad was viewed almost euphorically (DeZwager et al. 2005, for example)—linked as it was to the expectation that migrants would bring these savings with them on their return. This has now given way to a much more sober outlook. While return migration in the first decade of the new millennium could, following Cerase (1974) still often be characterized as a 'return of success', return migration since 2010 increasingly seems to fall into the category 'return of failure'. In practice, a wave of return migration of Albanians from Italy and, in particular, from Greece, has been triggered and may continue to gather considerable momentum. It is believed that 180,000 Albanians have returned from Greece alone in the last five years, a number that would correspond to a fifth of all emigrants[28] to Greece (Tirana Times, 5-11 October 2012, p. 7-8).

Returning to Albania has always been a component in the long-term life planning of many emigrants (cf. Labrianidis and Hatziprokopiou 2005). The option of returning home is one that people have kept open, especially those who migrated to European destinations in proximity to Albania, such as Greece and Italy. Life abroad is often not

---

28 Use of the term migration (and by extension the terms emigration and remigration) presupposes—according to the UN definition—absence from the previous place of residence lasting for at least one year.

accepted as permanent, but seen more as a stage in the life trajectory of individuals. A sojourn abroad mainly serves to fulfill a particular purpose, such as providing for a family that has remained in Albania or being able to maintain a certain standard of living upon returning there. Return migration, then, is not problematic in itself—earlier studies suggested that 56% of migrants (DeZwager et al. 2005, 21) were potential returnees—but can become so if its timing is inopportune and it takes place too early or too late in individual biographies. In the first case, the stay abroad may not have sufficed to generate enough capital. In the second, as in the case of families with adolescent children, the return may come at an awkward point in the life trajectories of family members.

From both a social and an economic standpoint, the key problem raised by return migration has its origins in Albania itself. The prevailing conditions affecting not only migration, but also daily life in the country have barely changed. Albanian politics and civil society are still characterized by corruption, clientele politics, and rigid and unreliable governance; these factors go hand in hand with a high rate of unemployment, a lack of individual life opportunities, an abundance of jobs requiring unskilled labor, all of which result in brain drain and brain waste. Those are precisely the factors that drove numerous Albanians to emigrate, and they have remained constants in Albanian society for two decades. This partially answers the question as to the outcome of the migration-development nexus; it would seem that it has not, thus far, been possible for Albania's 'migration society' to create the basis for long-term economic stability and the functioning of civil society in the country. This means that (possible) return migration is connected with a high degree of risk and uncertainty (Williams and Baláž 2011), comparable with the out-migration years ago.

ALBANIAN MIGRATION REVISITED: PHASES OF RECENT ALBANIAN (E-)MIGRATION

The beginning of the post-communist period in Albania witnessed a sweeping mobilization of society (Barjaba 2000). After the political changeover, migration represented an escape valve for structural deficits and individual needs and necessities that had accumulated over time. This applies both to internal migration (Barjaba and King 2005; Göler 2009; Doka and Göler 2010) and to emigration. As the first decade of transformation drew to a close, almost 750,000 Albanians had already left the country with its population of little more than 3 million (figure for 1999; Vullnetari 2007, 36). Of these, 500,000 had gone to Greece and 200,000 to Italy. In 2005, it was estimated that 1.1 million Albanians were emigrants (loc. cit.) and by 2010, the figure had climbed to 1.438 million (World Bank 2011, 54). In the early phase, migrants were often young, unmarried men who were willing—when necessary—to undertake the risks of illegal border crossings and live as illegal immigrants. Migrants to the Mediterranean region surrounding Albania generally held lower qualifications than the long-term emigrants who relocated to the USA or Canada. What had began typically as a back-and-forth labour migration took on a more permanent character after 1996/97, when the upheaval in Albania interrupted the country's economic and political transition and led to widespread and severe instability. Migration in family units and the reunification or starting of families abroad around this time demonstrate that the migration regime was becoming stable and life outside of Albania was taking on a more permanent character for many people.

REMITTANCES, RETURNEES, AND MIGRANTS' SAVINGS – HAS THE "MIGRATION-DEVELOPMENT-NEXUS" BEEN SEEN TOO OPTIMISTICALLY?

The most obvious and most timeless effect of emigration undoubtedly takes the form of remittances (Castles and Miller 2009, 59ff). These are duly given extensive consideration in the migration research literature dealing with Albania. 70% of migrants send remittances. The total volume of remittances sent rose from around USD 400 million (1994; DeZwager et al. 2005, 21) to USD 889 million (2003) before reaching its highest historical level of just under USD 1.5 billion in 2008 (World Bank 2011, 54). At times, it represented a fifth of the entire Albanian GDP—exceeding both the value of industrial production and the volume of direct foreign investment (DeZwager et al. 2005, 21). A figure of USD 1.285 million was estimated for 2010 (World Bank 2011, 54). This is still equivalent to a 13.7% share of GDP, although it does, at the same time, signal that the flow of private capital has fallen during the crisis period.

Research on how this money is spent has not yielded homogenous results (cf. King et al. 2011a, 277-279). The answer seems to depend strongly on regional, sectarian and individual contexts. In the agricultural sector, Müller and Munroe (2008) report that a 'rent seeking mentality' exists; agricultural production is abandoned in favor of living off what one or more family members can earn abroad. In contrast, Miluka et al. (2010) did not detect significant differences relating to the standard of technology in use or the income generated by 'migrant' and 'non-migrant' small farms. Similarly, it seems that only very minor differences, if any, can be established in relation to patterns of consumption and the consumer goods that households in receipt (or not) of transfers from abroad are equipped with (Arrehag et al. 2005). Remittances, then, are not necessarily useful as a criterion for identifying either those in poverty or the more comfortably off. Nevertheless, cash from abroad does constitute a considerable chunk of private budgets and "there is a corresponding risk of an over-reliance on remittances" (King et al. 2011a, 277). In the district of Korça for example, remittances comprised, on average, 35% of household income (Arrehag et al. 2005, 20). This finance thus constitutes a substantial part of the patchwork income structures that are typical for Albania (Göler 2005, 102). Together with state assistance, it often exceeds the monetary income generated *in situ* by families. Remittances play a particularly important role in providing a measure of social security in peripheral Albanian regions and for the material subsistence of the elderly population (Vullnetari and King 2008; King et al. 2011b). However, the hypothesis that this social security system was already vulnerable even in periods of economic success (Göler 2009, 493) is borne out by the most recent developments.

In addition to remittances, which are generally spent on consumption, entrepreneurship fed by capital from abroad forms a second and more important (because it is possibly more effective) pillar supporting the migration-development nexus. Returnees' business is widespread in South East Europe and did not begin only with the return home of guest workers from Yugoslavia. However, the intermeshing of migration and entrepreneurship seems to be tighter in Albania than anywhere else: a study on start-up businesses in the manufacturing sector (Göler 2007, 2012) showed that the establishment of a business had been preceded by emigration in 33 cases out of the 34 examined. This suggests that migration promotes the establishment of new enterprises and that a positive connection can be taken to exist between (e-)migration and economic development.

The first element in this causal chain is the generation of the necessary financial resources for setting up a business. In Albania, approximately 40% of the starting capital of new companies is earned through work abroad (UNDP 2000, 43). Nor should the transfer of technology and innovation in the form of knowledge acquired by emigrants be underestimated: the much-lamented brain drain and brain waste that goes hand in hand with emigration is mitigated to some extent by self-employed returning migrants. Such feedback effects can reach beyond the accumulation of capital and knowledge; some Albanian returnees had brought back the machinery needed for production from their host countries. They had bought the equipment second-hand which they had used abroad and were familiar with and imported it on their return. In such cases, it is preordained that the start-up companies operate in the same sector, or in a closely related one, and draw on proven technology and methods.

Some findings suggest that the migration-development nexus should not be interpreted particularly optimistically. One of the clear findings of the aforementioned study, which was conducted when Albania was booming and reflects the situation before the crisis, was the markedly low educational level held by many entrepreneurs. Only in a few cases did the new entrepreneurs have formal qualifications that were relevant to their respective sectors.

This trend was even more extreme in cases where individuals had founded companies outside of the sectors in which they had previously worked, often in areas in which they had little or no experience. As a rule, entrepreneurs invested in their own futures as self-employed businesspeople. Only in isolated cases did they act collectively (other than in family contexts), which would have made it possible to expand the resources available for founding their enterprises; pure equity investments were even more rare. This aversion to all forms of collective action, widespread throughout Albania, has its origins in the negative experiences of many during the communist and post-communist periods. The overall effect was that the capital stock of new companies was quite limited.

Most of these companies were, moreover, relatively basic, standardized manufacturing operations with little innovation in evidence. In light of the conditions outlined, it is clear that the small-scale and fragmented structures that have resulted from recent start-ups are largely uncompetitive in international terms. Most of these companies produce goods for the domestic market. This has at least had the economic effect of somewhat reducing the dominance of imported products that manifests itself even with regard to the most basic items. Finally, it is worth noting that an impressive degree of entrepreneurial dynamism has become evident, not least because of an all too frequent willingness to apply the principle of trial and error and an enormous tolerance of risk bordering on fatalism. The lack of a national re-migrant policy, the absence of state guidance, and the generally difficult conditions for the entrepreneurial activity of small and medium sized business have all also taken a certain toll.

An Albanian-Italian study prepared by the IOM (International Organization for Migration) shall be cited as a third empirical finding relating to the pre-crisis situation. This study established that Albanian migrants each saved an average of Euro 5,400 annually (DeZwager et al. 2005, IV and 61-64). In Greece alone, Albanians were thought to have amassed savings of over 2 billion Euros. At the same time, 56% of those surveyed stated their intention to return to Albania, on average 17-18 years after first migrating. The authors use this data to model a migration cycle according to which a wave of return migration would have been expected, as a long-term consequence of the first wave of emigration, for between 2010 and 2015, even without any crisis-related effects being factored in. The potential inflow of finance was valued at 10 to 15 billion Euros. As 40% of the returnees planned to invest money, it was anticipated that Albania would benefit from an investment reserve roughly of the order of 5 billion Euros.

A PRELIMINARY ATTEMPT TO TAKE STOCK: FROM PRE-CRISIS TO CRISIS MIGRATION

It can be established, then, that massive emigration after 1991 had both positive and negative consequences for Albania. Even with the hindsight we have today, the question remains open as to whether the resultant brain gain, or self-employed migrant entrepreneurship, was able to mitigate the effects of the previous brain drain and brain waste. The same applies to the question as to whether remittances were able to compensate for the generally poor economic situation, or the specific lack of social security provision by the state. Significant effects, in the sense of trends in economic development that are attributable to migration, became increasingly obvious from 2000 onwards. In the second decade of post-socialist transition, the country became markedly more stable and saw GDP growth rates of 5% to 10%. It can be assumed that this upswing was not related insignificantly to the effects of migration.

The same phenomena—emigration, remigration and circular migration—now need to be reassessed in the current third decade of Albania's transition and against the background of tectonic shifts in the choices facing people and the options available to them. At the level of individual choices made by migrants, the option of returning (Labrianidis and Kazazzi 2006) was always linked to a degree of freedom, but has become a dead end with limited room for maneuver sooner than expected for many. Headlines in Ekathimerini on September 12, 2011 like "The Greek crisis is forcing Albanian migrants to go home" are becoming commonplace in Albania's day-to-day media discourse and in the Greek and Italian media. How emigrants and return migrants cope with the new situation and what opportunities and problems result from the new constraints is a central question facing migration research. Our current state of knowledge suggests that the following thoughts could guide further consideration of the issues:

(1) The remigration currently taking place is not a completely new phenomenon, but one that draws on old and widespread paradigms for action. What is new is the current forced character of remigration, in particular from crisis-stricken Greece.
(2) Re-migrants leave a fundamentally altered (temporary) host society; at the same time, they encounter more or less unchanged economic, political and social conditions in Albania.
(3) 'New' returnees, such as those from Greece, bring influences from abroad back with them just as previous returnees did, irrespective of the now-altered conditions obtained abroad.

The central question now is whether these elements make the return easier or are more of a problem in the 'old new' home country. Can remigration in the Greek-Albanian context still be seen as a resource under the current conditions?

EFFECTS, PERCEPTION AND COMMUNICATION SURROUNDING CRISIS MIGRATION

The lives migrants lead are often more precarious than those of non-migrants. Phrases like 'First hired, first fired' (also cited by Gedeshi and DeZwager 2012) encapsulate their particularly high exposure to risk and their increased vulnerability. This is underscored by the fact that 26% of the Albanians employed in Greece are casually employed (Deutsche Welle 2011). What this means in practice is that they are employed on the black market, have no social safety net and are in particular, strongly affected by the impact of the crisis. Often enough, no option other than returning home remains open to them. The Greek newspaper Ekathimerini stated on September 3, 2011 that "The Greek crisis is forcing migrants to go back". The report cited the fact that 10% of the migrants living in Greece—most of them presumably Albanian—had already left the country.

The wave of return migrants that is now becoming apparent is mainly, but not exclusively, seen in negative terms in the media. A Deutsche Welle report from April 4, 2012 titled "Migrants leave Greece" described the situation of workers from Albania burdened with high debts and identified immigrants as particular victims of the crisis. This is in line with Gedeshi's findings on the situation of Albanians abroad, the potential return migrants, according to which the crisis has resulted in unemployment, but also and particularly to working hours being reduced, migrants being forced to switch to less skilled work, and a consequent decline in incomes. The average loss of income between 2008 and 2009 is estimated at 10.7% (Gedeshi et al., 247); this manifests itself particularly in people saving less. Initially, it seemed that migrants in Italy were more strongly affected, but the Greek crisis subsequently became much more acute in 2010. Various strategies for tackling the problem are mentioned in the study, mostly (still) formulated as options for remaining, although the possibilities of repatriating some family members or of entire households returning were already beginning to loom large for many at this point [29] (Gedeshi et al., 250).

However, the option of returning is also fraught with difficulties. In the case of families from rural villages, for example, their dwellings may be a state of disrepair and in need of investment - and this in villages that generally do not offer adequate opportunities for family members to earn a livelihood. Migrants often return to the time-consuming commutes over long distances they engaged in before emigrating in order to provide for their families at home. Given this context, it is understandable that many see their return to Albania not as a long-term decision, but only as a stepping-stone leading them on to one of the destinations in Western Europe that are now favored. These plans, in turn, are frequently thwarted by the difficulty of obtaining immigration documents and work permits.

Others opt to remain abroad in spite of the crisis. Shekulli takes up this theme, citing arguments like: "I'm not going back, the situation there is the same" (shekulli.com.al, March 29, 2012) and"I haven't sent anything to Albania for a year." The 'stayers', then, have reduced their expenditure and especially their remittances. This is echoed in a case from Italy mentioned by Gedeshi and DeZwager (2012, 251) involving a change in the direction of the flow of remittances ("I know of migrants that started to ask their families in Albania for money").

In relation to the effects in Albania itself, an increase in unemployment has been anticipated as a result of increased remigration (*Zëri i Amerikës / Voice of America*, February 19, 2012), and not only in relation to the south of the country. The "integration of children" has also been flagged as "difficult"; more than 260 children have already returned to Gjirokastër in southern Albania (*Zëri i Amerikës/ Voice of America*, 15 February 2012) and language barriers have created problems in local schools. This is only logical, since children born in Greece have possibly already attended school there and may well have spoken Albanian only at home, if at all.

More positive media coverage of remigration has focused mainly on the financial inflows and entrepreneurial input that might be expected from migrants: "The crisis in Greece means more investment for Albania", according to the pro-government Albanian newspaper *Gazeta 55* (April 1, 2012). *Shqiptari i Italisë* has reported on October 18, 2011 that "The Greek Crisis is bringing companies to Albania". This is more or less still the same status quo as in the period before the crisis (see above; Göler 2007); there are currently no indications, however, to suggest that the level of entrepreneurial investment in Albania is rising.

The *Voice of America* on 18 December 2010 has also picked up on another issue that highlights the complexity and the deep social roots of these processes: the return of Albanian migrants to the south of the country has, it seems, given added impetus to the process of obtaining retrospective planning permission for buildings erected informally (cf. Becker et al. 2005). A good 5% of the value of the building needs to be paid to the state as part of this process. The inflow of capital from abroad has expedited this process. In the district of Gjirokastër alone, 2000 buildings have now been registered.

---

29 The cited study covers the situation at the end of 2009, when Albanian return migration was just beginning to set in.

CONCLUSION

Against the general background of Albanian return migration, the personal migration experiences and resources of individuals, the context in which any possible return is embedded, and the future options that may be linked to that context are decisive. As the information we have at present is heterogeneous, any current assessment of the effects of the economic crisis on Albanian migration must necessarily arrive at ambivalent results.

This applies particularly to the question of the impact migration may have on development. Despite the changed circumstances of Albanian migration and its underlying motives, the key question as to the migration-development-nexus has not changed: the 'new' returnees, for example from Greece, continue to bring influences from abroad back with them, independently of the changed circumstances surrounding return migration. It is questionable whether these are all elements that make returning easier; return migration alone does not necessarily solve problems. The conditions and circumstances encountered by return migrants are decisive. Returnees both before and during the crisis period are equally embedded in a field with a large number of options and an equally large number of constraints. The reflux of capital with the associated level of investment and (re-)migrant entrepreneurship are still, now as then, harbingers of development for Albania. Little has changed, however, in relation to the lack of measures flanking these developments in the sense of a re-migrant policy. And it should not be overlooked that return migration (and the resulting cessation of remittances) undermines the foundations of a system of social support upon which many in Albania depend.

From an economic perspective, Albania can only profit from remigration: input from abroad still contains development potential for Albania, if only because the majority of returnees are of working age and many have extensive work experience. Examining the individual life trajectories of return migrants suggests, however, that the balance sheet may be more ambiguous. The key question as to the spatial and social differentiation of return migration remains to be addressed by geographical research. In this respect, Albania and its return migrants have now arrived at a *dangerous crossroads*.

REFERENCES

Apsite, Elina, Zaiga Krišjāne and Berzins Māris. 2012. "Emigration from Latvia under economic crisis conditions," *International Proceedings of Economics Development and Research* 31, 134-138.

---

30 A joint project carried out by the geography departments of the Universities of Bamberg and Tirana that will include interviews with returnees will supply more specific data here.

Arrehag, Lisa, Örjan Sjöberg and Mirja Sjöblom. 2005. "Cross-border migration and remittances in a post-communist society: return flows of money and goods in the Korçë district, Albania," *South Eastern Europe Journal of Economics* 1, 9-40.

Barjaba, Kosta. 2000. "Contemporary patterns in Albanian emigration," *South-East Europe Review for Labour and Social Affairs* 3, 57-64.

Barjaba, Kosta and King, Russell. 2005. "Introducing and theorising Albanian migration," in *The new Albanian migration*, edited by Russell King, Nikola Mai, Stephanie Schwandner-Sievers (Portland, Sussex: Academic Press), 1-28.

Becker, Hans, Alexander Blöchl, Dhimiter Doka, Daniel Göler, Merita Karaguni, Bernhard Köppen and Ralf Mai. 2005. "Industriesquatter in Tirana," *Europa Regional* 13/1, 12-20.

Castles, Stephen and Miller, Mark J. 2009. *The Age of Migration. International Population Movements in the Modern World*. New York, London: The Guilford Press.

Cerase, Francesco P. 1974. "Expectations and reality: A case study of return Migration from the United States to the Southern Italy," *International Migration Review* 8, 245-262.

DeZwager, Nicolaas, Ilir Gedeshi, Etleva Germenji and Christos Nikas. 2005. *Competing for Remittances*. Tirana: IOM.

Doka, Dhimitër and Göler, Daniel. 2010. "Migrimi në Shqipëri dhe ndikimi i presionit human në krijimin e parabarazive të zhvillimit rajonal dhe lokal," *Studime Albanologjike* 15, 279-287.

Findlay, Allan, Alistair Geddes and David McCollum. 2010. "International Migration and Recession," *Scottish Geographical Journal* 126, 299-320.

Gedeshi, Ilir and DeZwager, Nicolaas. 2012. "Effects of the global Crisis on Migration and remittances in Albania," in: *Migration and Remittances during the Global Financial Crisis and Beyond*, edited by Ibrahim Sirkeci, Jeffrey H. Cohen and Dilip Ratha (Washington: The World Bank), 237-254.

Germenji, Etleva and Milo, Lindita. 2009. "Return and labour status at home: evidence from returnees in Albania," *Southeast European and Black Sea Studies* 9, 497-517.

Göler, Daniel. 2005. „European Shrinking Regions. Applied Regional Geography in Peripheral Areas (with Case Studies from Albania and Germany)," *Studime Gjeografike* 16.

Göler, Daniel. 2007. „Entrepreneurship im Transformationskontext – Eine Analyse des regionalen Gründungsgeschehens in Südosteuropa (mit Beispielen aus Albanien und Serbien)," *Europa Regional* 15, 23-37.

Göler, Daniel. 2009. „Regionale und lokale Auswirkungen von Migration in Albanien," *Südosteuropa* 56, 472-499.

Göler, Daniel. 2011. „Returnee's Business in Südosteuropa: Remigration als Entwicklungspotential in Albanien?" in *Gesellschaften in Bewegung. Emigration aus und Immigration nach Südosteuropa in Vergangenheit und Gegenwart*, edited by Ulf Brunnbauer, Karolina Novinscak and Christian Voß (München, Berlin: Sagner) , 205-218.

Göler, Daniel. 2012. „Unternehmensgründungen und Entrepreneurship in den westlichen Balkanländern. Fallstudien aus Albanien, Bosnien-Herzegowina und Serbien," in *Inventer de nouveaux territoires. Comparaisons européenne*, edited by Jean-Baptiste Humeau and Martine Long (Angers: Presses de l'Université), 322-349

Kilic, Talip, Calogero Carletto, Benjamin Davis and Alberto Zezza. 2009. "Investing back home. Return migration and business ownership in Albania," *Economics of Transition* 17, 587–623.

King, Russell, Esmeralda Uruçi and Julie Vullnetari. 2011a. "Albanian migration and its effects in comparative perspective," *Journal of Balkan and Near Eastern Studies* 13/3, 271-286.

King, Russell, Adriana Castaldo and Julie Vullnetari. 2011b. "Gendered Relations and Filial Duties Along the Greek-Albanian Remittance Corridor," *Economic Geography* 87, 393-419.

Labrianidis, Lois and Hatziprokopiou, Panos. 2005. "The Albanian migration cycle: migrants tend to return to their country of origin after all," in *The new Albanian migration,* edited by Russell King, Nikola Mai and Stephanie Schwandner-Sievers (Portland, Sussex: Academic Press), 93-117.

Labrianidis, Lois and Kazazi, Brikena. 2006. "Albanian return-migrants from Greece and Italy: Their impact upon spatial disparities within Albania," *European Urban and Regional Studies* 13, 59-74.

Miluka, Juna, Carletto Gero and Benjamin Davis. 2010. "The Vanishing Farms? The Impact of International Migration on Albanian Family Farming," *Journal of Development Studies* 46, 140-161.

Müller, Daniel and Munroe, Darla K. 2008. "Changing rural landscapes in Albania: Cropland abandonment and forest clearing in the postsocialist transition," *Annals of the Association of American Geographers* 98, 855-876.

Nikas, Christos and King, Russell. 2005. "Economic growth through remittances: Lessons from the Greek experience of the 1960s applicable to the Albanian case," *Journal of Southern Europe and the Balkans* 7, 235-23-57.

UNDP. 2000. *Albanian Human Development Report 2000*. Tirana.

Vullnetari, Julie. 2007. "Albanian Migration and Development: State of the Art Review," IMISCOE Working Paper 18). Sussex.

Vullnetari, Julie and King, Russell. 2008. "'Does your granny eat grass?' On mass migration, care drain and the fate of older people in rural Albania," *Global Networks* 8, 139-171.

Williams, Allan M. and Baláž, Vladimir. 2011. "Migration, Risk, and Uncertainty: Theoretical Perspectives," *Population, Space and Place* 18, 197-180.

Worldbank. 2011. *Migration and Remittances Factbook 2011*. 2nd. Edition, Washington.

VASSILIS NITSIAKOS

ALBANIAN MIGRANTS TO EPIRUS (GREECE) AFTER 1990:
TRANSNATIONAL MIGRATION DECONSTRUCTED

THE ETHNOGRAPHIC CONTEXT

I would like to begin by relating a series of incidents that occurred during my ethnographic fieldwork along the Greek-Albanian frontier and especially on the Greek side, in the province of Konitsa (region of Epirus), in order to contextualize my argument as well as render the special atmosphere concerning the 'transnational space' created in the area after 1990.

First incident: On a beautiful day at the beginning of April 2002, wandering very near to the borderline, close to the border-post of Prosilio, which is around 10 km away from the town of Konitsa, I came across two Albanians on horseback returning to their village, Radat. They were coming from the Greek village, Agia Varvara, where they work, and hence, travel this road on a daily basis. They cross the border almost every day without any official permission, but with the consent of the local population, a fact to which local authorities turn a blind eye. From my research it came out that these men are almost daily visitors to the specific village offering a wide range of services from construction of any kind to gardening and even taking care of houses whose owners are absent. It happens that a relatively large number of Albanians from villages along the border commute on a daily or weekly basis to work in Greek villages across the border with or without the necessary documents.

Second incident: On Friday afternoon, during the spring of 2002, I was in the border zone village of Molyvdoskepastos. The border is about 500 meters from the village church, at the edge of the settlement. As we drink and chat with the villagers in a café on the central road, I observe a group of children, who look like school children, walking towards the border. I inquire about them and find out that they are children from the nearby Greek-speaking Albanian villages of Vllahopsilloterrë and Biovizhdë, who study in schools in Konitsa; they stay in residence halls and boarding homes during the week and return to their villages on the weekends, via the military outpost of Molyvdoskepastos, which functions unofficially as a customs point for the people of this area.

Third incident: In October 1996 a man from a Vlach village of Pindus, told me about an incident that occurred to him while he was transporting his animals by trucks from the mountain village to the winter pastures. A policeman belonging to the local patrol police stopped the trucks to check for illegal Albanian immigrants. Upon discovering one, the policeman arrested him in order to send him back to Albania and verbally insulted him. The owner protested against this behaviour explaining at the same time that the arrested man was a Vlach like himself, belonging as he said, to the most genuine part of Hellenism, and that the Greek state and its representatives should be more careful and sensitive towards them. After a long and very tense discussion and threats from the shepherd that he would protest to the police headquarters, the Albanian was released and joined the caravan on its journey to the plains. It is noteworthy that in all the pastoral villages of the wider area there are a great number of Albanian shepherds employed, who move along with the herds from the mountains to the plains and vice versa twice a year. In the first period of the Albanian exodus to Greece most of the shepherds employed in Vlach villages were Albanian Vlachs.

Fourth incident: In the summer of 1999 in my home village of Aetomilitsa, I heard, in the middle of the day, a noise and became aware of a strange commotion in the village. I sought to understand what was transpiring and witnessed various Albanians running away towards the mountain or trying to hide in village basements and huts. After a short while, I see a police car in the village square and some Albanians being arrested and led by the police to be deported via the customs station of Kakavia. During this time of year, about 40 Albanians work in the village as shepherds and that same number in construction sites. Most of them do not have the required documents, the so called 'papers', and, as a result, are considered 'illegal migrants'. In a discussion with the village authorities, I confirm what I more or less already know, that there exists a silent agreement with the police to tolerate the migrants, so that 'the village is serviced'. Every time something like this happens, it means someone has 'snitched' for personal reasons, usually revenge against a particular Albanian or even a fellow villager and so the situation is reversed for at least a few days. The village authorities, however, consider it their duty to renew this silent agreement with the police, even using their connections with high standing politicians. This is, after all, a common secret not only here but on a national scale. Views seem to be divided by self-interest as to whether so many Albanians should be staying illegally in the village, even though the majority is well served by their presence, especially shepherds and those building houses. There is a contradiction, though: while the villagers express a negative attitude and racist behavior whenever there is a problem with the Albanians, they are still the ones who invite the Albanians, employ them and, actually, complain if the police deport them. In any case, the community authorities take on the responsibility for the presence of the Albanians regarding the preservation of security and order in the village. It seems, somehow, that the border is transposed inside the limits of this frontier community, regarding the relocation and presence of Albanians, especially those from the area of Ersekë, behind Grammos.

Fifth incident: In the Winter of 2000, an elderly man from the village of Plikati fell ill and had to be hospitalized for several days in Jannina. His wife accompanied him, so a problem arose relating to the care of their few domestic animals. The solution came from a young Albanian from the village Rehovë, who offered to take the animals to his home on the other side of the border and keep them there until the return of the elderly couple.

Sixth incident: A few years after the violent opening of the Albanian border, public opinion in Jannina was preoccupied with a peculiar case of smuggling from the neighboring country. This phenomenon had been rampant for about a decade and had not been confronted (everything, from sheep, goats and other animals, to guns and drugs, crossed the border in various ways), but this particular case created a strong impression owing to the ingenuity it demonstrated. It was discovered that from a small village next to the border, where a large family of shepherds reside permanently, large quantities of milk were canalized into Greece via a plastic pipe and sold on the Greek market.

Seventh incident: In the early Spring of 2002 while I was working in my office at the University of Ioannina, I was very surprised to see before me a man from Leskovik (Albania), who had been sentenced to four years of prison for smuggling drugs and had also been banned from entering Greece. He asked me to intervene with the police headquarters so that he would be allowed to enter the country and go to the island of Paros for work. Apparently, he had crossed the border illegally and managed to come through Konitsa to Ioannina. I refused to do the favor he asked for and he was finally obliged to return to his home town. He explained to me, what I already knew, that it is very easy to cross the border and go to Konitsa, but less easy to have access to Ioannina, and even more difficult to proceed from there to the rest of Greece. It seems that in a way there are different zones where the entry of undocumented migrants and their movements are constrained in varying degrees of severity with the actual border looking more like a constantly shrinking and growing wave.

Eighth incident: My editorial from the local *Amarandos* magazine: "As in the rest of the country, in our village, too, the census took place. It is known that the villages have been deserted […]. This is why they tried to bring in populations from the cities, to present an adequate number of people and gain economic benefits […]. Personally, I am against the creation of a false image, because this way we miss the point of the matter and do not confront the root of the problem. And, of course, I do not measure everything according to the economic benefits, whereas those in charge of the census in our village fell into that trap. Anxious to assemble more people, they brought in Albanian immigrants both, legal and illegal, from Konitsa and Albania […]. The individuals registered in the village were 88, not including the soldiers whose number is secret. The Statistics department that gave me this information provides no more details about the nationality of those registered, so we do not know how many Albanians were registered. We do know, however, that we only have one, Ligor (Grigori) Rousta from Podes (Podë), who comes periodically, and very rarely his brothers, Yianni and Alfredo accompany him. Of the 61 Albanians found in the village, 7 were illegal and were discovered late in the evening by the police. In other villages, the census of Albanians was attempted, but they were thrown out violently (the matter made news on television) […]" (2001, 25-29).

Ninth incident: During my fieldwork, I came across many cases of families divided between the two countries after the border was sealed by the Communist regime of Albania at the end of the World War II. The incident that struck me the most was a family whose two children remained in Albania while their parents found themselves in Greece as they were in the winter pastures near Konitsa. In the interim, two more children were born in the family. When the border fell in 1991, the family was reunited, but the older children could not communicate with their younger siblings speaking Albanian and Greek respectively. Further adding to the irony is the fact that these siblings belonged to different nations.

THE HISTORY OF THE BORDER (1912-1990)

Let us now examine more specifically the history as well as the ethnography of the border and the space created around it, which means to define the specific characteristics of the ethnographic field.

The creation of the independent Albanian state in 1912 and the demarcation of the border line, which was concluded after the Balkan wars, occurred arbitrarily, vis-à-vis the ethnic and cultural state of affairs; the committees in charge met insurmountable difficulties in recording the national identities of the populations of the wider area because, with respect to a large part of the population, the ethnic mosaic was composite, the correspondences between objective facts and subjective self-definitions problematic and the identities and consciousness too fluid. It was, in other words, impossible to find a line that would divide these populations into two homogeneous categories, Greek and Albanian (Nitsiakos 2010).

The problem was not only the ethnically mixed communities and the geographical interpenetration between the various ethnic groups, but also the internal differentiation within groups of similar ethnological origin, mainly owing to the *millet* system, which used to distinguish and still, in a way, distinguishes the Albanians in particular. The distinction between Orthodox Christians and Muslims was decisive not only because it determined their position within the Ottoman dominion, but because it affected their ethnic identity, the basis on which their national consciousness developed during the dismantlement of the Ottoman Empire and the making of nation-states. The Orthodox Christian Albanians, who belonged to the *rum millet,* identified themselves to a large degree with the rest of the Orthodox population. While under the roof of the Patriarchate and later the influence of Greek education system, they started to form a Greek national consciousness, a process that was interrupted by the Albanian national movement in the end of the 19th century and subsequently by the Albanian state. Still, even within the community of the Christians, distinctions based on ethnic origin and language differentiation (Greek-speaking, Albanian-speaking, Vlach-speaking) persisted and the same was the case with the Muslim community, who were divided mainly on the basis of their particular dogma (Sunnis and Bektashis) (Skendi 1967; Clayer 2007).

For the above reasons, the border changed several times before it became fixed, but was questioned later, especially by the Greek state, leading to the notorious incidents connected to the so-called 'North Epirus issue' (declaration of independence, recognition of Greek minority, etc.). Even though the border was finally fixed by international treaties, the lack of correspondence between national borders and ethnological facts continued to be a problem, as ethnic groups and even kinfolk and families were divided between the two nation-states (Hart 1995 and 1999; Nitsiakos 2010).

During the period between the creation of the Albanian state and World War II, the border did not obstruct communication between the two sides. On the contrary, financial transactions and social relationships persisted, as well as cultural contacts, albeit with the required formalities pertaining to the crossing of the border, which was after all, not guarded particularly strictly. People continued to move from one territory to the other without difficulty (tradesmen came and went, shepherds moved with their flocks from their winter pastures to the highlands, women and men visited relatives on the other side, marriage exchanges continued between villages that traditionally used to form marriage alliances, and so on).

However, on both sides of the border, processes of population homogenization, through ideological and other state apparatuses, were a reality and, in time, the groups which represent otherness started feeling the pressure to become assimilated. In Greece, this process is easier both due to the fact that the state has been in existence for an extended period of time as well as the great influence the Church used to have on all the ethnic groups belonging to the *rum millet*. There was only a problem with the Muslim population, but this was also solved with the exchange of populations after 1923, when most of those who remained after the liberation of Epirus left, with the few who remained gradually decreasing in number, so that after World War II there were only a few Muslim families in Konitsa, some of whom are still there to this day (Nitsiakos 2010).

During the inter-bellum period as well as the era concluding with the foundation of the communist regime in Albania, there was a wave of relocations of Greek and Albanian Christians from South Albania to Greek Epirus, who became known as 'Vorioepirotes' (Greeks who come from the part of Epirus that was yielded to Albania and is since referred to by Greeks as 'Northern Epirus'). The 'Vorioepirotes' of Albanian origin have to a large extent a Greek consciousness and identity which is why they choose to come to Greece, where they are treated as Greeks. On the contrary, only Muslims who have developed Albanian national consciousness or who cannot identify with either Greeks or Turks leave Greece for Albania, which they choose owing to ethnic, linguistic and confessional affinity. Let us note here, that the flight of the 'Vorioepirotes' of both Greek and Albanian origin persisted—albeit to a much lesser degree—in the form of escape during the communist regime, despite the Draconian security measures on the border (Hart 1995 and 1999).

THE FALL OF THE BORDER (1990) AND THE NEW SETTING

With the collapse of the Albanian regime and the violent opening of the border in 1990, the two sides somehow reunited particularly kinfolk and families which had been divided. Financial transactions, social relationships and cultural contact between the two groups were reinstated and, most importantly, a great flow of population occurred, from the Albanian to the Greek side, and configured a transnational field of intense mobility, since, regardless of whether they settled permanently in the area of Konitsa or not, these people crossed the border with great frequency. Of course, produce and merchandise, ideas and mentalities crossed the border along with them, configuring a landscape of flows.

So, in this way, a zone of mobility, activities and flows was formed, which intersected the national border. This zone is not delimited, but possesses geographical features. It may present some flexibility, expanding or contracting depending on the relations that prevail at times between the two countries, as well as between the local communities on the two sides of the border. Still, it comprises a band of land, where relations appear generally different when compared to the relations between the two countries while being subject to constant negotiation. The idea of establishing a trans-border zone of free exchange, which is often discussed in public debates but has yet to be realized, apparently represents a demand for the institutionalization of a situation that tends to establish itself permanently, albeit unofficially, and with no consideration for the law and the border.

The borderline, (or the border as a physical presence), is a fact, but exists to be violated, in practice. This violation expresses an attitude of the border populations, to perpetually resist the boundary in their everyday life. So, sometimes the boundary can be compared to a sea wave that ascends and descends intermittently. However, there are points no one can go beyond as an 'illegal immigrant', objectively (i.e. due to strict border-patrols—after all the police itself has designated different zones of surveillance), but some obstacles are subjective (such as the lack of social, economic and cultural requirements—what we call 'symbolic capital'). For example, those occupied as shepherds move inside the area of the pastures. Those who work in villages nearby on unofficial agreements, move within the limits of those communities—they may dare a trip to Konitsa for some errands but go no further (Konitsa is the limit for many). For the bolder ones, the limit may expand as far as Jannina, but from Jannina to Athens the road is harsh if not impermeable, as it includes—but it is not limited to—strict controls.

The zone we are talking about is also a place of extreme intimacy, real and symbolic. Not only is the social and cultural environment familiar to those crossing the border from the nearby areas of Albania, but compounding this, human relationships are so personal they make this zone very secure for them. These interpersonal relations also involve individuals in public office and even some in charge of guarding the border and affect their attitude, rendering it more flexible. This is the case on both sides of the border, since on the side of Albania there are also guards whose task is to patrol the boundary. The following example is enough to illustrate this variety of relationship. In Radat, an Albanian village next to the border, I met one guard, who comes from that village and lives there. His father crosses the border illegally to work in the Greek village Amarandos. His son is obliged by his position to at least stop his father from crossing the border illegally. On the Greek side I have encountered many cases of Albanians without proper documents working and even staying in the homes of Greeks who occupy official positions in the state mechanism, sometimes even related to the guarding of the border. The interpersonal relations often acquire a moral undertone, disrupting the typical structure of relations and forming a field of mutual trust, which, as a rule, maintains order and security much more effectively than persecuting practices.

The above observations regarding the configuration of a broader zone of mobility and exchange around the border, though focused on the geographical dimension, pose questions of symbolic boundaries. The relation of the material and symbolic boundaries between the various groups who have lived, live and move around the national border is of special interest. While the negotiation of the geographical border, the borderline that was finally fixed, and the political border between the two national states took place in the context of specific procedures pertaining to the international juridical-political framework of settling differences related to border delineation, the negotiation of the symbolic boundaries between national but also ethnic groups in particular, consists of processes that cannot be confined to set frameworks or time scales. The incompatibility of the political border with the ethnological facts put the former in doubt, in principle and on an official level. This is a fact that affects the everyday private beliefs and negotiations of the relations and limits between the groups, whose historical presence in space variously cross-cuts the division that has been imposed from above on the two national groups that are supposed to be or appear homogeneous and 'pure' according to the dictates of national ideology.

So, while the arbitrary demarcation of the borderline, in the first place, and its subsequent sealing—for which the Albanian regime was responsible—provoked ideological and emotional reactions, as well as resistance amongst the populations who found themselves divided between the two states (the result being a struggle between symbolic and political boundaries), the opening of the border in 1990 compelled a renewal of renegotiations of relationships and symbolic boundaries. The most characteristic case is that of the Greek population who had stayed in Albanian territory and constituted the Greek minority (recognized or not by international treaties). The imposition and sealing of the border provoked political and ideological-emotional reactions in Greece. In particular, it led to the powerful ideological charging of this group as being excluded from the national corpus of the ethnic Greek population and the development of the well known irredentism, which kept alive the misgivings about the arbitrary demarcation of the particular boundary. Above all, it claimed the reproduction of the symbolic border, which opposes the political one. We observe here an oppositional relation and function of the two forms of border, tackled differently by the two national states. In the Greek case, there exists a tendency to remind and nurture this opposition through its ideological apparatuses and institutions of memory preservation, while the Albanian side tries in every way possible to undermine and gradually nullify it with assimilative policies. The opening of the border, on the other hand, while being hailed initially by the Greek side as a liberating event for the 'Northern Epirus brothers in bondage', allowing the Greek population of Albania to come into contact with the national body and the 'motherland', subsequently provoked negative reactions, resulting in the erection of new symbolic boundaries where the material ones had collapsed (Kassimis and Nitsiakos 1997).

Now, as for the Albanians themselves who cross the border, legally or illegally after 1990, the renegotiation of relations and symbolic boundaries between different ethnic and religious groups is of a multi-dimensional and composite nature. We can, however, observe that with the opening of the border, the movement of Albanian population to Greece as a migratory destination acquired an additional tendency to open up the symbolic boundaries as well, only this opening was one-sided. While different categories of Albanians tried to relax the symbolic boundaries and discover or imagine symbolic ties with the Greeks, so as to facilitate their reception and integration in Greek society, the Greeks raised mental walls of exclusion, regarding the Albanians' symbolic integration, because otherwise, one way or other, they did become part of Greek society, even if through their marginalization.

So, the symbolic boundaries are influenced by the function of the political borders, but their own function follows separate rules in the context of the conditions of negotiation of collective and individual identities, a phenomenon depending on the historical conjuncture and the various social situations.

THE POLITICAL ECONOMY

The relations formed in this trans-border context, cannot be understood unless they are examined with regards to the political economy of the particular mobility. The concept of asymmetry, the inequality between the two sides of the border is decisive for this. In the first place, the very movement of people from one side to the other is part of a dynamic that develops with the opening of the border, a dynamic that is determined by the tendency or pressure to leave the country because of the great political, social and economic crises and the attraction of Greece for its stability and prosperity in these same regards.

The flow itself being one way, directed from one side to the other of the border, indicates a relation of inequality between the two countries. Indeed, the violence with which the collapse of the regime is effected and the subsequent opening of the border and the, as a rule, undocumented method of entering Greece, makes this relation even more asymmetrical and places those who move in a much more powerless position, as they live and work illegally: their 'outlaw' status deprives them of all rights. Legalization improves their position but does not cancel the structural inequality that characterizes the phenomenon of immigration any way, as well as the quality of the immigrant. In any case, the effort of the immigrants to present aspects of identity that would facilitate their position and residence—proof of Greek roots or Christian faith, changes of names, etc.—demonstrates, precisely, how they experience this unequal relationship, which is further aggravated by factors pertaining to their otherness.

The trans-border zone is not exempted from this parameter, but rather, here immigrants are better qualified to alleviate the negative consequences of this asymmetry and inequality, owing to the historical and cultural affinity mentioned above. Moreover, the geographical proximity itself functions positively in this regard.

While the flow of people is almost exclusively in one direction, where goods are concerned the movement is reciprocal, but mostly from Greece to Albania. The few exchanges also bear the imprint of the above structural asymmetry and reflect the level of development of the two countries.

While primarily agricultural and dairy products—drugs and weapons being a separate matter—flow from Albania to Greece (mostly uncontrolled), there seems to be, in addition to money, a flow from Greece to Albania of a great gamut of material goods and products, from simple items of everyday use and consumption, to electrical equipment and cars.

The Greeks who go to Albania with purposes other than a simple visit are mainly tradesmen, whose presence once more manifests, in its own way, the same relation of inequality between the two countries. The denial of the Greek majority to engage in more permanent relations with Albania confirms a total rejection of the country's image and reproduces the perception of its inferiority. In any case, the trans-border zone of mobility condenses in its own way, though it also somewhat mitigates, the relations of inequality between the two countries.

THE ARGUMENT: TRANSNATIONAL MIGRATION?

From what has been said so far it is already obvious that my initial hypothesis about transnational migration, based on the fact that migrants move from one national territory to another creating a transnational space by crosscutting a national border, proved to be almost obsolete. Along with the notion of transnationalism, the very idea of migration had to be revised, since it was connected with a kind of methodological nationalism.

Let us first contend with the notion of transnationalism in relation to previous forms of migration, where there appears to be a total breakdown of social relations and cultural ties between migrants and their countries of origin, together with a parallel tendency of assimilation by the host country. According to the theory of transnationalism, in the new migration, the migrants' networks of social relations, their activities and patterns of life involve, on the whole, both host and home societies: a social field is being formed which links up the two countries irrespective of borders and geographical conditions, while the new immigrants live thus in between and form rather 'hybrid' identities. (Glick Schiller *et al.,* 1992, 1; Kivisto 2001, 552). Of great significance with regard to the further elaboration of the transnational conceptual model is Faist's contribution. He includes in the definition of the social field, or rather space, the circulation of ideas, symbols and elements of material culture. Space here "does not only refer to physical features, but also to larger opportunity structures, social life and the subjective images, values, and meanings that the specific and limited place represents to migrants. Space is thus different from place in that it encompasses or spans various territorial locations. It includes two or more places. Space has a special meaning that extends beyond simple territoriality; only with concrete social or symbolic ties does it gain meaning for potential migrants" (Faist 2000, 45-6).

Focusing on the 'transnational' space encompassing more or less the frontier along the Albanian-Greek border, I came to an impasse in trying to apply the concept of transnationalism, since due to the specific history and ethnography of the border and the border population described above, this notion obscured rather than helped illuminate the existing situation. Very soon I realized that the solution to the problem was to go beyond national identities and follow the practices of the Albanian migrants as well as the manner in which the locals responded to them. On this basis, ethnicity appeared to be a more useful category. Thus, I had to revise my initial conceptual tools and hypothesis. As a matter of fact, this revision was decisive. Despite the fact that national classifications are important and seem to play an important role in the everyday life and practices of the people, notions such as ethnicity and ethnic identity proved to be more important. I realized, in other words, that I had to scratch the surface of national relations and identities and understand how ethnicity works.

This decision was enhanced by the fact that another ethnographic study in an adjacent area came up with a similar *problematique.* The French anthropologist, Gilles de Rapper, giving the title "new transnationalism?" to the concluding chapter of a relevant publication noted: "Emigration and the opening of the border have brought a change in the local conception of identity: the Albanian-Greek opposition has given way to a more complex 'bricolage' based on memory of the *kurbet* and on a cultural and geographic proximity, and this can be seen as the marker of a new situation of transnationalism between Greece and Albania. This is the way in which the Lunxhots respond to the challenge of gaining access to the Greek labor market" (2005, 192). He emphasizes the fact that while national classifications still persist, in order to understand the everyday reality of people with respect to the migrants' conduct and strategies, it is necessary to take into account other, more ambiguous and fluid categories such as ethnic identities. It is not easy, however, he concludes, to determine the extent to which this re-emergence of ethnicity is caused by the configuration of a transnational space due to migration, where antagonism is expressed in ethnic terms, or whether it is a reaction to the nationalist propaganda of the communist era.

It is not easy to provide an answer to the above question unless a thorough examination of the history of the border is undertaken and issues concerning ethnic groups and boundaries are touched upon in the context of the frontier ethnographic landscape where people live, manipulate relations and negotiate identities under specific historical conditions that form a dynamic political economy around and across the border.

Broadly speaking, the new setting is a typical configuration of transnational migration, but this term is not of particular utility if we are to understand the actual attributes of the relations and flows that take place on the social level, which intersects the national border. The geographical and cultural proximity of the two areas on both sides of the border, the composite character of ethnic relationships, the historical background of the social and economical relations involved but also of the translocations and relocations from the one area to the other, the fluidity of identities in the past but, to a certain degree, in the present as well, with respect to a large part of Albanian population (mainly the Orthodox Christians), do not allow us to approach the migratory phenomenon in nationalist terms, namely assuming a national 'purity' and homogeneity, which presupposes the existence of national identities, consolidated in time and space and coinciding with the physical territory of the nation-states. This means that the concept of transnational migration is rather problematic and inadequate for the study of the specific phenomenon and that we have to, on the one hand, transcend the transnational framework that pertains to the existence of nation-states, and attend to the level and the context of ethnic relations, which intersect the national ones.

On the other hand, the very concept of migration itself is to be also revised, since it is inextricably related to the phenomenon of the nation (Ventura 1994; Tsimouris 2009; Karagiannis 2006). While with the term 'migration' we refer to any form of population relocation from place to place, from an agricultural area to another or an urban centre to another, from city to city, from country to country, etc., its use is associated, as a rule, with the movement from nation-state to nation-state. This is why when we refer to relocations within the borders of a state we have to use the term 'internal migration'. Even though almost all kinds of relocation, even temporary ones, have been recorded in history as a social problem and are inscribed in the collective consciousness as traumatic experiences, the parting with the country of origin in particular and the settling in another state is further negatively charged with the ideas of deprivation of a homeland, severing from the national body, uprooting from the land of one's forefathers and forced integration with another county and another nation; by definition, the immigrant becomes a national 'other', a stranger.

The critical approaches to nationalism and the new 'constructivist' theories of the nation clearly influenced the discussion on migration and migrant populations, but did not necessarily lead to an epistemological revision of the basic study tools of the phenomenon, or, most importantly, a radical questioning of the structural connection of the national with the migratory phenomenon and a re-adjustment of the conceptual and methodological framework itself. I contend that the symbolic dimension of this field that intersects, together with geographical borders, the boundaries of national wholes, is of great consequence to the construction of new identities: new identities that force us to re-define the terms we customarily use to approach national identities and, furthermore question even the very notion of 'hybridity'. It is obvious in this context that the idea of 'hybridity' cannot be valid since it presupposes some 'pure' identities in the first place, which when mixed produce the new hybrid character. As a matter of fact, underneath the surface of national identities there are hidden multiple combinations of fluid ethnic, religious and local identities, which acquire great importance in the new setting of trans-border mobility and prevent us from approaching them in terms of hybridity as it is defined in the context of the transnational migration discourse.

It is very interesting, indeed, to examine the way various 'pre-modern' bonds are activated in the context of trans-border mobility, but, also, the way the subjects themselves confer meaning to them. The very definition of these bonds presents special interest, in the sense that they are basically ethnic, since they concern the common ethnic origins of the groups concerned, while now their members belong to different national wholes, being Greek or Albanian. The formation of modern, 'pure' national identities and the ideology of nationalism generate difficulty in the classification of these bonds, as is the case with any kind of identification, which, when compounded with any other social and psychological consequences it may elicit, may yield an identity crisis as well. This is the case not only with minority ethnic groups such as the Vlachs, but also with the ethnic Greeks and ethnic Albanians, especially the Orthodox Christians. With respect to the ethnic history of the wider geographical area where the two nation-states were created, and especially the wider zone where the national border was demarcated one can ignore neither the existence of different ethnic groups nor the interpenetration of the two dominant ones, which finally constituted the two nation-states.

Looking more closely at the facets of the everyday trans-border mobility of Albanian citizens to the area of Konitsa (Epirus), one can discern a series of different forms of mobility. To mention the most important ones: Families settled in Konitsa or surrounding villages, who visit their home on the other side of the border very often (they keep their houses there and many of them have elderly parents whom they leave behind); families who have settled in Greece but visit their places of origin only occasionally, due to the distance; men or women who work during the week in the area and visit their homes in the weekends; mainly men, who come for work and return on a daily basis (from the Albanian villages very close to the border); schoolchildren who attend classes in schools in the area, stay in halls of residence or boarding houses in Konitsa and visit their homes on weekends and holidays; elderly people who divide their time between Albania and Greece where their children live; people who work in both countries depending on the season (e.g. construction workers who spend the winter-saison in Albania occupied in various agricultural of construction jobs, while in Greece the demand for such work decreases); and, finally, men and women who are married to Greek citizens and live in the area permanently.

So we observe great mobility, but also a differentiation between the various categories, which are fluid themselves, since individual and family strategies change in time, depending on the objective facts of the job market but also each family's developmental cycle. On the other hand, given that there is not only geographical proximity but cultural affinity as well, the conditions of Albanians in Greece are nothing like one would expect in a truly foreign land. And this affinity is traced back to the time before the sealing of the border after World War II, when the two sides of the border used to communicate in various ways and the old unity had not broken down, despite the imposition of the national border after the Balkan wars and the foundation of the Albanian state (business transactions, social contact, even marriages continued throughout the period between the wars).

To conclude, instead of using the term 'transnational migration', I prefer the term 'trans-border mobility', because it overcomes methodological nationalism while at the same time makes the concept of the real as well as the symbolic border (Barth 1969; Wilson and Donnan 1998) central in understanding the ethnographic context of the mobility across the border which characterizes the presence of Albanian citizens in the border area of Konitsa (Epirus).

REFERENCES

Barth, Fredrik. 1969. "Introduction", in *Ethnic groups and boundaries: The social organization of cultural difference,* edited by Fredrik Barth (Boston: Little, Brown and Company), 9-37.

Clayer, Nathalie. 2007. *Aux origins du nationalism albanais.* Paris: Karthala.

De Rapper, Gilles. 2005. "Better than Muslims, not as good as Greeks. Emigration as experienced and imagined by the Albanian Christians of Lunxhëri," in *The new Albanian migration,* edited by Russel King, Nicola Mai, Stephanie Schwandner-Sievers (Brighton-Portland: Sussex Academic Press), 173-194.

Faist, Thomas. 2000. *The volume and dynamics of international migration and transnational social spaces.* Oxford: University Press.

Glick Schiller, Nina and Linda Basch and Cristina Blanc Szanton. 1992. *Towards a transnational perspective on migration: race, class, ethnicity, and nationalism reconsidered.* New York: New York Academy of Sciences.

Hart, Laurie Kain (with K. Budina). 1995. "'Northern Epiros': The Greek minority in southern Albania," *Cultural Survival Quarterly* 19(2), 54-63.

Hart, Laurie Kain. 1999. "Culture, civilization and demarcation at the northwest borders of Greece," *American Ethnologist* 26(1), 6-23.

Karagiannis, Evangelos. 2006. "Metanastevsi-thiethikotita-kinitikotita. Paratirisis pano stin erevna dhiethnikis metanastevsis [Migration-transnationalism-mobility. Comments on research about transnational migration]" *Sighrona Themata* 92, 23-30.

Kassimis, Chryssa and Nitsiakos, Vassilis. 1997. "I elliniki mionotita tis Alvanias: Metavasi i katastrofi? [The Greek minority of Albania: Transition or catastrophe?]" *Ipirotika Chronika* 32, 353-371.

Kivisto, Peter. 2001. "Theorizing transnational immigration: A critical review of current efforts," *Journal of Ethnic and Racial Studies* 24/4, 549-577.

Skendi, Stavro. 1967. *The Albanian national awakening 1878-1912.* Princeton, New Jersey: Princeton University Press.

Tsimouris, Giorghos. 2009. "Anthropologhikes prosegisis tis metanastevsis sti metapolemiki Elladha: Orismenes ipothesis ghia mia arghoporimen schesi" [Anthropological approaches to migration in post-war Greece: Some hypotheses for a belated relationship], in *Opseis anthropologikis'erevnas* [Facets of anthropological research], edited by Dimitra Gefou-Madianou (Athens: Ellinika grammata), 293-313.

Ventura, L. 1994. *Metanastevsi ke ethnos* [Emigration and nation], Athens: EMNE - Mnimon.

Wilson, Thomas M. and Hastings, Donnan (eds.). 1998. *Border identities. Nation and state at international frontiers.* Cambridge: Cambridge University Press.

PART THREE

THE TRANSFORMATION OF THE FAMILY IN THE POST-COMMUNIST 'ALBANIAN SPACE'

KARL KASER

FAMILY AND KINSHIP IN ALBANIA: CONTINUITIES AND DISCONTINUITIES IN TURBULENT TIMES

INTRODUCTION

Stereotyping 'the Albanian family' has a long-standing tradition, which shows ethic and emic dimensions. The etic dimension has been fuelled by the neighboring peoples and their intelligentsia, who have considered the closely tied Albanian family relations and high fertility rates to be threatening to their own ethnic survival as well as by western scholars, who point at the Albanian family and certain features of it as an archaic reminiscence of a world the West has lost. Many Albanians, however, are also convinced that they practice a unique family life, which they stamp 'the' Albanian family. The fact that Albania proper had been isolated for almost half of a century from the outside world has contributed to this emic as well as ethic prejudices and stereotyping. Albanian scholars investigating their family structures were and still are delighted to discover specific social institutions that allegedly separate them from the Slavic world and from the West and scholars from the West have been satisfied discovering allegedly exotic social institutions even in Europe, which reifies western identity.

Northern Albania, Kosovo and the areas of Western Macedonia with an Albanian population are usually portrayed as constituting the last holdout in Europe and in the Balkans where the multiple family household[31] has 'survived', although its number has been decreasing rapidly since World War II. This kind of statement is not completely wrong, although it misses historical and cultural contextualization, which has to be taken into account.[32] The reasons for this 'surviving' phenomenon in Albanian contexts are manifold. Although it is almost exclusively spread over Albanian territories, one cannot seriously argue that this is an ethnic characteristic. Extremely unstable and unfavorable political and economic conditions of the country and of the Albanian populations in Kosovo (see Rrapi 1995; Reineck 1991; Backer 2003) and in Macedonia (Brunnbauer 2004a) as well as weak state institutions have been among the most prominent reasons for the perpetuation of large family units. The late demographic transition from a stage of high to low fertility and mortality rates—which seems to be a general Muslim phenomenon—accompanied by a significant population increase, which has been reversed in recent years, is another reason.

This paper focuses on the Albanian kinship structure, family and household features in Albania proper as it was constituted as an independent state by the Great European Powers in 1913. There have been differences in the political, economic and legal con-

---

31 The definition of the complex family household here is a household composition that consists of two or more related conjugal family units. The basic formation unit is an agnatic core (father, sons, brothers, male cousins). The extension of the family household can be vertical and/or horizontal.
32 Contextualization is claimed, for instance, by Michael Mitterauer's ground breaking article (Mitterauer 1996) with regard to the Balkans.

texts with respect to the family in Albania and Yugoslavia since this time and therefore the history of the Albanian family follows divergent tracks in the course of the 20th and early 21st century. Whereas the complex family structures among the Albanian population in former Yugoslavia were left relatively untouched by Tito's regime, Enver Hoxha's regime in Albania practiced a brutal policy of suppression of the traditional way of life. Especially the traditional family and kinship structure was exposed to Communist ideology. Whereas in former Yugoslavia labor migration to the Western markets for the Albanian family became a reality which Albanians have slowly been able to become acquainted with since the 1960s, for the population of Albania, the sudden opening of an until then isolated country in 1990/91 involved many families redefining them as 'transnational household' or breaking apart. For most Albanian families labor migration of one or more family members has become a pre-requisite for their economic survival.

In earlier publications I have stressed, primarily on the basis of qualitative data from the 19th and early 20th centuries, the hypothesis that the traditional Albanian family model belonged to the area of distribution of the multiple patriarchal Balkan family household, which was widespread over Albania, Northern Greece, Macedonia, Western Bulgaria, Serbia, Kosovo, Montenegro and Bosnia-Herzegovina. This household structure was questioned by legal measures such as an enforced socialist family law and socioeconomic processes such as industrialization and urbanization, which resulted in the dissolution of large family compounds in the second half of the 20th century (Kaser 1995, 265-471; Kaser 1996, 375-386). The structure of multiple family households comprises its fragmentation and nuclearization, since it has always been exposed to processes of fission and fusion, has to split into several nuclear units before it grows again and regains its typical character. This implies the existence also of nuclear families in any given society with a predominant complex household structure. There may even be a higher percentage of nuclear families than multiple family households. But even then the majority of the population may live in multiple family households. Therefore, the transformation from a tendency to form multiple to a tendency to stay in nuclear families does not constitute a radical break with the past. A strong cohesion of kinship and family relations is not a monopoly of multi-generational and horizontal family and household extension.

The 20th century was one of the most turbulent centuries in Albania's history. It included state formation, nation building, King Zog's dictatorship, a bloody war of resistance against the axis-powers' domination in the course of WWII, the oppressive Communist regime, a rough period of transition as well as significant socioeconomic transformations such as urbanization, industrialization, de-industrialization as well as internal and external migration in the second half of the century and at the beginning of the 21st century. It is common knowledge that family and household are not only exposed to these kinds of processes but constitute significant actors in these processes. The aim of this paper is to investigate continuities and discontinuities of household formation and reproduction as well as of family and kinship ideology in the course of this turbulent century from the beginning of the 20th to the beginning of the 21st century. One decade ago, I outlined a first rough profile of Albania's family history in the 20th century (Kaser 2000). Meanwhile, a series of fresh studies has been conducted, which enable us to specify this preliminary profile.

One of the methodological and theoretical tools applied here in order to rationalize family and kinship structures in Albania proper is the relationship between state, household formation and relevance of kinship. As already elaborated in more details elsewhere (Kaser 2010, 422-23), a basic differentiation between a tributary and an interventionist character of the state is useful in this regard. Without the ambition of claiming universal validity of this model, at least Europe's social relations in history have been co-shaped by the states' and empires' character families are embedded in. To summarize: tributary states or empires, which showed no ambition to intervene in the everyday practice of its population but were primarily interested in its tributes, taxes and loyalty constituted a fabric of strong family and kinship relations, whereas interventionist states were ambitious to establish an intensive relationship between the population and the public institutions. Whereas the tributary state did hardly mediate the social relations of its population, the interventionist state did. This model was further elaborated for the Balkan region by U. Brunnbauer, who differentiates between milieus of openness and closeness in pre-modern times. Whereas the milieu of openness resulted in weaker kinship and family ties in the eastern Balkans, the milieu of closeness resulted in extended kinship agglomerations, pronounced patriarchal values and intense family solidarity in the western Balkans (Brunnbauer 2004, 445-47).

Having this in mind, Albanians' household formation practices and their family-centered value system constitutes not a miracle any longer, since the region belongs to a tributary state system inherited from the Ottomans and to the milieu of closeness of the Western Balkans. The Communist period represented a harsh interventionist system in combination with an isolationist strategy. Not accidently, this system intervened in family and household structures historically completely unknown in its intensity. The tributary 'The winner takes it all'-political system (Kaser 2003) of post-socialist Albania is, again not accidently, accompanied by a phase of re-traditionalization and re-patriarchalization of society.

In the context of this theoretical and methodological background, this paper intends to explore in its first section the formal family structure at the beginning of the 20th century as point of departure. In its second section, the severe impact of the interventionist Communist state and socioeconomic change on family structures will be analyzed. The third section will explore the adaption of family structures to the constraints of the weak post-socialist state and massive emigration while the last section will focus on the persistence of patriarchal family and kinship values as well on the advantages and disadvantages of Albania's family centeredness.

FAMILY AT THE BEGINNING OF THE 20TH CENTURY

Until the 1950s, when the communists began to intervene in the traditional household structure and family composition, rural household formation was shaped by a set of rules that was adapted to the predominant tributary state system and a milieu of closeness in the north and a more open environment in the south of the country. At the beginning of the 20th century, the majority of rural population, which constituted more than 80% of the population, lived in multiple family households. Several factors determined the form of a multiple family household structure: among them the residence of the newly married couple and the timing of the household fission were crucial. In the rural areas of the Western and Central Balkans the principle of patrilineality was usually strictly observed. This required patrilocality as a residence arrangement after marriage. Thus the agnatic kin constituted the core of the traditional household, and wives had to be married in.

Whereas the formal structure of the multiple household was also widespread in Croatia (Grandits and Gruber 1996, 477-496), Balkan family households shared additional ideological elements that Croatian households usually did not share: a distinctive patriarchal cultural background, a patriarchal variant that can be called Balkan patriarchy (Kaser 1992), strong blood ties and ancestor worship (Kaser 1993)[33], patrilineal ideology, bride price, blood feuds and a patrilineal kinship structure (Kaser 1995, 167-263). This excluded other forms of living arrangements than marriage and included women's virginity at marriage; to be divorced from the husband or to receive an inheritance portion was inconceivable.

Until 1918 our information about family composition in Albania is dependent on ethnographic evidence mostly from the second half of the 19th century, which is not always very reliable. The overall picture is of a homogenous distribution of large multiple family households in the northern part of the country and its initial disintegration in the southern part. The earliest evidence stems from the French geographer and traveler, A. Boué. He reports about the habit of the Albanian highlanders to live in large family units under one roof. Up to 16 conjugal units would have lived together (Boué 1889, 346). In the middle of the 19th century, J.G. von Hahn gives information about the joint property among the members of such households and the tradition of keeping the household undivided over generations together. The largest households he allegedly observed were among the tribal confederation of the Mirdita in the north of the country with 70 to 80 members (Von Hahn 1854, 180-81) S. Gopčević also visited Mirdita—but about 25 years later. He reports household sizes of about 50, 100 and even 200 members. The reason for these large sizes was that the households did not split for generations (Gopčević 1880, 408; Gopčević 1881, 317). Another report from the same region gives us details about a household consisting of about 100 members spread over 8 houses; 60 household members were able to carry weapons (Kaser 1995, 270).

The first Albanian census, taken by the Austro-Hungarian occupation forces in WWI, covers almost the whole territory of Albania[34] and provides with a first quantitative picture of household composition, which does by far not prove the mentioned ethnographic encounters. The census whose results enable household arrangements to be reconstructed was taken in 1918 by the statistical department of the Austro-

---

33 In this regard a very odd article of an author of Albanian origin should be mentioned. Doja (Doja 2010) calls this kind of heuristic procedure a "savant" effort of western scholars (i.e. historical anthropologists at Graz University) to stereotype Albania population by "anecdotic typical models" (Doja 2010, 352). He places them close to Albanians communists, Albanian ethnographers of the communist period, the German kulturhistorische tradition and the Viennese Kulturkreislehre, which, of course, is pure invention. He blames the author of this contribution of producing a "myth of many children, high fertility rates, and complex family structure" in north Albanian society by using the results of a research project conducted by this very same author. Doja quotes parts of my published texts selectively and 'proves' my alleged errors by other texts of mine, which he quotes correctly.

34 For a detailed description of the census material see for instance Kera and Pandelejmoni 2008, 128-29, Gruber 2008, 140-42 and Kaser 2000, 47-48.

Hungarian army, which had been occupying most of the country from 1916 to 1918.[35] This material, more precise than the following censuses taken by the Albanian authorities, had not yet been researched and used for the reconstruction of Albanian family history until the beginning of the 21st century. S. Gruber and R. Pichler were the first to have collected data about carefully selected villages and cities and provided a first comparative analysis (Gruber and Pichler 2002).

Coming to the results of this study it should be stressed that the experience of spending the first years of a marriage in multiple family households was shared by many younger Albanian couples. In the mountains and in some villages of the plains the time-span in which a person was part of a joint family household was even much longer. In five settlements an absolute majority and in three villages a relative majority of the people lived in multiple family households. Only in two of the neighborhoods of Shkodra was the majority of the population living in nuclear families (Ibid, 355). On the basis of this data selection the authors conclude that the joint family system was predominant in rural Albania at the beginning of the 20th century (Ibid). Marriage was almost universal; the mean age at marriage of women was below 20 years, but completely unexpected 25 or higher for men. In the case of Gruber's and Pichler's data set, it was 18 for women and 28 for men (Ibid. 360). Female heads of household were rare; in practically all the cases they were widows, who lived with underage sons (Ibid, 364). The chance of forming a multiple family household was relatively low and confined by demographic accidents. At age 50, 24% of men had no son and 33% only one son. Only the remaining 43% had at least two sons, who could therefore become the starting point for a multiple family household with lateral extension (Ibid. 371).

One year or so after the publication of this first study, E. Papa and G. Kera, who had been collaborating with Gruber in census data entry and analysis, were able to present a first overall picture. According to this data, the singulate mean age at marriage for rural women was 18.0 years and for rural man 25.8 years. Whereas 86.1% of the female population was married at the age of 24 years, 65.6% of the male population was still single at that age (Papa 2003, 81). This means late marriage for men and a considerable age gap between age at marriage between women and men of almost 8 years, which strengthened male domination and the patriarchal order (Gruber 2009, 233-34). Household size was much lower than the data given in the ethnographic encounters: it differed between 5 and 6 persons per household on the average in all districts except in the Puka region which had a mean household size of 6.7 persons. Only 8% of all family households had more than 10 members. Surprisingly, the majority of rural households were nuclear (39.7%), 23.1% were extended and 31.1% were multiple family households, which, however, comprised with 49.6% the majority of the population. 16.9% of household members were cousins, which means that household division in every generation was not the rule (Ibid, 238-242).

Urban household structures did not deviate significantly from the rural ones, since most of the cities had kept a rural character. Only approximately 12% of the overall population was urban (Gruber 2008, 142). The age at marriage for urban men was even 4 years higher than in the countryside. It ranged from 18.2 to 20.9 (women) and from 26.9 to 34.2 years for men (Gruber 2009, 234). Therefore, many women became

---

35 Seiner 1922 and Seiner 1922a. The census was organized by an expert on statistics, the Graz-based Franz Seiner.

widows at quite a young age: in the age group 40-44 years one third of all wives were already widows (Gruber 2008, 144). Marriage was practically universal also in urban milieus, except Shkodra, where 7.2% of women and 14.7% of men remained unmarried until the age of 50. One of the reasons for this high percentage of celibacy was due to the Catholic portion of population with its share of clergymen and nuns (Kera and Pandelejmoni 2008, 132). Urban households were smaller and less complex than rural ones (Gruber 2009, 238). 56.2% were nuclear, 20.7% extended and only 12.8% multiply structured. 56.2% of the urban population lived in nuclear households and 24.6% in multiple family households. The distribution of the nuclear family was weakest in Tirana and Kruja and highest in Shkodra. There were practically no registered household members not related to the household head (Ibid, 239-242; Gruber 2008, 143). Orthodox Christians and Muslims had quite similar household structures, whereas the proportion of Catholics living in multiple households was only half that of Muslims and Orthodox Christians (Gruber 2008, 144).

Which conclusions can be drawn from the results of the first Albanian census?

- The average household size was much lower than expected; this was also due to the fact that the First Demographic Transition, entailing increasing fertility rates, began approximately one decade or so after the census was taken;
- Approximately 50% of the population lived in multiple family households, which did not split in every generation;
- The age at marriage was low for females but surprisingly high for males, especially in cities; therefore, the number of widows was high;
- Marriage was universal, except in the biggest city of the country, Shkodra;
- Marriage arrangements were patrilocal;
- One quarter of husbands died without having a son and successor;
- The formal patriarchal matrix was widely spread over the country; the only significant exception being the city of Shkodra;
- Household formation was neither confessionally nor ethnically determined;
- There is—given the formal household structures reflected by the census—no significant difference between rural and urban settings; this is also due to the fact that at the beginning of the 20th century Albanian cities, with the exception of Shkodra, had a rural character;
- Neither the traditional urban household became the matrix of the urban household one century later nor was this the case with the rural household.

HOXHA'S REGIME AND THE IMPACT OF COLLECTIVIZATION ON THE FAMILY

Albania's socioeconomic development in the interwar period remained relatively stable, which means continuation on a poor developmental level. There were hardly any remarkable impulses for changes of household formation and family relations. The urban share of the population did not increase from 1923 to 1938—on the contrary, it dropped slightly from 15.9 to 15.4%. Only in wartime (until 1945) did this share increase to 21.3% (1945). However, this was not a result of accelerating economic dynamics but of the desire for security in insecure times (Sjöberg 1991, 34-35). Key industries did not work, except the bitumen extracting mines at Selenicë with approximately 500 workers. The rest of industrial production was mostly based on raw materials from agriculture and livestock farming. However, no dairying industry of any importance had emerged; the processing, distribution and sales of dairy products were carried out by the owner of the flocks themselves (Ibid, 34).

After the takeover of power by the Communist Party, socioeconomic development gained momentum. From 1945 to 1988, the rural-urban population flow intensified. In 1988, the rural share of population decreased from approximately 85% to 65%, whereas the urban share increased to 34.4%. The share of urbanized population would have been higher if the regime would have given permission for free movement (Ibid, 51-52). The industrial sector generated 43.3% of the national income by 1985, but the country remained poor with a GNP per capita of $380 by the end of the communist regime (Gjonca, Aassve and Mencarini 2008, 262-63).

When the Communist Party of Albania came into power by the end of 1944, an attack on the traditional ("reactionary") mentality, behavior patterns and forms of social life was officially announced. Especially the 'patriarchal family' was exposed to Communist modernization measures. Whereas the South Albanian regions—the population of which was very pro-Hoxha and had supported the Communist partisan movement against the Italian and German invaders and internal rivals—was relatively easy to win for this program, the population of the regions in the north was strongly opposed to the new regime. This is why the regime began to formally destroy the tribal structures and institutions after the mountainous population had widely resisted the Communist take-over of the government from the very beginning (Neuwirth 1995, 28-29). However, it seems that the Communists were not able to change the traditional family ideology and household structures rapidly.

This can be demonstrated by a small case study taken from the North-Albanian region of Dukagjin, north of the Drini River. We conducted field work there in the Summer of 1993 and were allowed to copy family-related data for the year 1950 from the register books of the four villages of Abat, Pepsumaj, Plan-Gjuraj and Than-Plan, which belonged traditionally to the tribal areas of Shala, Shoshi and Kiri.[36] When we compare the percentages of the agnatic core (which is represented by the categories 'household head', 'father', 'father brother's son', 'brother' and 'sons'), 46.1% (1918) and 44.9% (1950) show a practically unchanged constellation over time. What is interesting here is the difference in the husband-wife bond, the frequency of which according to Gruber and Pichler is expected to increase, giving way to a weakening of the patriarchal order. This data showed a move to the opposite direction: a percentage of 19.4 in 1918 compared to 14.5 in 1950. Maybe this result is accidental, but in any case the data does not indicate a disappearing patriarchal order. This is no argument against Gruber's and Pichler's findings, since the general trend can be opposed to a regional constellation in the Northern highlands of Albania.

---

36 Although the traditional tribal organization had been destroyed as mentioned above, a vivid consciousness can still be observed to which tribe one belongs.

Although this data represents only a small Albanian region, it represents insofar a general trend as we have clear evidence that the Communist party functionaries in the first few years were not able to force the large household complexes to split up despite this being their defined goal. With the onset of collectivization they found the necessary tools. Whereas this process had already been introduced in South Albania in the 1950s, in the above mentioned Dukagjin region it began only in the late 1960s/early 1970s. For this region we have details as to how the complex households were destroyed. Among others generally two methods were applied:

1) To support certain household forms by granting them economic advantages. As a result of collectivization, only 300 square meter of private land was allotted to each household. For a household consisting of 20 or 30 persons this was almost nothing. When 5 or 6 conjugal units divided, 5 or 6 times as much land was allotted. The attractiveness of a household division was increased by a system of free rations consisting of coffee, sugar, oil etc. Each household of the co-operative was provided with a free ration independent of how large it was. The ration was big enough for a nuclear family but not for a large complex household.

After a few years, all the complex households, for instance, in the village of Abat had divided. But this was not the end of the patriarchal order. In most cases the household division was only formal. The household was officially declared as divided and the conjugal units were separately registered. In many cases the household as a corporate unit continued to work in its traditional form under changed circumstances: The money individually earned in the co-operative was put together in the traditional manner and the now informal household head administrated and distributed it. This was relatively easy as there was no large geographic distance between the stem house and the newly constructed ones. In several cases even no separate houses were constructed; the members explained to the administration that they were financially unable to construct new houses (Kaser 1995a, 138-40).

2) The second method to achieve household division was the application of violence. Family members who resisted the dissolution of the household were forced to emigrate and were settled in distant co-operatives. In 1993, I met five brothers in Dukagjin who had been forced to leave their joint household in 1968. Despite the distances between their new residences they never stopped considering themselves as one household. The oldest of the brothers acted as household head and was responsible for the distribution of the money. When one of their sons married, all the brothers contributed to the marriage feast. When I met them they were just considering reuniting their joint household spatially after 25 years of separation.

This example is one of the rare cases of still existing multiple family households. Their distribution is confined to the remote mountainous areas in the northern parts of the country like the region of Dukagjin. To this extent, communist politics has achieved its aims. But more generally speaking, as Pichler points out, traditional social forms as well as the customary law were wiped out formally, but in social reality traditional values and kinship ties remained intact; a syncretistic overlap of traditional and modern social structures was the consequence (Pichler 2003, 97).

One of the continuities from pre-modernity to socialist modernity was the universality of marriage. People without family were considered poor and handicapped. Divorced couples were rare and stigmatized. One of the most significant discontinuities was that the state provided people with sufficient income and took over many of the traditional functions of the family. A new form of patriarchy, state or party patriarchy was aimed at substituting traditional patriarchal structures. The socialist regime considered, in not only a metaphorical sense, society to be family, and the Party as father. Socialist society was conceptualized as a classical patriarchal household. The result was a patriarchal household-state, which etatized even birth and the foetus. The female body became an instrument of the reproduction constraints of the state like the reproduction of patrilineality in agrarian society. Socialism redistributed male and female roles in household, socialized considerable parts of reproduction, and took over certain functions of the patriarch (Kaser 2008, 143). People had an enormous amount of leisure time, which they used for communication with relatives and friends. Clearly women experienced the communist economic and social system differently. Many of them were at work which had not been the case before, and had to come to terms with the management of work and household. However, many of them received their own income and enjoyed good training, which were completely new experiences.

Household formation became independent from the household head's death, the newly married couple established its own household upon marriage. Neolocality was only limited by the enormous population increase until the 1960s. Polygamous marriage arrangements, however scarcely practiced in previous times, were not allowed any longer (Nicholson 2006). Another continuation of the past was age at marriage for both sexes. In 1950, the mean age at marriage for a female was 22.0 years, while in 2000 it was only 23.0 years. The same applied for men, with a mean age at marriage of 27.7 years in 1950 compared to 28.1 years in 2000 (Gjonca, Aassve and Mencarini 2008, 278). However, fertility began also to decrease, which will be discussed in more detail in the next section. Mortality rates decreased significantly, which extended marital life and allowed many to enjoy a new experience: the grandparent-grandchildren relation. One can conclude that the interventionist state reorganized family life to a significant degree. But did the socialist regime leave a modern family by European standards, when it was forced to abdicate?

THE IMPACT OF POST-SOCIALIST POLITICAL AND ECONOMICAL TRANSFORMATION ON THE FAMILY

This situation favorable to the family changed considerably with the collapse of the Communist regime. The political and economic transformation of Albanian society since 1991-92 has had a significant impact on formal aspects of the Albanian family. In this regard, a new era of Albanian family history began. Economic liberalism reshaped the entire society and seemingly also its central social institutions such as the family. The constraints of the new conditions, especially the almost complete breakdown of the social security institutions, led to an enormous social disparity among the population—the highest in the Balkan region. More than half a million people live in extreme poverty (a situation, when people can expend less than $1 per day per person) and almost one half of the population lives under the poverty-line of $2 per day (Kaser 2003a, 393). At the same time Albania's GDP has been growing fastest from 1990 to 2007 compared to all other European countries (Wikipedia 2011). This might cause both tensions as well as solidarity among family members.

The question arises, whether the newly established economic framework can provide the general conditions for a break-up of the family? The answer depends at which segment of family life we are looking. If we look at the traditional household composition of the multiple family household with its patriarchal arrangements, we have to conclude that this definitely has become history. The census of 2001 reveals 5.4% of the total number of households in the country, which share a common dwelling and have a shared economy. The rural share is 6%. This still seems to be a relatively high proportion, but the data is obscured by the fact that it does not become clear whether they constitute stem families or joint family households.[37]

If we look at other factors that have an impact on family life[38], the picture becomes more complicated. As already mentioned, the census of 1918 indicates that marriage was universal in the countryside as well as in the urban milieu, except the city of Shkodra with a relatively high proportion of celibacy. The census, however does not allow for calculating the general fertility rate of the country (Kera 2003, 23-26). It does permit us to calculate the mean number of children of married and widowed men and women in the parents' household at the moment the census was taken, which does not reflect fertility rates because daughters were married out. What can be stated is that about three men out of four were able to secure the continuation of the family by giving birth to a surviving son. Because of the high male age at marriage half of the men were living with a son only at an age of more than 40 years (Ibid, 33-34).

At the end of the communist period, marriage was still universal with only 3.2% of men and 1.4% of women being not married by the age of 50 (Falkingham and Gonça 2001, 310). Recent data demonstrate that marriage is still almost universal. In absolute figures the number of marriages increased between 1980 and 1999 from 217,000 to 273,000 and the crude marriage rate (marriages per 1000 population) is very high, which did not decline between 1980 and 1999 remarkably, namely from 8.1 to 8.0. European marriage rates were slightly higher in some places such as Liechtenstein (8.7) and remarkably higher in Cyprus (14.0) but significantly lower in most other countries (Eurostat 2002).

Alternative forms of marriage, such as cohabitation are practiced only on a very low scale. Pre-marital sex and cohabitation also hardly exists; the cohabitation rate in 2003 was only 0.2% (population at age 15-29). Therefore, childbirth outside of marriage practically does not occur, which is reflected by a percentage at 0.5% (Falkingham and Gjonça 2001, 310; Aassve, Gjonca and Mencarini 2006, 19; Lerch 2011, 16; Aassve, Gjonca and Mencarini 2006, 288). There is an increase of divorces; however, Albanian divorce rates are still at the bottom of the European scale. Whereas Sweden leads Europe's list with a percentage of 54.9 of divorced marriages (2002), Albania enjoys still a very low divorce rate of 10.9%. However, the percentages of Bosnia (5%), Macedonia (5%) and Turkey (6%) are much lower (Divorce Magazine 2002; Eurostat 2002).

The age of women's first sexual intercourse in Albania remains relatively high compared to other European countries. Data indicate that the proportion of women who experienced sexual intercourse before the age of 18 was 10% for women aged

---

37 The household is defined "as a group of persons living together in one dwelling and who have a joint economy".
38 Migration, of course, has a considerable impact on family life and family composition. However, this complex phenomenon needs separate analysis.

between 40 and 44 and 16% for women aged between 20 and 24. The average age for first sexual intercourse for women was 21.1 years, only a few months younger than the average age of first marriage at 21.9 years (Aassve, Gjonca and Mencarini 2006, 288), which indicates that they would marry their first sexual intercourse partner.

With respect to fertility we cannot expect the same high level as decades ago, but the question is, whether Albanian fertility rate does equate with the rates of other European countries. The answer is yes. Generally, the onset of the First Demographic Transition among Muslim populations in the Balkans and the Near East was considerably late compared to Europe's Christian populations. Whereas the transition among the Christian Balkan population began in the 1880s with a population increase, this was the case among the Muslim populations only half a century later. This means that Muslim populations began to increase, when Christian populations already began to decrease. The reasons for these divergences are manifold; a high percentage of illiteracy among Muslim populations, especially among women was one of the most prominent reasons (Kaser 2011, 222). In 1945, Albania (as well as the Albanian population of Kosovo and Macedonia) had the highest fertility rate in Europe with an average of more than six births per woman. However, in the interventionist Communist period fertility fell to around three children per woman, despite the pro-natalist bio-politics of the Hoxha-regime and the absence of modern contraception and abortion. Fertility rose during the 1950s and reached a peak with almost seven children per woman around 1960. In the 1970ies a steady fertility decline began, which continues to the present. However, at the end of the communist period, fertility was still high compared to the neighboring Balkan countries (Falkingham and Gjonça 2001, 310).

This process was accompanied by a slight increase in the age at marriage and the date of first birth for women in 1990 compared to 1950. This, however, was not the reason for the decline in fertility. The reason was simply the intensified practice of traditional contraception methods such as withdrawal and coitus interruptus, the success of which indicates a decrease of patriarchal behavior (Ibid, 313-15) and an increase of young women's education and their inclusion in the work-force. Universal education and the increased involvement of women in agricultural and industrial production was a result of the Party's 'glorious struggle to emancipate women'. The regime provided equal educational access to boys and girls across all levels of education and by 1990 the share of women in higher education was 51.3% with the percentage of women in the work-force being 45.1%. This reduced the time a woman could spend with her children. With better education, the value of children in terms of family labour was also reduced. All these factors had a negative impact on fertility (Ibid, 317).

The reduction of fertility during the 1990s was also due to the delay of the second and third births; there was no change in timing of first birth. The first birth used to occur within the first year after marriage (Aassve, Gjonca and Mencarini 2006, 4). Whereas the total fertility rate in 1990 was 3.0, it was 2.2 in 2004 and only 1.6 in 2008-09 (Ibid, 10; Measure DHS 2010). Within less than two decades, the fertility rate halved. There was a relatively sharp break in fertility as a consequence of the crisis in 1997. During the subsequent political and economic consolidation, the more highly qualified strata began to postpone their marriages and births. Since the beginning of the 21st century, the First Demographic Transition seems to be completed with a decline in fertility to sub-replacement levels. The fertility rate in Tirana is only 1.0 (2010). The obvious reason is that women began to retreat from universal motherhood and/or to delay family formation. Whereas in 2000 70% of women married before the age of 24, in 2007 only 40% did. The different socioeconomic strata began to behave differently. Whereas lower-skilled women maintain their traditional family formation patterns, highly-skilled women begin to postpone marriage and child-bearing (Lerch 2011, 9-14). The question arises whether fertility decline is a result of changing family values or vice versa, if declining fertility rates have a sustainable impact on family values.

FAMILY AND KINSHIP IDEOLOGY

The northern mountainous areas had constituted the backbone of Albania's patriarchal ideology, which was supported by the rule of customary laws, which only was wiped out temporarily by the communist regime. Zogu's government was not successful in establishing a rule of public law in the region before. Unlike the southern parts of the country, where the patrilineal descent group was only weakly established, the patriarchal order was much milder and the traditional self-governing institutions, which had worked under the rule of customary laws, had been already destroyed by the end of the 18th century, the traditional social order in the north remained practically untouched until the communists destroyed it by force. The patrilineal descent groups here were characterized by tribe-like organizations, which basically practiced exogamy and controlled defined territories. Whereas in the south, the descent group's consciousness comprised only three or four subsequent generations, the importance of the male bloodline in the north could comprise ten or more generations. Whereas in the north, the milk line, i.e. the bride's line, did not become kin with the male bloodline of the husband upon marriage, in the south kinship runs through the male as well as through the female line (Pichler 2003, 104-107; de Rapper (to be published). This does not mean that north and south reflects radical different societies but rather variants of a pronounced patriarchal order.

In communist times, the power of the former tribal leaders and the tribes' informal self-governing bodies was destroyed, but it remains doubtful whether this was also the case with the accompanying patriarchal ideology, which could not be wiped out so easily. Although solidarity among and cohesion of the members of the patrilineal descent group seemed to be weakened, the principles of patrilineality and patrilocality are still constitutive for household formation, rules of customary laws are still applied and ancestor worship is still practiced (Kaser 1995, 142-148). Via internal migration processes from the rural areas to cities such as Shkodra, Tirana or Elbasan, this ideology and customary behaviour has been transported into urban settings. Nowadays, Albania's cultural context appears to be oscillating between a return to tradition and the development of new influences from neighboring Europe, channeled through external migration (Lerch 2011, 7). Most of the post-socialist societies seem to experience a phase of re-patriarchalization based on traditional values.

In the first decade of transition due to economic crisis, social anomie and extremely weak institutional bodies, people increasingly began to more intensely rely on extended kinship structures in order to establish a form of economic and social security. This brought about a re-traditionalization of society, which primarily spelled negative effects for women's freedom. Women became subject to stricter controls in order to prevent family dishonor. Gossiping, the parents' fear for their daughters' security and for potential love affairs at school resulted in pulling them out from school. Many of them never returned and were married early. In addition, a traditional pattern was strengthened, namely an increasing age at marriage of men because of their time they spent abroad before union formation. The widening gap between the husbands and wives thus restricts female empowerment within couples. The social pressure on women to reproduce was increased by patrilocal and multigenerational living arrangements in urban areas and especially in Tirana, which were caused by the high costs of apartments under liberal market conditions. This explains at least partly the maintenance of traditional fertility behavior among the lower strata of society (Lerch 2011, 14-16).

Islam is considered to constitute the framework of re-traditionalization in Muslim societies since the Islamic Revolution in Iran in 1979. Approximately 70% of Albania's population is considered to be Muslim. However, in all of the post-socialist countries in the Balkans a remarkable revitalization of the Muslim and Orthodox religions can be registered. This is also the case in Albania, where in the first decade after the fall of communism religiosity was low. At the turn of the century, the percentage of people who declared themselves religious believers jumped from 43.4 (1998) to 65.2% of the overall population (2002) (World Values Survey 2009)—a proportion, which is still relatively low. Taking this into consideration, the re-emergence of religiosity did not contribute significantly to this process of re-traditionalization.

As in other post-socialist countries, the fall of the regime affected the public sphere. By contrast, the private sphere represented continuity with the past and remained the main source of livelihood during the transition, especially for women who withdrew *en masse* from the labor market (Lerch 2011, 7). Unemployment among women is higher vis-à-vis men with a rate of 28% compared to 18.8% for men with female income being only approximately 50% that of male income (2004). The percentage of housewives has increased to 47% for women 15 years and over. When asked whether being only a housewife is fulfilling, approximately 45% of the Albanian respondents agreed or agreed strongly in 2000. This agreement, however, was lower than in the other Balkan countries (Kaser 2008, 215). This relatively low approval probably reflects an economic situation in which a single male breadwinner usually cannot provide for a sufficient household income (Aassve, Gjonca and Mencarini 2006, 4; Kaser 2011, 217).

Albanian society has remained traditional in terms of sexual behavior (Ibid, 10) as already mentioned before. The use of contraceptive methods fits this observation and is far from indicative of a Second Demographic Transition (Lerch 2011, 16). For instance, although 90% of Albanian women know about modern contraception methods, only 8% of married women use those (2002); 67% of females and 74% of males report withdrawal as the main means of contraception (Ibid, 19). From 2002 to 2008-09, the percentage of modern contraceptive-use inclined to 11%; surprisingly, there is no significant difference between urban (10%) and rural (12%) married women (2008-09 Albania 2009).

With regard to family values, change is noticeable on a low scale. In 1998, only 1.1% of Albania's population thought that children were not necessary for a woman to be fulfilled. Four years later, in 2002, already 7.2% shared this view. What is striking is the growing number of Albanians, who think that marriage is an outdated institution. Whereas in 1998, 5.1% agreed to this statement, in 2002 8.2% agreed. This corresponds roughly with the approval of women as single parents, the percentage of which increased from 9.7 (1998) to 11.1% (2002). Equally interesting is the response to the question addressed by the World Value Survey in 1998: "If you were to have only one child, would you rather a boy or a girl?", 51.3% opted for a girl and only 32.2% for a boy, 13.2% remained undecided (World Value Survey 2009).

Kinship ties have been adapted to the new challenges. They seem to be weaker than at the beginning of the 20th century, but kinship networks function in reformulated ways nowadays. Migration plays a significant role in this reformulation of kinship ties since it extends them over regions and state borders and mobilizes countryside to city-exchanges and vice versa. Extended kinship relations, in Albanian contexts, still constitute the basis for informal transactions and the solution of economic and everyday problems in a society, which is tributarily and fragmentarily organized.

Ideas such as the common good in Albania are clearly not as expressed as in Western and Central European democracies. Albania shares this attitude with its neighboring Balkan countries, where civil societal structures also hardly exist and the degree of societal fragmentation is also high. Economic, social and political relations are family-centered as almost everywhere in the region. Trust exists only among kinship members, and actions aim at defending and expanding group interests and resources at the expense of other individuals and groups. Rapid enrichment is possible for strong family and kinship groups. The political system is controlled by more powerful groups and can become another resource for their own enrichment (La Cava and Nanetti 2000, 45).

Such a constellation is good for the group's survival but extremely negative for societal cohesion. A World Bank-study characterizes this situation by the term 'vulnerability gap'.[39] Due to the inability of traditional kinship networks as well as the post-socialist governments to bridge the societal fragmentation a series of social vulnerable groups have emerged, which are exposed to human abuse and widespread violence. Contrary to poverty, vulnerability is caused by low social cohesion in Albanian society, which cannot be improved simply by economic measures. The study published in 2000 identifies seven vulnerable groups: youth at risk of abandoning school, institutionalized and abandoned children, young men at risk of criminal behavior, young men at risk for drug addiction, abandoned elderly, and women at risk for gender abuse (young women at risk for prostitution and adult women without male protection). Especially vulnerable according to this study are divorced women without children; it is difficult for them to remarry, to return back home or to live alone. Their family of origin considers them a shame and/or economic burden (Ibid. 1-5, 36).

The World Bank considers the implantation of the idea of social capital a necessary prerequisite for enhancing community action in order to provide for public good at various levels. The exemplary differences between familialism and social capital can be roughly sketched as follows:

---

39 La Cava and Nanetti 2000. The study is based on fieldwork conducted in 1997-98.

Table 1: Familialism versus social capital (Ibid, 46)

Familialism	Defining elements	Social capital
Of group members	Trust	Among non-group members
Group cohesion	Values	Community solidarity
Defence of group	Actions	Civic engagements
In-group resources	Outputs	Public goods
Haves and have-nots	Outcomes	Diffused and self-sustaining development
Social exclusion	Societal goal	Social inclusion
Rapid enrichment	Political strategy	Cumulative improvements
Group members	Actors	Community members

This critical approach towards family and kinship-centrism demonstrates a double-edged sword. It provides for necessary instruments and a means for people to survive in critical moments in history but it undermines the foundation required for a modern democratic state to be established.

In conclusion, this paper has attempted to outline the most important stages undergone by Albanian rural and urban families in the course of the 20th and at the beginning of the 21st century. Continuities and discontinuities characterize the history of the Albanian family in this turbulent period of time. The hypothesis of an existent homogenous 'Balkan family' pattern that until the Second World War allegedly was widespread over the Western and Central Balkans including also the Albanian family, has been challenged, but much more research has to be done in order to clarify distinct household formation patterns in various Balkan regions in time and space. The most remarkable discontinuity consists in family size and household composition. The nuclear family became the almost exclusive pattern already in the communist period and the average number of children decreased roughly from six to two.

It was the concept of the Albanian Party of Labor and its interventionist methods of rule that pushed the family in the direction of modern forms but not necessarily in the direction of modern family values and sexual behaviour. To a certain extent, Party politics conserved traditional family values by giving family formation absolute priority in its ambition to increase Albania's population. The protected family life became seriously challenged by the new constraints of market economy following the abdication of the communist system. Whereas during the subsequent two decades political and economic life was instable, the new state's institutions remained weak and future became non-predictable for the crisis-shaken population, family and kinship cohesion was kept intact to an astonishing degree. One could state that the turbulent century only altered family size and household composition but did not question traditional family values and universality of marriage. Sexual behavior with an emphasis on female virginity and a low rate of use of modern contraceptives are rather signs of continuity rather than of discontinuity.

REFERENCES

2008-09 Albania. 2009. "2008-09 Albania Demographic and Health Survey. Fact Sheet," accessed February 29, 2012,
http://www.measuredhs.com/pubs/pdf/GF16/GF16.pdf.

Aassve, Arnstein, Arjan Gjonca and Letizia Mencarini. 2006. *The highest fertility in Europe – for how long? The analysis of fertility change in Albania based on Individual Data*. ISER Working Paper 2006-56. Colchester: University of Essex, accessed February 29, 2012,
http://www.iser.essex.ac.uk/files/iser_working_papers/2006-56.pdf.

Becker, Berit. 2003. *Behind stone walls: changing household organization among the Albanians of Kosova*. Prishtina: Dukagjini Publishing House.

Boué, Ami. 1889. *Die europäische Türkei*. Vol.1. Vienna: Kaiserl. Akademie der Wissenschaften in Wien.

Brunnbauer, Ulf. 2004. *Gebirgsgesellschaften auf dem Balkan: Wirtschaft und Familienstrukturen im Rhodopengebirge (19./20. Jahrhundert)*. Vienna-Cologne-Weimar: Böhlau.

Brunnbauer, Ulf. 2004a. "Fertility, Families and Ethnic Conflict: Macedonians and Albanians in the Republic of Macedonia, 1944-2002," *Nationalities Papers* 32, 565-598.

De Rapper, Gilles. 2012. "Blood and Seed, Trunk and Hearth: Kinship and Common Origin in Southern Albania," in *Albania. Family, Society and Culture in the 20th Century,* edited by Andreas Hemming, Gentiana Kera and Enriketa Pandelejmoni (Wien, Berlin: Lit), 79-96.

Divorce Magazine. 2002. "World Divorce Statistics," accessed February 29, 2012, www.divorcemag.com/statsWorld.shtml.

Doja, Albert. 2010. "Fertility Trends, Marriage Patterns, and Savant Typologies in Albanian Context," *Journal of Family History* 25, 346-367.

Eurostat. 2002. *First results of the demographic data collection for 2002 in Europe*, accessed February 29, 2012, http://www.eds-estatis.de/en/downloads/sif/nk_03_20.pdf.

Falkingham, Jane and Gjonça, Arjan. 2001. "Fertility transition in Communist Albania, 1950-90," *Population Studies* 55, 309-318.

Gjonca, Arjan, Arnstein Aassve and Letizia Mencarini. 2008. "Albania: Trends and patterns, proximate determinants and policies of fertility change," *Demographic Research* 19: 261-292, accessed February 29, 2012, http://www.demographic-research.org/Volumes/Vol19/11/19-11.pdf.

Gopčević, Spiridion. 1880. "Ethnographische Studien in Ober-Albanien," *Dr. A. Petermann's Mitteilungen* 26, 405-420.

Gopčević, Spiridion. 1881. *Oberalbanien und seine Liga*. Leipzig: Duncker & Humblot.

Grandits, Hannes and Gruber, Siegfried. 1996. "The Dissolution of the Large Complex Households in the Balkans: Was the Ultimate Reason Structural or Cultural?" *The History of the Family* 1, 477-496.

Gruber, Siegfried and Pichler, Robert. 2002. "Household structures in Albania in the early 20th century," *The History of the Family* 7, 351-374.

Gruber, Siegfried. 2006. "The Quarters of Shkodra in 1918: Differences and Similarities," *Ethnologia Balkanica* 10, 141-158.

Gruber, Siegfried. 2008. "Household structures in urban Albania in 1918," *The History of the Family* 13, 138-151.

Gruber, Siegfried. 2009. "Household Formation and Marriage: Different Patterns in Serbia and Albania?" in *Families in Europe. Between the 19th and 21st Centuries. From the Traditional Modell to the Contemporary PACS*, edited by Antoinette Fauve-Chamoux and Ioan Bolovan (Cluj-Napoca: Cluj University Press), 229-247.

Hahn, Johann G. Von. 1854. *Albanesische Studien*. Jena: Friedrich Mauke.

Institute of Statistics. 2001. *Preliminary Results of the General Census of Population and Housing, April 1, 2001*, accessed February 29, 2012, www.instat.gov.at/repoba/zyra_shtypit/prel_engl.thm.

Kaser, Karl. 1992. *Hirten, Helden, Stammeskämpfer. Ursprünge und Gegenwart des Balkanischen Patriarchats*. Vienna, Cologne, Weimar: Böhlau.

Kaser, Karl. 1992a. "The Origins of the Balkan Patriarchy," *Modern Greek Studies Yearbook* 8, 1-39.

Kaser, Karl. 1993. "Ahnenkult und Patriarchalismus auf dem Balkan," *Historische Anthropologie* 1, 93-122.

Kaser, Karl. 1995. *Familie und Verwandtschaft auf dem Balkan*. Vienna, Cologne, Weimar: Böhlau.

Kaser, Karl. 1995a. "Jede Menge Familie," in *Albanien. Stammesgesellschaft zwischen Tradition und Moderne*, edited by Helmut Eberhart and Karl Kaser (Vienna, Cologne, Weimar: Böhlau), 133-149.

Kaser, Karl. 1996. "Introduction: Household and Family Contexts in the Balkans," *The History of the Family* 1, 375-386.

Kaser, Karl. 2000. "The History of the Family in Albania in the 20th Century: a First Profile," *Ethnologia Balkanica* 4, 45-57.

Kaser, Karl. 2003. "'The Winner Takes It All': Tribal Aspects of Albania's Political Culture," in *Political culture in the Baltic Sea Region and in Eastern Europe*, edited by Walter Rotholz (Berlin: Aland-Verlag), 145-151.

Kaser, Karl. 2010. "Patriarchen, Machos und Beamte: Varianten europäischer Sozialbeziehungen," in *Kontinuitäten und Brüche: Lebensformen – Alteingesessene – Zuwanderer von 500 bis 1500*, edited by Karl Kaser, Dagmar Gramshammer-Hohl and Elisabeth Vogel (Klagenfurt: Wieser Verlag = Wieser Enzyklopädie des Europäischen Ostens, vol. 12), 421-549.

Kaser, Karl. 2011. *Balkan und Naher Osten. Einführung in eine gemeinsame Geschichte*. Vienna, Cologne, Weimar: Böhlau.

Kaser, Michael. 2003a. "Die Nationalökonomie Albaniens im Transformationsprozeß," *Österreichische Osthefte* 45, 379-395.

Kera, Gentiana. 2003. "The Albanian Population Census of 1918: Basic Statistics and Analyses" (Diploma thesis, University of Graz).

Kera, Gentiana and Pandelejmoni, Enriketa. 2008, "Marriage in urban Albania (during the first half of the twentieth century)," *The History of the Family* 13, 126-137.

La Cava, Gloria and Nanetti, Rafaella Y. 2000. *Albania: Filling the vulnerability Gap*. Washington: The World Bank (= World Bank Technical Paper 460).

Lerch, Mathias. 2011. "Fertility decline in Albania: interplay with societal crisis and subsequent consolidation" (paper presented at the Population Association of America

Meeting 2011, Washington DC, March 31–April 2, accessed February 29, 2012), available at: http://paa2011.princeton.edu/download.aspx?submissionId=111667.

Measure DHS. 2010. "Demographic and Health Service," accessed February 29, 2012, http://www.measuredhs.com/publications/publication-GF16-General-Fact-Sheets.cfm.

Mitterauer, Michael. 1996. "Family Contexts: The Balkans in European Comparison," *The History of the Family* 1, 387-406.

Neuwirth, Hubert. 1995. "Geschichte muß sein," in *Albanien. Stammesgesellschaft zwischen Tradition und Moderne*, edited by Helmut Eberhart and Karl Kaser (Vienna, Cologne, Weimar: Böhlau), 17-30.

Nicholson, Beryl. 2006. "Women who shared a husband: Polygyny in southern Albania in the early 20th century," *The History of the Family* 11, 45-57.

Papa, Enriketa. 2003. "The Albanian Population Census of 1918: Household and Family" (Diploma thesis, University of Graz).

Pichler, Robert. 2003. "Gewohnheitsrecht und traditionelle Sozialformen in Albanien," *Österreichische Osthefte* 45, 97-110.

Reineck, Janet S. 1991. *The past as refuge: gender, migration, and ideology among the Kosova Albanians* (PhD diss., University of California).

Rrapi, Gjergj. 1995. *Savremene albanske zadružne porodice*. Belgrade: Filozofski fakultet.

Seiner, Franz. 1922. *Ergebnisse der Volkszählung in Albanien in dem von den österr.-ungar. Truppen 1916-1918 besetzten Gebiete*. Vienna, Leipzig: Hölder, Pichler, Temsky (= Schriften der Balkankommission, Linguistische Abteilung XIII).

Seiner, Franz. 1922a. *Die Gliederung der albanischen Stämme*. Graz: Author's edition.

Sjöberg, Örjan. 1991. *Rural Change and Development in Albania*. Boulder: Westview Press.

Wikipedia. 2011. "Lists of economies by incremental GDP from 1980 to 2010," last modified on September 23, http://en.wikipedia.org/wiki/List_of_countries_by_GDP_growth_1990%E2%80%932007.

World Values Survey. 2009. "World Values Survey 1981-2008 Official Aggregate v.20090901," accessed February 29, 2012, www.worldvaluessurvey.org.

ERMIRA DANAJ

FAMILY IN ALBANIA AS A PRIMARY SOLIDARITY NETWORK

INTRODUCTION

The aim of this paper is to explore the Albanian family beginning in the early 1990s following the fall of the communist regime, the main characteristic of which was a centralized state with a formal full social protection system. In the aftermath of the communist regime, Albania has experienced significant socio-cultural, economic and political changes, which have notably transformed the social and cultural networks. The principal developments in this transitory period were the opening of the country to external influences and a new multiparty political system, established as a first step toward a Western-style democracy; the new market economy began to introduce new rules regulating the supply and demand of work, housing, goods and services, etc. In a country where almost everything was controlled by the communist state, these developments resulted in periods of acute discomfort, high unemployment, problems in the education system and other related social and economic issues (Danaj, Festy et al. 2005, 7;79). In the past two decades since the collapse of the communist regime, Albania has witnessed massive flows of external and internal migration, massive privatization, the collapse of a massive pyramid scheme in 1997, a minimalist welfare state, political instability, etc. In lieu of these developments, families have assumed a strong role in attenuating the shock of poverty inherited from the communist regime; the high unemployment after 1990, in line with mass privatizations and the collapse of agriculture and industrial sectors, the housing difficulties, etc. Two decades after the fall of the communist regime, one may observe that the mutual support among family members is still very strong, and that informal channels of support function better than the state social provisions and assistance.

The family, as the primary social institution, is based on a functional support and reciprocity among family members, whereas state solidarity is mainly contractual, whereby social support, solidarity and reciprocity are formal (Bawin-Legros and Stassen 2002, 258). This implies that state solidarity and its related social provisions and assistance are formally regulated and should be organized in the same manner for everyone. Contrary to this, solidarity and reciprocity within the family is more flexible and informal and the rules for such a brand of solidarity and reciprocity are set amongst family members (Ibid.). This means that the internal family rules concerning solidarity and reciprocity lack the dimension of 'in the same manner for all', which is the main characteristic of state solidarity as a formal contract between the citizens and the state. Consequently, the replacement of state solidarity with a family/kinship support network will result in an unequal development instead of an equal distribution which characterizes a proper social welfare state (Ibid. 245, 248, 252, 258, 259). A strong social welfare state helps to combat inequalities created by the market and passed from generation to generation by the family. Weak welfare states rely on the market to produce and distribute wealth and on family support for individuals who need help. In the case of Albanian society, the fall of the communist regime in the early 1990s and the weakening of the central government led to the inevitable strengthening of the role of the family as a central social network.[40] Although the participation of the state grows, its importance regarding social support is residual, and the family is more than ever the main source of social support (Danaj, Festy et al. 2005, 80). Such is the case of the Albanian family of the past two decades.

The paper draws from a critical review of the literature and previous studies on social welfare state, socio-economic developments and migration dynamics in Albania and in the region. Additionally, this paper makes use of the current official data regarding socio-economic developments in Albania such as that available from the Census of 2001 and 2011 as well as the results of the Living Standards Measurement Survey 2002-2007. The main constraint with such resources is that the data from the Census conducted in 2011 by the Albanian government are still general as only the preliminary results have been published thus far. The paper has the following structure: (i) an analysis of the major dynamics of the social welfare state in Albania after the early 1990s, which is then followed by a critical overview of the main socio-economic transformations that occurred in Albanian society over the past two decades. The intention here is to explore the characteristics of the state social support and solidarity in Albania as it has developed during the transitory period towards the consolidation of democracy as well as to be able to compare such characteristics with the features of the social welfare state in the previous regime; (ii) the part of the paper engages in an in-depth analysis of one of the most significant socio-economic developments in Albania, i.e. internal and international migration, which has had a major impact on Albanian society. International migration and internal demographics are at the heart of economic, social, and cultural change in Albania over the past decades (King 2005, 133); (iii) this section of the paper offers a brief overview of the Albanian family structure and its essential characteristics in an attempt to contextualize the role of the family in contemporary Albanian society as the principal provider of social solidarity and support. Such a role will be explored in terms of remittances, which is why migration plays a crucial part in the current socio-economic developments in Albania; support in finding employment and housing for young generations; as well as in terms of the lack of consolidated state social policies and state solidarity for vulnerable groups such as children, elderly and/or sick persons.

WELFARE STATE DEVELOPMENT IN POST-COMMUNIST ALBANIA

Albania was the last country in the Eastern communist bloc to overthrow its communist regime only doing so in 1990. Despite the fact that during the communist era Albania experienced the highest degree of isolation from external influences compared to the other communist countries in Eastern Europe, the change from one political sys-

---

40 The role of the family in Albanian society was central even during the communist regime, even though the centralized state controlled almost all aspects of social life. In this vein, the state provided formal social support for its citizens and as a result Albanian society was characterized by a complementarity of family and state support and not by a substitution.

tem to another was not violent as it was in Romania. The events which marked the early days of the transition from communist regime to a new political system in Albania were the citizens' protests in the capital and in other major cities as well as the students' hunger strike, which is deemed to be one of the most significant moments in this period of significant political transformations. However, this apparently peaceful changeover of political systems was accompanied by difficult economic and social conditions and by a harsh transformation from a centralized to a free market economy. The growing pains switching to capitalism were equally intense, exposing the population to massive unemployment, uncontrolled demographic movement and a degree of government laissez-faire hard to distinguish from economic and judicial anarchy (De Waal 2005, 5).

Despite their common communist legacy, the Eastern European countries followed different development paths after the early 1990s: some countries, such as Poland and later on Albania, adopted a residual and familial model of social welfare state; other countries, such as the Czech Republic, despite the implementation of the free market economic reforms, have maintained some crucial elements of the social welfare state (Fultz et.al. 2003, 19, 20, 29). However, in general terms the level of faith in state solidarity, the social policies introduced by the state and the overall social landscape in the post-communist countries is lower than in the Western democracies (Fenger 2007, 25). The system of social security and the overall social welfare mechanisms implemented in post-communist countries have been relatively weak due to the lack of resources and the deterioration of the public institutions' capacities to adopt, design and implement social policies (Bartlett and Xhumari 2007, 8). Therefore, currently it is very difficult to situate the post-communist welfare states within any of Esping-Andersen's[41] or any other well-known types of welfare state. On the other hand, the empirical analysis does not show a distinct, specific type of post-communist, welfare state which developed only in the post-communist countries. In this sense, post-communist welfare states are merely characterized by lower levels of their govern-

---

41 According to Gosta Esping-Andersen the welfare state models could be clustered in three regimes/ideal types: the liberal/residual welfare state, the corporatist/conservator or Bismarck welfare state and the social democratic/universalist welfare state (Esping-Andersen 2006, 167-169; Merrien et al. 2005, 178). The liberal regime is characterized by means-tested assistance, modest universal transfers or modest social-insurance plans. The protection is offered to the most marginalized and weakest persons and is associated with stigma. In the corporatist regime, according to Esping-Andersen "the liberal obsession with market efficiency and commodification was never pre-eminent and, as such, the granting of social rights was hardly ever a seriously contested issue. What predominated was the preservation of status differentials; rights, therefore, were attached to class and status" (Esping Andersen 2006, 167). In this regime the redistribution is weak, the right is associated to class and status, and the social services for the family and children are weak (Merrien et al 2005, 179); under a strong influence of the Church, trying to preserve a traditional family-hood, social insurance in this regime excludes non-working wives, and family benefits encourage motherhood; the principle of 'subsidiarity' serves to emphasize that the state will only interfere when the family's capacity to service its members is exhausted (Esping-Andersen, 2006, 168). The social-democratic regime is characterized by a high level of social protection and a high level of redistribution. We do not find here a dualism between state and market, between working class and middle class, but a model that would promote an equality of the highest standards, not an equality of minimal needs as we saw in the other regimes. The right is associated to the citizenship not to the class and status (Merrien et al 2005, 179); the social services allow independence within the family and allow women to choose work rather than the household. According to Esping-Andersen the emancipation is not only addressed to the state but also to the family, and the principle is not to wait until the family's capacity to aid is exhausted, and not to maximize dependence on the family, but capacities for individual independence (Esping-Andersen 2006, 169).

mental programs and their particular social contexts (Fenger 2007, 27). As far as the Western Balkans is concerned, Albania, Macedonia and Kosovo have relatively low levels of social security and social protection expenditure overall, having followed a liberal economic policy involving meaningful reductions in government budget deficits. In contrast, Croatia, Bosnia and Herzegovina, Montenegro, and Serbia have followed a more traditional corporatist model with relatively high shares of public expenditure in proportion to GDP (Bartlett and Xhumari 2007, 25).

Since 1993, every Albanian government has applied the distribution of cash payments to poor families as the sole instrument of poverty alleviation in the country. This instrument was first designed at a time when the country was facing a complete collapse of the former political system and when extreme poverty was prevalent across the country (Bartlet and Xhumari 2007, 8). The economic assistance distribution scheme is a major instrument for the administration of social problems during the transition period but it offers minimal guarantees in support of poor families. The economic assistance scheme, which represents an economic program in cash transfers in support of the poorest section of the population, was launched in 1993 based on Law 7710, dated 18.05.1993 "On Social Protection and Assistance". Under this law and other by-laws, the right to economic assistance applies to families which have inadequate or no income at all. Economic assistance is a means-tested social assistance program for urban families with no independent source of income and rural families with small plots of land (Papps and Danaj 2005, 3; Bartlett and Xhumari 2007, 8, 22). Economic assistance still remains the primary state policy for the reduction of poverty, while there is still no official established minimum living standard. The amount received by families in the economic assistance scheme is much lower compared to the minimum living standard in Albania as established by various non-governmental organizations working in the area of social policies. Based on the regulations introduced by the Ministry of Labor, Social Affairs and Equal Opportunities within the framework of the law on social protection and assistance, the amount to be distributed to families in the economic assistance scheme is calculated based on the number of family members, but cannot exceed 7,500 Lek per month (approximately 60 Euro per month)[42]. This is the total amount that a family in need received from the state every month to cover all living expenses. Whereas, as will be shown in the following section, the average monthly amount from remittances varies from 70 to 115 Euro (Agenda 2011, 3), i.e. this amount is higher than the maximum amount that a family in need receives from the state in the form of economic assistance.

The system of social protection and economic assistance in Albania is conceptualized in such a way that it refers only to the support and assistance provided to marginalized groups in society such as Roma, street children, victims of trafficking, victims of domestic violence etc. In lieu of this situation, whereby the social protection from the state is residual, family/kinship plays a crucial role in social and economic support and solidarity. This implies that the lower the extent of the social welfare state, the greater the role of the family as solidarity network in regards to the support and protection of the elderly, children, social and economic assistance and so on.

---

42 Figures are available at the official website of the Social State Service which is the responsible institution for the administration of the Economic Assistance Scheme in Albania. Accessed July 14, 2012, http://www.shssh.gov.al/ndihma-ekonomike/grupet-perfituese.

MIGRATION IN ALBANIA

As stated above, migration has been (one of) the most significant processes in post-communist Albania. According to De Waal "[…] the two commonest survival strategies since the end of communism have been migration abroad and descent from mountain villages to plains and plains towns" (De Waal 2005, 241). Albania experienced the highest level of internal and international migration after the fall of the communist regime compared to other post-communist countries in Eastern Europe. This is mainly due to the fact that the communist government in Albania imposed absolute control over the internal and external movement of its citizens and the country was almost completely isolated from the rest of the world. The massive international migration outside of the country has a major impact on the economic, social and political transformation of the Albanian society. The international or external migration served as the driving force of the internal demographic movements (De Waal 2005; Agolli et al. 2011), whereby through the remittances and other forms of support from emigrants, their families and relatives in Albania started to move from the periphery and isolated countryside areas towards urban areas and the major cities in Albania.

According to the World Bank, nearly 1.5 million Albanians, that is almost half of the resident population of Albania, have emigrated between 1990 and 2010 (Vullnetari 2012, 15; Gedeshi and Jorgoni 2012, 6).

In 1997 Albania experienced the most dramatic crisis after 1990, the collapse of several pyramid schemes which affected almost two-thirds of Albanian families who in turn, lost most of their savings (Gedeshi and Jorgoni 2012, 7). Unofficially, it is estimated that Albanians lost around 1 billion dollars in this scheme. After the collapse of this scheme the country went through a chaotic period with almost a complete lack of state control.

Based on the preliminary results of the Census 2011 data the population of Albania in 2011 is 2,831,741[43] compared to 3,069,275 according to the 2001 Census. This means that there has been a population decrease in Albania of 7.7% in about ten years. According to INSTAT, this is supposed to have been to the result of large scale emigration and a decline in fertility from 2.1 in 2001 to 1.4 in 2008 (INSTAT 2002; MoLSAEO 2012, 26).

Emigration, internal migration and demographic movements in Albania are strongly related to each other, despite the fact that the processes are highly complex and individuals and families are involved in various forms in these movements (Vullnetari 2012; De Waal 2005; Agolli et al. 2011). Internal migration in Albania after 1990 was characterized by a total lack of official policies governing it. During this period, there was no control over the free movement of people. The movement that happened was accompanied by a massive, chaotic, and disproportionate development of the urban

---

43 The Census is the complete count of all dwellings, households, and residents at a single point in time (census moment), together with the record of some of their characteristics 'Usual residents' are all persons who are usually resident in Albania, regardless of their citizenship and whether or not they are present at their usual place of residence at the census moment or temporarily absent providing that this absence is not longer than 12 months. Only persons who have resided in the place of usual residence for a continuous period of at least 12 months prior to the census moment; or who arrived at their place of usual residence during the 12 months prior to the census moment, with the intention of staying there for at least one year, shall be considered usual resident(s) (INSTAT 2011).

zones in comparison to the rural areas. It is argued that "[…] as well as failing to organize emigration or tackle corruption and crime, the Democratic government took no steps to organise the growing demographic trend to descend from mountain regions to the coastal plains. In 1995, President Berisha made his 'fytyrë nga deti' (face towards the sea) proclamation, officially recommending what was already a fait accompli. This was a feeble attempt to present the unstoppable bid for economic survival by mountain villagers descending to squat on coastal plains, as if it were part of a state instigated program. The subsequent absence of measures to regulate this influx was defended as a freedom of movement policy (*lëvizje e lirë*), intentionally laissez-faire." (De Waal 2005, 9). The lack of government control and regulation of the internal demographic movement served as a political instrument to conceal the major economic problems that families were facing in Albania, to eclipse the lack of development strategies and adequate social policies and to keep the population calm and hopeful of better social and economic prospects to come with the new political and economic system in place after the 1990s.

Internal migration toward the urban centers led to a decline of 13% in the rural population when comparing the 2001 Census with to the previous Census in 1989. According to the data from the Census in 2001, urban population has markedly increased due to internal migration, from 33.5% in 1979 and 35.7% in 1989 to 42.1% in 2001 (INSTAT 2002). In the previous period (1945-1990) the rural population had actually increased by 20%. Not only did the population move from the villages to the towns, but also from the mountainous regions to the hillside areas, from the more remote areas to the urban countryside, and from rural areas with a cold climate and little arable land to villages with a milder climate and more cultivation opportunities (Galanxhi et al. 2004). According to the data from LSMS 2005, about 16% of households nationwide are headed by individuals who have moved since 1990. In the majority of cases, it was individuals and not entire families who moved, and only 5% of households moved together in the same year between 1990 and 2004 (World Bank 2007, 31). The trends show that internal migration rose between 1990 and 1998, and then declined thereafter. Since 1998, the flow has decreased sharply, and appears to be stabilizing at approximately 20,000 individuals per year (Ibid. 32). Due to the internal movement of population toward urban and central areas, the population of the capital (Tirana) alone is estimated to have risen from 200,000 in the early 1990s to approximately 800,000 in 2005 (Caro 2011, 32). According to INSTAT, "[…] for the first time in the history of population censuses in Albania, the population in urban areas is larger than the population of rural areas. According to 2011 census preliminary results, 53.7% of the population lives in urban areas and 46.3% in rural areas". There is an increase of the urban population from 1,294,196 inhabitants in 2001 to 1,521,907 inhabitants in 2011, while there is a decrease of the rural population from 1,775,079 in 2001 to 1,309,834 in 2011 (INSTAT 2012). This shows that the internal movement in Albania has continued with an important pace even during this last decade.

FAMILY SOLIDARITY INSTEAD OF STATE SUPPORT

Clarissa de Waal argues that: "Emigration has eased the problem of unemployment and produced remittances so substantial that this money has sustained the households of the unemployed at home. The scale of emigration (greater proportionately than from any other former communist country in Europe) and the level of remittances have enabled the state—weak, distant and indifferent—to avoid tackling the main obstacles to political and economic advance [...]. Internal migration, emigration, emigrants' remittances and savings have prevented Albania from collapsing. At the same time, Albania's leaders have for the most part hampered development, partly through misguided interventionism, mainly through laissez-faire."[44] In the context of a 'laissez-faire' state, individuals and families have found their coping strategies mainly through mobility, international migration and internal demographic movements. Family support and solidarity have functioned not only through the provision of cash for family members, but also through the use of family/kinship network to find job opportunities, to cope with housing problems and the lack of other social services. In lieu of a very weak social welfare state in Albania, family networks remain the only solidarity nets that are the main coping mean in the difficult transition period in the country, but at the same time these nets reinforce inequalities in society (Danaj, Festy et al. 2005, 79-80).

Economic aid versus remittances

According to recent studies regarding the internal and external movements, apart from the remittances from emigration, a small percentage of the economic support for families and relatives in Albania is also covered by the money transfers from internal migration (Agenda 2011, 3; Vullnetari 2012, 172). Consequently, this paper will take into consideration, despite their respective percentages, remittances from both internal and external migration. Remittances are considered to be a major element of migration not only for the countries of origin, but also for host countries.[45] Remittances have played an essential role in Albania and they constitute one of the major elements of financial support for families in need and in deep economic problems, thus contributing to the reduction of poverty levels in lieu of the lack of social state policies and state solidarity (Vullnetari 2012). In 2004, the World Bank pointed out that the flux of

---

44 Clarissa de Waal, presentation at the Second International Conference in the framework of the Regional Research Promotion Program, June 2010, Durrës, Albania.
45 Remittances can be looked upon as the payment that the source country receives in exchange for lending its human resources. However, the relationship between economic development and inflow of remittances is ambiguous and research in this field has pointed out that remittance flows can have both a positive and a negative impact on the recipient country (Arrehag, et al. 2005; Vullnetari 2012). A recent report on the role of remittances on women's employment in Albania shows that there is a negative correlation between remittances and women's employment, and this increase with the marital status of 4)women and child rearing (Agolli et al. 2011). This is shown also from additional studies in other countries where the recipients of remittances have the tendency to not be engaged in paid work (Agenda 2011,

remittances from emigrants abroad reached 13.5% of the Albanian GDP, three times higher than the net foreign direct investments in the country and twice as high as the Official Development Assistance obtained by the Albanian government (Agenda 2011, 2). According to the study conducted by the Agenda Institute on the impacts of remittances in Albania (Agenda 2011), the average annual remittance from the European Union countries is €1,400, whereas from the United States of America it is approximately $830. This shows that on average every family receives $70 per month or €115 per month.

Drawing from the recent studies and research on the role of remittances in Albania, it is argued that the main use of remittances in Albania has been for: basic daily needs, food, clothing, utilities, to expand/build a house and for family celebrations such as 'weddings, funerals and religious celebrations'. Only a small portion have been used for investing in economic activities and these businesses are small with limited productivity and often informal (Gedeshi 2008; King and Vullnetari 2010; Agenda 2011). Remittances have improved the living conditions of households, but have had a limited role in creating sustainable work opportunities. 'Investment in farming' holds 6th place in the ranking for the use of remittances, and 'investment in non-agricultural businesses is 14th placed, being reported only by 2.6% of respondents (Vullnetari and King 2010, 25). Whereas, considering the research conducted by the Agenda Institute in 2011, which shows that the main use of remittances is for food and basic needs, for 73% of the families receiving remittances (Agenda 2011, 3). Thus, remittances are mainly used for living expenses, for funding the missing services (social, health, education, and infrastructure), and not for investing or savings, etc.

The importance of remittances for Albanian families is obvious when considering that 60% of Albanian families, with monthly income no more than 30,000 Lek, have a crucial and vital need for the money transfers from relatives abroad. Approximately 55% of the Albanian families that receive regular remittances are settled in rural areas, whereas 45% are settled in urban areas in Albania. The families in the rural areas receive approximately 63% of the overall amount of remittances from abroad. 77% of the families receiving remittances from abroad consist of 1-4 family members, which is the typical Albanian family structure based on the Census of 2011. Close family members are the ones to send more money transfers compared to other relatives. Young people/offspring working and living abroad typically send more money transfers to their parents and family living in Albania. The research of the Agenda Institute shows that 65% of the money transfers through remittances are carried out by young people/offspring sending money to their parents and only 10% are covered by husbands and/or wives (Agenda 2011, 8). Another important feature of the recipient family of the remittances from abroad is the monthly income they receive in Albania. More than half of the recipient families had average monthly income of no more than 30,000 Lek, without including here the money received through remittances. For these families, i.e. 51% of the overall families receiving remittances from abroad, the amount received from money transfers is crucial for maintaining their living standards. The research of the Agenda Institute also shows that half of the families receiving remittances are composed of family members who are unemployed or retired. For families living in the district of Tirana, remittances are even more significant. For 80% of these families, remittances are vital to their existence and for 39% the remittances are highly important. This is due, to some extent, to the internal demographic movements from rural and isolated areas towards the urban zones of the capital, Tirana, where one finds the highest level of population density.[46]

It is important to stress that the lion's share of the remittances received by Albanian families are used for basic living expenses such as food (65% of the families), which is then followed by health service expenses. Only 11% of the recipient families manage to use the amount received through remittances efficiently, i.e. for expenses and savings at the same time. Also, only 3% of the Albanian families use remittances for business and other types of investments. These figures show that the remittances are of crucial importance for the day to day living expenses of Albanian families, including health service expenses. In principle, health service provision is a public service, i.e. offered for free by the state and covered through the social and health insurance scheme, but in practice Albanians pay for health service provisions through informal payments to doctors and nurses or by going to private clinics and hospitals (World Bank, 2003). In this light, given that remittances offer a way-out for the economic problems at the micro level (individual and family level) and not at the macro level of overreaching long-term governmental social and economic policies, there is the risk that the reduction of remittances will bring about negative effects for Albanian families and Albanian society as a whole. The Albanian government is urgently facing such problems owing to two main reasons: first, the natural cycle of remittances, i.e. remittances will gradually decline as emigrants establish their households abroad; and secondly, the financial global crisis coupled with the most recent Euro zone crisis. Consequently, the flux of remittances, which used to be even higher than foreign direct investments, is gradually falling since 2008 (Agenda 2011, 19).

The use of remittances to cover daily basic living expenses can be observed in internal money transfers as well. Only a small percentage (9%) of Albanian families receive internal money transfers and the majority of these families (more than 50%) who benefit from local remittances are settled in rural areas, whereas the senders live and work in Tirana. 84% of such local or internal money transfers are used to cover food expenses and 60% are used to cover health service expenses, whereby 16% goes for specialized medical care. Only a quarter of the recipient families manage to save some money from the remittances. None of the recipient families use the amount received from internal or local remittances to invest in business or other forms of enterprise.

Drawing from the above figures and evidence, remittances have played a cardinal role in the survival of the Albanian families in lieu of harsh economic and social conditions in the transition from communism to democracy. Remittances have had both positive and negative effects in Albanian society. For instance, they have played an important role in the amelioration of living conditions, housing and health care for Albanian families in both urban and rural areas (Caro 2011; Vullnetari 2012), but at the same time they have had negative impacts on the employment opportunities for women (Agolli et al. 2011). Despite such contradictory effects, the main impact of remittances over the past two decades in Albania has been to fill the gap created by the lack of adequate social and economic policies in reducing poverty, improving well-being and living conditions, regulating internal movements and advancing social and

---

46 According to the preliminary results of the Census 2011 (INSTAT 2012) the density in Tirana in 2011 is 10,533 inhabitants per km² while the average of the country is 98.5 inhabitants per km².

health services etc. "The trajectory of change has been clear enough. Thanks to emigrant remittances, life inside most flats and some rural houses has become more comfortable with the acquisition of new sofa beds, television sets, washing machines, refrigerators, electric cookers and radiators. But while families with members abroad can afford to improve some aspects of their indoor standard of living, the public side of life, the leaking municipal water and waste systems, the overloaded degraded electrical network, is outside their control" (De Waal 2005, 14). As argued by De Waal (2005) and Vullnetari (2012), the solutions to the economic and social problems in Albania offered by remittances are short-term micro level ones and do not offer sustainable development in Albania.

Employment

Unemployment remains high in Albania, especially for young people and women. Amongst the youth the rate is significantly high for both sexes (between 15% and 27% depending on the age group of young people). Throughout the 30-59 age group, the women's unemployment rate remains significantly higher compared to that of the men, due mainly to their withdrawal from the labor market and retirement at home to care for children and the elderly (MoLSAEO 2012, 67-81), as will be explained further in this paper. Returning to the high unemployment rate for young people and difficulties in finding work, it appears as though these difficulties have increased the role of the family and family networks, which have a central role in the process of job searching, while the marginal importance of labor offices reflects the difficulty of the state to regulate the labor market.

According to the Living Standard Measurement Survey in 2002, only 9% of young people under 30 find their jobs through the labor offices, while 49% find it through friends and relatives. Among the unemployed youth seeking employment, the role of informal networks is even greater: 68% use information from family and friends, 21% rely on the Labor Offices and 3% start their own 'businesses'. Those who remain, in small numbers, look for a job in newspaper ads, etc. (Danaj and Festy 2007). The labor offices in Albania are intended to support job-seekers with the right information about the needs of the labor market, to facilitate communication between employers and job-seekers and to provide the proper training and qualifications for job-seekers. As mentioned above, such a role has been very weak, but remains unchanged. According to the Labor Force Survey 2009, the overwhelming majority of young people continue to report "family relations and friends" as the main source while looking for a job (MoLSAEO 2012, 67-81) and not state labor forces. Family/kinship relations still serve as network of support for the employment of young people as opposed to official state networks.

Residential autonomy and housing[47]

Another important dimension that emphases the role of the family as an essential support provider instead of state policies, is the support provided for housing. Before the communist regime, young people lived with their parents until marriage. Given the important role of the family, living alone was stigmatized. Normally, the wives would live with their husband's parents. In 1918, 75% of unmarried men aged 30 and 55% of married men were living with at least one parent, despite the high mortality rate for elderly parents (Gruber and Pichler 2002). After 1944, despite the importance of state social policies, residential independence did not become common place among the young before marriage. After marriage, it was the responsibility of the state to find accommodation for the young couple, in line with the state policy for strengthening of the nuclear family. But, with economic hardship, inadequate housing became a major problem, forcing young couples to live with their parents, usually the parents of the bridegroom.

In 1993, after the fall of communism, the state decided to privatize the housing sector and apartments were sold for insignificant amounts to their occupants. Parents of the young people of today have become owners of their homes. Since then, the market was completely liberalized and it has become extremely difficult to buy an apartment, especially for young people. In addition, the state no longer is responsible for finding housing for young couples. With the liberalization of the housing market, prices are extremely high. It is harder than ever for young people to become independent and live alone. The proportion of young people who live alone before marriage is low in Albania and this is due to the traditional way of envisioning the family, but also the very difficult economic situation of young people, which are the most-effected by unemployment, making it impossible to afford renting or buying an apartment.

Table 2: Single young people living with their parents (p. 100 single people in each age group).

Age	Men	Women	Total
15-19	93.7	93.8	93.8
20-24	92.3	93.1	92.6
25-29	87.6	89.0	88.1

Source: 2001[48] Population and Housing Census, INSTAT

According to research conducted by an international team of the Council of Europe about youth policies in Albania in 2009 young people continue to live with their par-

---

47 This section borrows its main elements from the report published by INSTAT, Albanian Institute of Statistics: Danaj, Ermira, Patrick Festy, Aida Guxho, Marinela Lika and Edvin Zhllima. 2005. Becoming an adult. Challenges and potentials of youth in Albania, Tirana: INSTAT, 97.
48 Data for housing refers to the 2001 Census as the complete results of the 2011 Census have not yet been published. It will be very important to compare after the two sets of data. However, if we refer to the CoE research report of 2009, it can be noticed that the trends remain the same.

ents. The report shows that: "It was too expensive to live independently and so young people continue to live with their parents, often even after getting married. Parents and families were usually accepting of this—it was part of tradition with a family-centered culture—but young people were less and less enamored with being 'trapped' in this way" (CoE 2010, 22).

Table 3: Married young people living with their parents (p.100 married young people in each age group)

Age	Men	Women	Total
15-19	70.1	63.0	63.4
20-24	60.3	49.1	51.4
25-29	46.1	32.0	37.5

Source: 2001 Population and Housing Census, INSTAT

The percentage of young married couples who live with their parents is certainly lower than that of young singles, but it is also remarkably high. The results are not very different from those recorded a century ago, when 55% of men aged 30, married, lived with their parents. Relying on more recent reports than the Census of 2001, the vast majority of young people in Albania live with their immediate or extended families, until and often beyond the time they get married. It is frequently explained as being a result of the Albanian tradition, "even if it has now become too expensive to do otherwise in Tirana" (CoE 2010, 39). On the other side, there are no state policies concerning housing, especially of young people. According to the same report of CoE, "housing, in the Albanian National Youth Strategy is conspicuous only by its absence" (Ibid.). There are no initiatives for supporting young people by a controlled/affordable renting system or by crediting facilities. In this context, specifically that of the absence of state support, family remains the provider of support for young people.

Social services and women's paid and unpaid work

During the communist regime, social policies and the state in general focused to a large extent on the family, i.e. providing support through social and economic policies to families including child care benefits and maternity leave scheme, complemented by a state-sponsored system of crèches and kindergarten. In addition, the prices for a number of essential products for children were subsidized by the state (Fultz et al. 2003). When analysing the developments of social welfare state in post-communist countries, it is observed that the reduction in social policies has primarily affected the mechanisms previous in place to support families and as a result women have been negatively impacted by these changes in social policies. The withdrawal of women from income-generating activity to the household to take care of children and family has turned out to be convenient for post-communist countries with minimal social welfare provisions.

When analysing the main indicators of the labour market in Albania, one may observe that the inactivity rate refers to the percentage of persons who, in principle, are available for the labour market but are neither registered as employed or unemployed. There is a pronounced gender difference in the inactivity rates of females and males. According to LFS 2009, the inactivity rate was 26.7 for men and 48.2 for women (MoLSAEO 2012, 67-81). This is affected by many factors including difficulties in finding a job with a regular contract, insurance, suitable working conditions and adequate salaries. In addition to this, there is a lack of social services regarding support and assistance provision for young people, elderly and disabled or sick persons. Statistical data shows that the level of unemployment and withdrawal from the labour market rises with the increase of the 'family responsibilities', which are deemed to be exclusive to women who are to answer for taking care of both children and household, whereas men provide income, according to a traditional production/reproduction division of duties.

In a study conducted in 2008 on the unpaid work of women within the household, the majority of the women participating in the study argued that the main reason for their withdrawal from the labour market and income-generating activities was to take care of children due to a lack of support for childcare and maternity leave from the government. The lack of adequate public crèches and kindergarten as well as the expensive rates of private childcare institutions force women to abandon employment in order to take care of children at least until the children are old enough to attend school.[49] However, once the children are ready to attend school and women are available to work, it is almost impossible to find a job and to adapt to the demands of the labour market. Other important aspects which were identified in the meetings with women in ten different cities in Albania were the low salaries and the inappropriate working conditions. The women participating in the study argued that it was more convenient for them to stay at home to take care of children rather than sending them to private kindergarten, which cannot be afforded because of very expensive rates. At the same time, they consider the public kindergarten as unsafe for their children due to a lack of appropriate conditions (Danaj, Plaku et al. 2008). In addition, it is important to mention that the lack of social and economic support for elderly and/or sick people, which is covered mainly by family members and family solidarity networks rather than by the state. There are private institutions offering care for the elderly and/or sick but Albanian families cannot afford them given their difficult economic conditions.

Referring to the economic situation of women it must be emphasized that few other elements lead to a better understanding of their dependency: incomes, property right and entrepreneurship. Regarding the property rights, the major issue is about land and recently the issue of legalization of illegal settlements in the suburbs of the big cities mainly in the center of Albania. Unfortunately there are not sex-disaggregated data about property which is one of the main issues raised recently by various reports. However, the last report on property and gender (Stanley and Di Martino 2012) provides some useful material for further analysis on this issue. In 1991, land in Albania was distributed based on Law 7501, called the land reform. "Each rural family re-

---

49 We are referring only to the circumstances of women living in the urban areas. In rural areas, women are deemed to be self-employed given that their families hold land in the form of private property. At the same time, in rural areas social support infrastructure for children or elderly people is even more problematic than in urban areas in Albania.

ceived a portion of the land based on the size of their household. The land was designated the private property of the family. While only the head of the household's name appears on the land certificate, the land reform allotted agriculture land as family ownership and not individual ownership. As such, each family member is considered a co-owner of the land" (Stanley and Di Martino 2012, 4). And in order to improve the life and work prospects of women in Albania, in 2003 the Albanian Family code (Law Number 9062 Adopted May 8, 2003) was adopted and it stipulated complete equality between men and women before the law in terms of rights and responsibilities. However, even with the adoption of the Gender Equality Law in 2008, the situation, in practice remains quite difficult for women. Based on the same report, "property is registered only in the name of the head of household (which in Albania is the eldest man of the household). The land titling process does not include registering both spouses. After divorce, the majority of Albanian women re-joins their parents household and do not pursue their right to joint property acquired during the marriage. Besides tradition, one of the reasons for this situation is the lack of earning opportunities and financial resources among Albanian women to initiate legal procedures (lawyer expenses, courts taxes, etc) [...] estimates of the percentage of Albanian women informed, or aware of, the benefits of having joint property registration is still low at 30%, and perhaps lower in rural areas. Even well-educated women in urban areas are not familiar with their rights to land and property and do not enforce those rights regularly" (Stanley and Di Martino 2012, 5-6).

Another issue strongly noticed recently concerns the legalization of illegal settlements in the suburbs of the big cities, settlements built mainly following the internal movement of the population during these last twenty years. Based on the existing legal framework, the property should be entitled to all the members of the family as per the family certificate. However, the practice is quite different, with the property registered only in the name of the head of household. According to the figures from the records of civil register in Albania in the vast majority of cases (90%), the registered official head of the family is a man (MoLSAEO 2012, 80) When it comes to entrepreneurship, officially women own 25.7% out of 106, 477 business in the country (the majority of which are small businesses). There is an important unequal spatial distribution with 61% of registered businesses led by women being concentrated in Tirana and Elbasan. In 2005, only 17% of all agricultural businesses nation-wide were directed by women, despite the fact that agriculture remains the main sector of employment for women (MoLSAEO 2012, 79). These data and information show that in Albania women are in a much more difficult economic situation and their dependency on the family (husband/parents) is dramatically important.

CONCLUSIONS

Albania in the early 1990s was in a state of drastic political, socio-cultural and economic transformation which strongly affected its population by bringing about economic and social hardship. In these crucial moments of dramatic changes, one of the main developments was the application of radical free market economy policy, which led to a shrinkage of the public and expansion of the private, whereby the market is considered to be the only regulator and becomes the 'only game in town' (Klein, 2008). The shock therapy policies of the free market economy were implemented in Albania and as a result the social welfare state was toothless. In this sense, the individuals and their families were left on their own to cope with economic and social hardship (De Waal, 2005). In lieu of the minimal social welfare state and the difficult economic conditions, the large flux of emigration from Albania towards the European Union countries and the United States offered a way-out for many Albanian families and households by providing economic support in the form of remittances. The remittances from emigration were complemented by local money transfers as a result of internal migration movements from rural to urban areas, from isolated countryside towards major cities in Albania. Apart from remittances from internal and external migration in support of the living expenses of the recipient families in Albania, the role of the family as the primary solidarity network is also seen in the case of housing for young people in the form of co-residence with parents; finding employment through family/kinship networks rather than through the labour offices; providing support and care for children, the elderly and/or sick in lieu of the lack of proper social policies on the part of the government. These functions are mainly performed by women who are forced to withdraw from the labour market and have remittances from the emigration abroad as their major source of income. These are some of the most essential aspects whereby the family serves as a substitute for the social policies (or lack thereof) offered by the government. It is important to point out that individuals and families in Albania have managed to cope with harsh social and economic conditions due to the support received through remittances and the solidarity of family/kinship networks. However, this is a micro-level solution based on individuals and families and not on the macro-level of government social and economic policies, which in the long-term should offer sustainable development through social welfare policies. In this sense, the reduction of the remittances is followed by economic difficulties for Albanian families, who can find it hard to afford the daily costs of life. What is more concerning is that the lack of proper social and economic policy in the framework of a minimalist social welfare state can widen and reinforce social inequalities. Statistical data shows that there has been a reduction of the level of poverty in the period between 2002 and 2008, but this was not followed by a reduction of inequalities in Albanian society. On the contrary, social inequalities remain a major concern. Family support, solidarity and reciprocity are very important within the Albanian family structure and for Albanian society at large, but they cannot substitute state solidarity and its role in the provision of social services. Referring to Bawinn-Legros and Stassen (2002) it is important to emphasize that the differences between family and state allow them to be complementary, but not to substitute or exclude each other.

REFERENCES

AGENDA Institute. 2011. *Efektet e rënies së remitancave në Shqipëri* [The effects of the reduction of remittances in Albania]. Tirana: AGENDA Institute

Agolli, Mimoza, Ani Plaku and Ermira Danaj. 2011. "Dealing with integration- the case of internal migrants in Albania" (paper prepared in the framework of the Regional Research Promotion Programme in the Western Balkans (RRPP) 2009-2010).

Arrehag, Lisa, Orjan Sjoberg and Mirja Sjoblom. 2005. "Cross-border migration and remittances in a post-communist society: Return flows of money and goods in the Korçë district, Albania," *South Eastern Europe Journal of Economics* 1, 9-40 (http://www.asecu.gr/Seeje/issue04/sjoberg.pdf).

Bartlett, Will and Xhumari, Merita. 2007. "Social security policy and pension reforms in the Western Balkans," *European Journal of Social Security* 9 (4), 297-322

Bawin-Legros, Bernadette and Stassen, Jean-Francois. 2002. "Intergenerational Solidarity: Between the Family and the State," *Current sociology* 50 (2), 243-262.

Caro, Erka. 2011. "From the village to the city-Adjustment Process of Internal Migrants in Albania" (PhD diss., Rijksuniversiteit Groningen).

Council of Europe. 2009. *Youth policy in Albania - Conclusions of the Council of Europe international review team.* Strasbourg: Council of Europe Publishing

Danaj, Ermira and Festy, Patrick. 2007. "Le parcours des jeunes Albanais: entre choix individuels et contraintes institutionnelles [The course of Albanian young people between individual choices and institutional constraints]" (paper presented at the International conference «Jeunes, dynamiques identitaires et frontieres culturelles» in Hammamet (Tunisia) 16-17 February).

Danaj, Ermira, Ani Plaku, Milva Ekonomi and Zamira Cavo. 2008. *Unpaid care work in Albania.* Tirana: ASC.

Danaj, Ermira, Milva Ekonomi, Elda Dakli, Eglantina Gjermeni, Monica Budowski and Marcus Schweizer. 2004. *Gender Perspectives in Albania.* Tirana: INSTAT.

Danaj, Ermira, Patrick Festy, Edvin Zhllima, Milva Ekonomi, Aida Guxho and Marinela Lika. 2005. *Becoming an adult- challenges and potentials of youth in Albania.* Tirana: INSTAT.

De Waal, Clarissa. 2005. *Albania today – A portrait of post-communist turbulences.* London: I.B. Tauris in association with the Centre for Albanian Studies.

Esping-Andersen, Gosta. 2006. "Three worlds of Welfare Capitalism," in *The Welfare State Reader*, edited by Christopher Pierson and Francis G. Castles (Blackwell Publishing), 161-174

Fenger, H.J.M. 2007. "Welfare Regimes in Central and Eastern Europe: Incorporating Post-Communist Countries in a Welfare Regime Typology," *Contemporary Issues and Ideas in Social Sciences* 3(2), (http://www.learneurope.eu/files/9913/7483/4204/Welfare_regimes_in_Central_and_Eastern_Europe.pdf.)

Fultz, Elaine, Marcus Ruck and Silke Steinhilber, eds. 2003. *The Gender Dimensions of Social Security Reform in Central and Eastern Europe: Case Studies of the Czech Republic, Hungary and Poland*. Budapest: International Labour Office.

Galanxhi, Emira, Philipe Wanner, Janine Dahinden, Elena Misja, Mathias Lerch and Desareta Lameborshi. 2004. *Migration in Albania*. Tirana: INSTAT.

Gedeshi, Ilir and Jorgoni, Elira. 2012. *Social Impact of Emigration and Rural-Urban Migration in Central and Eastern Europe* (Final Country Report, Albania, European Commission).

Gedeshi, Ilir. 2008. *Introducing Migrant City Tirana, Albania* (paper presented at the Migrant Cities Conference, Glasgow, 25 November).

Gruber, Siegfried and Pichler, Robert. 2002. "Household structures in Albania in the early 20th century," *The History of the Family* 7, 351-374.
http://census.al/Resources/Data/Census2011/Instat_print%20.pdf

INSTAT. 2002. *The Population of Albania in 2001. Main Results of the Population and Housing Census.* Tirana: INSTAT.

INSTAT. 2012. *Rezultatet paraprake të Censusit të Popullsisë dhe Banesave 2011* [Preliminary results of the Population and Housing Census 2011] published on the website of INSTAT, www.instat.gov.al

King, Russel. 2005. "Albania as a laboratory for the study of migration and development," *Journal of Southern Europe and the Balkans*, 7(2),133-56

Klein, Naomi. 2008. *The shock doctrine – the rise of disaster capitalism*. New York: Picador.

Merrien, Francois-Xavier, Raphael Parchet and Antoine Kernen. 2005. *L'Etat Social [Welfare State]*. Paris: Armand Colin.

MoLSAEO and UNWomen. 2012. *National report on the status of women and gender equality.* Tirana: MoLSAEO and UNWomen

Papps, Ivy and Danaj, Ermira. 2005. "Policy Impact Analysis: Distribution of Economic Assistance Block Grants" (policy paper prepared in the framework of the progress report of National Strategy of Social and Economic Development in Albania, Tirana: DfID).

Stanley, Victoria and Di Martino, Samantha. 2012. *Assessing Land Administration Project's Gender Impacts in the Western Balkans*. Country Case Studies: Albania, Bosnia-Herzegovina and Montenegro, World Bank report (available at: http://siteresources.worldbank.org/INTECA/Resources/landgenderassessment.pdf).

Vullnetari Juli. 2012. *Albania on the move: links between internal and international migration.* Amsterdam: Amsterdam University Press

Vullnetari, Juli and King, Russell. 2010. "Gender and Remittances in Albania: Or 'Why Are Women Better Remitters than Men?' Is Not the Right Question." (Working Paper No 58, Sussex Centre for Migration Research, University of Sussex).

World Bank. 2003. *Albania Poverty Assessment.* Report No. 26213-AL.

World Bank. 2007. *Albania: Urban growth, migration and poverty reduction, a poverty assessment.* Report Nr. 40071- AL.

CAROLIN LEUTLOFF-GRANDITS

THE "SOCIAL GLUE" OF WEDDING FESTIVALS IN KOSOVO'S SOUTH: LINKING THE VILLAGE TO MIGRATION AND RESHAPING GENDER AND SOCIAL RELATIONS

INTRODUCTION

In the rural region of Opoja in southern Kosovo as well as all over Kosovo, marriage festivals represent the most important social gatherings and are celebrated within a large group of guests, first of all relatives. More specifically, the wedding remains in most cases the issue of the groom's family and his kin, stressing the male line of ancestry. By celebrating 'at home', in the groom's house, or in a wedding hall in the home region, they also stress the patri-locality.[50] The importance of patri-locality also applies to many migrants, who celebrate their wedding 'at home', amongst relatives, even if the groom and his family had migrated away years or even decades before. In the Opoja region, people largely practice village or at least *fis*[51] (the patri-lineal kin) exogamy, while at the same time most marry within the region, which includes those who have family roots in Opoja, but who migrated to or were even born in western countries.

Based on the fact that migrants hold an important position in weddings, either as groom, bride, or as guests, most weddings are held in summer (July or August), when migrants return home for holiday. Driving through Kosovo in summer, the roads are packed with cars displaying a white towel on the windshield wiper—a symbol that the cars belong to a wedding party (and should not be stopped by the police). The cars belong to the family of the groom, who is proceeding to fetch the bride in order to bring her home and celebrate the wedding. This habit includes many migrants, who come with shiny cars and western license-plates and who often take an especially active role in the staging of the wedding festival. Taking these observations as a starting point, I want to explore the various forms and meanings of wedding festivals and the social roles, the social status and the future perspectives which are negotiated there. In which way do wedding festivals contribute to family and kinship cohesion, and in which way do they support family fragmentation and individualization? I want to particularly examine the role of migrants in weddings and ask in which way migrants act as agents of social change or as preservers of family and gender values or of both.

I seek to argue that weddings are events in which the different experiences and perspectives of locally based villagers and migrants are brought together and harmonized again—at least for a certain moment in time—and a vision for a joint future is created. In fact, while migrants and villagers have a very different social profile as well as future vision and occupy sometimes even contradicting time-space coordinates, ex-

---

50 See for the traditional patri-local, complex households in the Balkans also Kaser 1992, 1995, 2000 and 2008, in Kosovo see Rrapi 2003.
51 See for the meaning of *fis* also de Rapper 2012.

pressed in views that migrants are living in the 'advanced West' while 'Kosovo is lagging behind', or that migrants 'lose time' while stranded in limbo as asylum seekers in the West, the weddings are events in which this non-simultaneity and a-synchronicity can be overcome. In times in which the community is under pressure owing to continuous outmigration and severe economic insecurities, weddings represent events which create security and a strong sense of community as well as a gender specific order. More broadly, I want to argue that weddings held in the circle of relatives are events which recreate the unity of the trans-local kin and stress the importance of the male descent line.

However, weddings are also events at which the position of single members of the community can be redefined, and the status of the groom and bride and their families as well as other members can be increased. At the wedding, the relations between groom and bride and, more generally, gender roles are newly ascribed and defined. Thus, weddings enable change and transformation in the community, with the way weddings are celebrated and their impact on family and gender relations being rather diverse.

In the Opoja region, some villagers pride themselves on the traditional way weddings are still held there, following the arrangement between families staged according to decade and likely even century old customs of patrilocality. They stress that in Opoja, weddings are lengthier and more traditionally celebrated than in other regions of Kosovo. Other villagers stress that wedding festivals have changed enormously and have become an arena of individualization and consumerism, in which the impact of the patri-lineal kin loosens, while the focus on the bride and groom increases. In fact, there are two different forms of wedding celebrations in the Opoja region: those which are celebrated at home, in the yard of the groom's house, and those which are celebrated in a restaurant or wedding hall, which line the main streets on the outskirts of the towns and partly also of villages in Kosovo, and which host between 300 and 1000 guests. In the Opoja region, the celebration in a restaurant is often added to the wedding held at home. The coexistence of these two ways to celebrate a wedding also express the simultaneity of the contemporaneousness of transformations in Kosovo and in the Opoja region itself as well as the different perspectives of migrants and those who remained at home, as well as of young and elderly villagers.[52] By celebrating in two different ways, the people of Opoja pay tribute to these complex and often contradictory transformations, and try to create a simultaneity and liability in a rather insecure time.

That a wedding can be seen as a ritual in which social transformations can be channeled has already been highlighted by Victor Turner (2005). With a ritual which is staged as a 'social drama', a repositioning of single members inside a community can be achieved, status can be (re-)created and more broadly, a community can be re-established and transformed. For migrants who are not physically present in community, such a ritual can be very important for reclaiming membership and status. For a villager who marries a migrant, the wedding is a ritual which offers a new, promising future abroad. For the community in general, the transformative power of the ritual is

---

[52] See for the concept of simultaneity in transnational social fields also Levitt (2004), who understands simultaneity as "living lives that incorporate daily activities, routines, and institutions located both in a destination country and trans-nationally".

of high symbolic meaning, as it links the village to migration and at the same time recreates and reshapes social structures and values.

Next to the symbolic and social meanings, weddings in Kosovo also encompass economic and legal aspects which act upon the community and can be described as a 'total social phenomenon' (Mauss 1968) in the way that it touches upon all aspects of social life. In fact, due to the high costs involved, weddings greatly determine the future possibilities of the household and its individual members by linking the village to migration and therewith to the decade or even century long lifeline. But they also shape future possibilities by keeping this money from being invested in other assets, such as education or commercial ventures. The legal aspects can be grasped when considering that weddings are often seen as binding from the side of the families, even if they are not accompanied by a civil wedding, and become a way to overcome the restrictive immigration policies of western countries, as marriage migration is at the moment the only secure way of creating long term perspectives abroad.

Research for this paper is based on multi-faceted socio-anthropological fieldwork in the region of Opoja in Kosovo as well as in migrant destinations between 2010 and 2013.[53] I want to analyze various weddings in the Opoja region to which I have been invited myself, have been told of or which I have watched together with villagers as well as migrants on DVDs, as well as many conversations about these weddings with villagers and migrants.

The article is divided in four sections: In the first section, I will shortly introduce the historical context of wedding festivals within the region of Opoja. In the next section, I want to concentrate on the social staging and economy of weddings and the links between wedding festivals, migration and future perspectives. In the third section, I want to describe in more detail the renegotiation of gender, social roles and social status during a wedding held at home, while in the final section I wish to concentrate on weddings celebrated in restaurants and their social impacts on community building, social status and transformations.

HISTORICAL CONTEXT

In the Opoja region, as well as in other areas of Kosovo and Macedonia, international (as well as national) labor migration to German speaking countries has played a considerable role since the late 1960s, being for a long time, primarily a male migration. Many migrants who came from rural areas lived in complex and patri-locally organized family households consisting of elderly parents with several adult, married sons, their wives and children and partly also unmarried siblings.

The social and economic effects of the widespread labor migration amongst the Albanian villages in the south of Kosovo have been best described in the PhD thesis of Janet Reineck (1991), who did fieldwork in the region of Opoja in the late 1980s. She showed that male migrants became the guardians of traditional values and spearheaded the 'freezing' of patriarchal values in rural Albanian villages in Kosovo. The money

---

53 This article is based on the FWF-financed research project „The Kosovo family revisited" (Project Number P 22659-G18) headed by Karl Kaser in collaboration with Eli Krasniqi and Tahir Latifi, to whom I am very grateful.

migrants earned was sent to their fathers, who would invest in weddings, land and housing as well as consumer goods in order to create a better living standard at home. At the same time, marriage ceremonies stressed the patriarchal order.

Until the 1990s and even beyond, girls were married to boys from the region following the arrangements of their parents, which meant that they often were not involved in the decision making process. More generally, the marriage had more an economic than a psychological function, as the bride was first of all seen as a source of labor as well as the mother of the children she would give birth to for the groom's family. Furthermore, the wedding established not only a union of the couple, but a union of two agnatically un-related families, who would respect each other as well as cooperate with each other (Backer 2003, Reineck 1991, von Aarburg and Gretler 2008, Pichler 2009a, see for the Turkish context also Schiffauer 1991).

Based on patri-locality, the bride moved at her wedding from her own parental household into the household of the groom and his family. While the departure of the bride was therefore a rather sad moment for the brides' family, and was celebrated quietly, the groom's family started with the celebrations already days before the bride arrived in the groom's house. The climax of the wedding festival was the fetching of the bride from her paternal house by the cousins of the groom, and her arrival in the groom's house. Until the 1990s, the whole village was invited to the wedding celebration on this day. Young men, who went abroad in order to contribute to the household finances, left their wives and children at home, in the household of their parents or brother(s) (Aarburg and Gretler 2008, Pichler 2009a).

From the 1990s on, especially after the end of the war in 1999, this migration system changed, as not only men, but also women and children started to migrate. In the 1990s, this was based on the deteriorating economic condition and the decreasing security situation in Kosovo, in which the Serbian dominated regime openly discriminated against Albanians and excluded them from all public institutions, including administration, schools, services and also most state owned firms. At that time, Albanians founded a parallel system, but unemployment and insecurity remained high.

In the ethnic crises of the 1990s, family reunion however did not mean that migrants stopped caring for their brothers and parents at home. It goes without saying that at that time, weddings of Albanians in Kosovo were celebrated rather low key, as it was too dangerous to have large festivals. In various cases which were reported to me, the wedding took place even while the groom was abroad, as it was too dangerous for him to return. Furthermore, weddings were partly celebrated without the music of the *Magjup*-Orchestras[54], as it was said that the Magjup collaborated with the Serbs. Therewith, an important element which made the 'traditional' wedding festivals so distinct was missing.

Some scientists (Schmidt 2008, Luci 2005, see for Albania also Schwandner-Sievers 2001) argue that the ethnic conflict in Kosovo brought with it a re-partiarchalization of the rural Albanian communities. In the Opoja region as well as in most other regions, many girls were taken from school after the obligatory eight years. In Opoja, they then concentrated on embroidery and needlework (*paje*)—mainly small table clothes—until they married. The needlework was presented to the family of the

---

54 Magjup is the Albanian name for Roma, Ashkali and Egyptians.

groom at marriage, and the size and elaboration would tell something about their diligence and industriousness.

After the bloody escalation of the conflict in 1998 and the ensuing NATO intervention in 1999, which put an end to the Serbian dominated regime in Kosovo, the situation in Kosovo changed again dramatically. Albanians reacted with euphoria to the establishment of a new administration in which they constituted the majority from the end of the war in 1999 on, and weddings, house building activities as well as investments boomed. At the same time, however, unemployment rates remained very high particularly among the youth (above 50%) (Fitze 2007), which again led to frustration and anger from a considerable part of the Albanian people, while others have become economically very successful. This controversial economic climate created feelings of competition and a lack of solidarity and brought new values of individualism, which stand in contrast to those of kinship and community values, and created a desire for external migration (Leutloff-Grandits 2010; cf. for the youth in Serbia also Erdei 2011).

The wish to migrate was however also connected to the phenomena of globalization, as nearly each and every village household today has internet access and many people—especially the young—have a Facebook account and spend a considerable amount of their day online. On their Facebook sites, they create imaginations and aspirations of a life abroad, and can give themselves another, alternative identity, one which enables them to earn money, of which they can in part also contribute to the finances at home (cf. for the influence on virtual media on imaginations also Appadurai 2004, 2005).

As after the war, other forms of migration such as asylum and labor migration were limited, marriage migration became therewith a new strategy for villagers to leave to western European countries and to realize their imaginations, which is why some young people in Kosovo wish to find a partner who lives abroad and who is willing or able to take them abroad. Some young male villagers also used other forms of mobility, such as the participation in an educational program at a university abroad, which promised a successful future, but also undocumented migration, which did not promise much of a future abroad, but rather the chance to earn money for a limited time.

From the side of migrants, an important reason for the renewal of family ties through marrying someone from home was based on the fact that Kosovo Albanian migrants were often not very well integrated in their destination countries not least owing to the many legal barriers they met in the 1990s, and remained attached to their birthplaces and families.[55] For migrants, marrying a spouse from 'home' was a strategy to remain connected to where they came from and their relatives.[56] Many children of migrants therefore celebrated their weddings at home; in a more or less 'traditional way' some also with a celebration in a wedding hall, too. It was however clear that they wanted to take the spouse abroad, in order to stay there together.

Through Kosovo Albanian weddings, villagers and migrants are therewith reconnected. Family ties are renewed and distances between family members in migration destinies and at home have been at least ideologically smoothened—which is the

---

55 See for the reasons of maintaining transnational ties also Glick Schiller, Basch and Blanc-Szanton 1997. See also Nieswand (2011) who stresses that transnational connections are also linked to the 'status paradox of migration', meaning that migrants lose status abroad, while they gain status at home.
56 See Pichler 2009b, who describes this by referring to Albanian migrants from Macedonia.

"social glue" (Vertovec 2004) of wedding festivals, or the re-establishing of the life line between villages and traditional migration destinies. With abundantly celebrated weddings, villagers invested in the community, the kin group as well as into their individual status. Through trans-border weddings, villagers and migrants are therewith re-connected.

In the following, I want to describe the staging of such a wedding in the Opoja region and explain the significance of migration as well as the importance of the family in conducting such a festival.

LINKING WEDDING FESTIVALS, MIGRATION AND FUTURE PERSPECTIVES

Linking marriage and migration

In one of the weddings I took part in the summer of 2011, the groom had been abroad for 10 years already, first as an asylum seeker and later as a student at an Austrian university. Rani was the youngest of three sons of the household and was preparing to marry a woman from a neighboring village. While an asylum seeker in Germany, he had a long-term relationship to a German woman, but in 2008, the German state deported him. Back in his home region, his eye had caught on a young woman from his region, who was the best friend and neighbor of his cousin. Soon afterwards, the engagement was arranged between the two families with the counseling of his aunt who acted as *msit* (a marriage broker or matchmaker).

From the day of engagement onwards, the family of the groom had to send gifts (*teshat*) to the bride on all bigger holidays, like Bajram or Women's Day, as this was customary in the region. The buying of gifts, either dresses or jewelry, involved high costs, and it was clear that the wedding should ideally be scheduled sooner rather than later, as a long waiting period would necessitate purchasing more presents and would therewith add to the already high costs of the wedding (see also Reineck 1991: 80-91).

The way the wedding was planned was not discussed at length between Rani and his parents, as it was clear to Rani that his parents envisioned a wedding for him in the yard of their home, in the way in which his two brothers had also married a few years earlier, following the war. This meant that the wedding would last three days and the family of the groom and of the bride would celebrate in most parts separately.

On the groom's side, about 400 guests were invited to the wedding, most of them relatives. This included first of all the families of the *mahalla* (the agnatically based neighborhood) who were regarded as blood relatives, the daughters of the house with their families as well as the relatives of the in-married women, the "kinship by milk" (Backer 2003). In all cases this also included migrants who belonged to the aforementioned families and who visited their home region for the summer and partly especially for the wedding.

The costs for the wedding days—for the *Magjup* musicians who played traditional drums and wind instruments, for the food during the joint meals and the costs for the cooks who prepared the meals, the renovation of the house and the furnishing of the bedroom, as well as the gifts to the bride—involved several thousand Euros in total.[57] As generally within a wedding which is celebrated within the grooms' house, gifts in kind of money from guests are rather minor, the wedding is mainly financed by the closer circle of the groom's family. In this way, the inviting family 'destroys' financial means or makes themselves dependent in order to abundantly celebrate the wedding of the son and increase its own status in the community.

In Rani's case, his parents and brothers did their best to contribute to the financing of the wedding, but it was still clear that Rani had to pay the lion's share of the costs for the wedding and all the gifts involved, as his father had been unemployed indefinitely and his two brothers could hardly finance the housekeeping costs for the local household. In order to earn the money needed for the wedding, Rani had to migrate again, as at home the possibilities to earn money were very restricted for him. He luckily received a student visa for Austria in order to earn an MA in mechanics. This was a great chance for him as an MA degree from Austria would offer him much greater life prospects in Kosovo as well as aboard. However, Rani had no time to concentrate on his studies, as he had to earn money for his wedding. When I asked him why he would not postpone his wedding and first finish his studies, or why he would not make a small wedding in order to free himself from costs, he said that his parents wanted it to be this way and they could not be swayed, as he was supposed to marry at this age, and in this manner. He also did not question the financial burden which his wedding imposed on him, as he said that he invested with it into his own future: His marriage would be stable and would last his whole life, and he had not to worry about a divorce as German couples did. In his eyes, a wedding was a necessary step in his life which promised stability and family continuation and which was therefore worthy of investment.

Like Rani, other young men from the village had also migrated with a student visa or illegally in order to support their own family, and to finance their wedding and save enough money to build a future.

The preparation of the wedding as a family affair

That the wedding was a family affair was however also noticeable in the organizational involvement of the family. In fact, while Rani was abroad, the other household members took over the organization of the wedding, which was a clear family task. In order to prepare for the wedding, Rani's two sisters in law, partly together with his bride, went on various shopping tours in the nearby town of Prizren in order to purchase the bridal necessities. Apart from a very elaborate white wedding dress, which the bride was to wear on her wedding day, they also bought another more simple white wedding dress and some evening dresses and combinations, which she would wear in the afternoons and evenings, when welcoming guests of the in-married family, or for festivities. They also bought a traditional wedding costume, which consists of a *dimia* (Turkish style trousers of nine to twelve meters of fabric), a *dajlama* (a long, embroidered, velvet jacket) and a *delek* (a short, embroidered, velvet jacket). Last but not

---

57 See for similar investments in Albanian weddings in Macedonia in the new millennium Pichler 2009b.

least, they also bought various shoes, gold jewelry, underwear, night dresses, bedclothes, makeup, and hairspray. Altogether, they spent near to 10,000 Euros.

Furthermore, his sisters in law as well as his mother engaged in knitting flowers for the blouse of the *dimia* as well as flowers for the headdress, which are generally both very complicated requiring one or more days per flower. The engagement in embroidery was in fact a very widespread action for women who belong to the generation which has only an eight year school education owing to being educated in the 1990s.

Also the male members of the groom's household heavily engaged in wedding preparations and incurred many expenses. Rani's brothers together with his father spent weeks renovating the house. As one of the brothers was a carpenter, he also made the furniture for the new bedroom. The brother then also bought a new car from money he had earned from his wood-working, which could be used by all (male) household members, and would be the car in which the bride was fetched. In short, the whole family worked for weeks and months in order to finance and prepare for the wedding, which was also the case in other families.

The staging of the wedding

The weddings in Opoja nowadays are still celebrated in the yard of the groom's house and follow a relatively homogeneous pattern. The *fis*, the close kin, which is represented in the territorial organization of a *mahalla* as a group of families originating from the same male ancestor, as well as all female relatives and their in-laws take part in the groom's wedding, ranging from old to young, male and female. Generally, the weddings are celebrated for three days, which were staged in the following way:

On the first day of the wedding, all the gifts for the bride were exhibited in one of the guest rooms of the groom's family house, and all members of the *mahalla* and family were invited to look at them and to celebrate, sing and dance.

On the second day, the male members of the family, the father, brothers, uncles and cousins of the groom, but not the groom himself, brought the gifts for the bride to the bride's family. In exchange for the gifts, the groom's relatives received the brides' needlework (*paje*) as well as gifts for the whole family. The arrival of the male family members was then followed by a festival with a joint meal, music, singing and dancing.

The bride however celebrated on this day her *kanadjegji* (farewell) at home, together with her close friends as well as all other women from the *mahalla* and her female relatives, inviting them for lunch. From the late afternoon on, the bride also exhibited the clothes and jewelry as well as the other gifts which she had received from the groom's family from the day of the engagement on, and the girls of the *mahalla* helped the bride to arrange the gifts as representative as possible.

The third day was the climax of the wedding, as at noon, all guests of the groom's family, several hundred people, were invited for lunch, and in the afternoon the whole *mahalla*—everyone who had a car—went to fetch the bride from the neighboring village and then celebrated the arrival of the bride jointly in the yard of the grooms' house.

Most weddings in the region were held in a very similar manner, so long as the groom or bride had migrated and married at home or that none of the spouses lived abroad. Nearly all families in the region also invested a great amount of money in the wedding of their sons, even if they could not afford it, so that—as some villagers remarked critically—status differences could not be seen during the wedding. In fact, families oriented themselves on what others had done, and sometimes even tried to be a bit better. Being inclined to invest in 'sameness', and offer the same as the neighbor did, families entered a 'wedding competition' and went into debts for the wedding of their sons.

This again put pressure on sons to go abroad or to stay abroad in order to finance their wedding or the wedding of their brothers. Therewith, the celebration of costly weddings was intimately bound to the future prospects of the families in Opoja, as the weddings consumed a high sum of money which could have been used for different purposes, too. What looked as it would be the same and symbolized equality and community was in fact bought expensively, especially for those families which had less economic means. As in the case of Rani, the financing of the wedding was also highly linked to the future prospects of migrating family members themselves.

Weddings as a family and community affair and as a generational conflict

Not all migrants had such an uncritical position to the wedding like Rani and did not mind going into debt for it. Instead, they pointed to disagreements with their parents as well as their spouses in terms of the organization of the wedding. Osman, another migrant who also studied in Austria and became engaged to a woman from the region marrying in a similar fashion like Rani while still studying, said openly that he did not want to spend so much money on the wedding, and that he had discussed it various times with his parents and his bride, but that his parents did not want to have a small wedding with less guests lasting only one day, as this would have affected their status at home. His bride—although having graduated from the faculty of Economics in Prishtina—understood him in principle, but she did not want to be the first bride who would abstain from jewelry and dresses, as the exhibition of the dresses was still an important status marker in the village community and they would have gossiped about her. He therefore adhered to his family, which put high pressure on him, raising conflict along gender and generational lines.

So everything stayed the way it was; only Osman began to grow worried. He desperately wanted to succeed in his studies, as this was the dream he wanted to build his future on, but as he had borrowed a great deal of money in order to finance the wedding, he had to work hard to be able to pay back the debt. Because of this, he saw his plans at the university and with it all dreams for the future endangered. He worried that without success at university, he would also lose his permission to stay in Austria. Without this permission, he would have to return home where he would be unemployed, and without employment, he would not be able to pay back his loan. Another effect of this wedding was that he could not fetch his wife, as she was not able to work abroad at the beginning, meaning that she would have posed additional costs for him. At home, she was one of the very few women who had taken up employment in a newly opened supermarket, bringing with it an income of 250 Euro, which was very welcome for the household. In short, with this wedding, Osman had received heavy burdens on his life. The wedding was still first and foremost a collective family endeavor, in which he had to step away from his individual wishes and aims, at least as soon as his individual aims conflicted with those of the family.

Like Osman, also other migrants had to adapt their plans to the aims of the family. Florim for example, another migrant from the same *mahalla*, had plans to study at home, but as money was short, he went illegally to Italy in 2009 in order to earn money for his household and his studies to come, as well as the costs for the study of his younger brother; about 300 Euro a month. Luckily, he was able to legalize his stay and worked hard in order to reach his goals as soon as possible. During one of his visits home, he became engaged to a woman (who had been chosen by his mother) from one of the neighboring villages. His wedding took place the following year, for which the family had to draw a loan from the bank in order to cover the relatively moderate costs of about 10,000 Euro, of which 'only' 3,000 Euro were spent on gifts for the bride.[58] In order to repay the loan, Florim went abroad again after his wedding, while his wife remained with his parents as it was difficult to organize papers for her. Then, his brother also became engaged, eager to marry soon, posing again high costs for the family. As his brother did not draw an income, Florim was burdened with financing the gifts for his brother's bride, as well as shouldering the costs for his wedding. Because of this, he will most likely remain a few more years abroad, however, after one and a half years of marriage his bride could finally join him. It is still undecided if they plan to stay abroad or if they will return and manage to build up a livelihood in Kosovo. Reviewing these examples makes clear that marriage and related family obligations still foster migration. Migration is therefore not necessarily a way to start an individual life, even if the spouse joins in, but may still be experienced as a family endeavor.

Weddings as a means of gaining status and their social and economic costs

The wedding of Isuf, who came to Germany in 2004, after his father, who had been abroad since 1992, had fetched him together with his brother and mother, shows again that migrants can also be the initiators for local 'wedding competitions'. They may be willing to invest in weddings in order to achieve status in the local community, to 'buy themselves in', even if this is at the costs of a hard life abroad.

In fact, in 2010, Isuf had married a woman from a neighboring village who had migrated to Italy after the war. The wedding was however not celebrated in Germany or Italy, but in Opoja, and involved high costs of about 25,000 Euro, of which the enormous amount of 15,000 Euro went to gifts for the bride, and especially to the traditional costumes of the region. As in the case of Osman and Rani, this was largely decided by the parents, who wanted to have a proper wedding which expressed their social status. This included expensive gifts to the bride[59] and a celebration in a restaurant. The costs however, imposed a bitter burden on the family. The groom's father

---

58 This was also based on the fact that Florim's mother had tailored and embroidered the traditional dimia as well as the other elements of the wedding costume, which altogether costs up to 5,000 Euro.
59 While many brides—hailing from abroad or from local villages—like the dresses, jewelry and traditional costumes and like to wear them for the wedding festivals, there are also brides who do not want such dresses and gold jewelry, only accepting them at the wish of their mother in law.

had alongside his regular job with the German railway a cleaning job and worked 12 hours per day in order to repay the loan, with his wife and son supporting him as well.

Generally, many families did not avoid any costs for the wedding, which especially in the case of migrants seemed quite questionable as they partly invested in goods which seemed to be of little practical use for the couple itself. In the case of Isuf's wedding, this, for example, also included the renovation of the house they owned jointly with their uncle in the village, even though they lived in Germany most of the year.

More generally, these investments hold an important social meaning for the migrant family, as they want to be able to demonstrate that they belong to the local community not only today, but also down the road. They want to demonstrate that they are successful, individual and modern, while at the same time appreciating and caring for traditional rituals and family values. Migrants who were still members of a complex household at home therewith also invested into the assets of their brother(s) and their families, while those migrants whose household was already divided often invested in houses which were then empty during the year, but which symbolized the presence of the migrant in the community.

Weddings however also could be a reason to postpone the division of households, as the costs of weddings would eat up the possibilities for other investments. Shpirt for example, who had three sons, organized three weddings of about 15,000 Euro each, which means that he spent nearly 50,000 Euro on weddings—a sum with which one could easily build a house in Kosovo, or even two for, as others remarked critically. Having the money spent on weddings, he still shared a house and household with his three sons and his wives and children, although the clear aim was to divide the household as soon as possible, as it was considered (too) large—which was however delayed. Others therefore tried to pool the weddings of the sons and marrying them off jointly, so that weddings with two grooms were no exclusion, but rather a rule. This however again posed a burden on those who wanted to marry earlier but had to wait for a brother.

Viewing these cases, it becomes clear that the expensive wedding costs unite the groom's family, while they narrow more individualized life options, such as in this case, the successful attendance of a university in Austria or Kosovo, or other investments in education or the economy.

As most weddings are celebrated in the summer, when the migrants are present, migrants visit several weddings and also pay visits to relatives during this time home, meaning that participation in weddings and visits to relatives are the dominating experiences of home (cf. also Pichler 2009b).

BETWEEN PATRIARCHAL COMMUNITY BUILDING, RE-NEGOTIATION OF GENDER ROLES AND THE CREATION OF INDIVIDUAL STATUS AT THE WEDDING

Dress codes as signifiers of women's roles

The weddings celebrated in the yard of the groom's house follow a relatively homogenous pattern and are mostly celebrated in a gender divided form. While the female guests remain in the yard of the groom's house, the male guests gather mainly in a neighboring yard—in many cases the yard of the grooms' uncle. Only at the arrival of the bride, both groups join, culminating in festive dancing. Gender and generational roles are however not only spatially, but also symbolically expressed. In this regard, the dress code of women is especially interesting, as it speaks to the different 'official' assignments of social roles of women in the families and in the community.

The unmarried young girls wear tight jeans and blouses, and sometimes also short skirts or dresses, not differing much from the teens in western countries.[60] In this way, they stress that they still do not fill an official position in the family network, but that they have the relative freedom to style themselves as they wish. The tight clothes are furthermore a sign that gender relations are in rapid transformation and that arranged marriages are not very widespread. Instead, choice and therewith also bodily appearance became very important and a way of individual distinction, which serves as an expression of an aspired modern lifestyle and an attraction to the men.

Women who have recently married into the *mahalla* arrive in one of their abundantly decorated white wedding dresses, which they had worn to their own wedding. In this way, they stress their position as a *nuse*; a young in-married wife in the blood related *mahalla*, in which the new brides are exhibited as a kind of 'common property' of the patrilineage (*fis*) at this occasion. The fact that the new brides are lavishly styled and decorated also stresses their value and the status of the individual families into which these women married. Having several other young women in white wedding dresses, the new bride is surrounded by other 'brides' of the *mahalla*, who all wear similar lavish wedding dresses and look as enthralling as the bride. This is also a way of taking the individuality away from the new bride as critically remarked by a migrant woman on her visit to one of the weddings. After arrival, *nuses* are then placed into a row of chairs on which they sit and wait for other guests to come, who they then welcome with the *temena*, a ritual hand gesture which is the special bridal greeting.

Women who have been married for several years and who have born children wear their traditional *dimias*, and a *delek*, as well as a blouse with flowers, which they received at their own wedding. This costume, which is part of the groom's gift to the bride, costs up to a few thousand Euros and is topped with an abundance of gold jewelry—all given to the bride at her wedding—as well as an elaborate hair style. During the wedding celebrations, sisters in law often also wear the same *dimias*, especially when they still live in a complex household together. In various cases, this was the gift of one of the brothers in law. As soon as he is still considered to be a member of the

---

60 However, women living in urban areas highlight that their compatriots in the villages dress more conservatively, as they wear mostly trousers and not skirts.

complex patriarchal household, he is supposed not to give a present only to his wife, but also to the wives of his brothers. In fact, buying a new *dimia* for one's wife and her sisters in law is a visible investment into the social status of the family, as it means that they will collectively wear the new *dimia*s at the next wedding occasion and will stress that they belong together and therewith to a strong family.

However, most married women do not stay in their traditional costumes for more than one or two hours, but change their dress and then appear in very elaborate evening dresses, often with much embroidery and glitter, and of course high heels. In this way, also for married women, there is a chance to catch up with a 'Hollywood-outfit'. Women, who do not like their traditional *dimia*s, as they find them too old-fashioned and uncomfortable, also shorten their time of wearing them as much as possible.

In fact, the young, in-married women of the house, the *nuse*, and partly also some of the female guests, change their dresses several times throughout the evening, presenting themselves first in a traditional dress, then changing into a 'modern' evening dress, only to present another costly evening dress about two hours later. By changing clothes they catch the attention of other women. Clothes therewith become a means to upgrade the status of the family, but also to express the individuality and the modern taste of the woman and also create competition. The fact that women do not in most cases earn wages themselves, but depend on the financing of their husbands, seems not to restrict their lavish styling—but shows that this performed 'individuality' is in fact a collective family endeavor, with rather strict rules of social behavior.

There were however also boundaries of individualism—although these boundaries were rather flexible and a matter of interpretation. One woman, who appeared with glaring red hair while wearing a *dimia*, was criticized by some other women who did not find her outfit appropriate. Another bride had a 'too urban hairstyle' for her wedding, as it was said to make her snobbish and less respectful to the groom's family. What was clear was the fact that women spend quite much money on hairdressers (although in some complex families, female family members took over this job) and therewith created costs for each and every wedding they took part in. The strong importance of weddings and the high costs involved also resulted in a larger wedding economy evidenced in the proliferation of hair salons, boutiques for wedding and evening dresses and jewelry and the massive construction of wedding halls, as will be discussed further below.

The middle aged and older women, who already had married their sons off, wear a simple white blouse and a black skirt or a simple *dimia* with a blouse as well as a headscarf. Having the highest status as a mother in law, they do not have to invest in their outfit any more, but rather take care of the outfit of their daughter(s) in law. Like the elder women, most married men are not especially festively dressed and do not attract much attention on the female side, as they are mostly out of sight and remain in a neighboring yard.

In the following, I would like to examine the various stages and rituals of the wedding in more detail including the negotiation of gender roles and community building on different levels; the family, the *mahalla* and the village.

Wedding festivals as expressions of community solidarity, gender roles and social status

For the organization of a wedding in the groom's yard, the close family—which includes the brothers and cousins of the household head who mostly live close by—must cooperate, as they have to share their living space in order to place and host all guests. The yard in which the men celebrate belongs in most cases to a close relative of the inviting family and is in the immediate neighborhood. In cases of conflict between the relatives, this space can be denied to the inviting family which can then become a matter of gossip and can negatively impact the inviting family as well as their relatives.

The cooperation and support of the *mahalla* is necessary for the joint lunch at the groom's house on the third day of the wedding, at which all guests, several hundred persons, are invited and which is taken divided along gender lines: the men eat first, followed by the women and children. For this lunch not only the women, but also the girls and boys of the *mahalla* help in the preparations, serving and cleaning.

The *mahalla* girls are engaged throughout all three days of the wedding in ritual singing for the groom. With their songs about the virility of the groom and his *fis* (close male kin), *farefis* (wider male kin) and even the whole village, performed in a small circle dance, they create a festive atmosphere and contribute to the local community building process and the status of the inviting family.

Another method of community building is reached with the traditional circle dance (*valle*) headed by a close member of the groom's family, in which many guests and family members, especially women and girls, take part over all three days of the wedding. The dance lasts at least an hour, with some dropping out of the chain and others joining in. The never ending circling with the same kind of movements creates a feeling of union, in which the dancers merge into a common body. This dance is also especially appreciated by migrants, who take an especially active role in it. In fact, migrants are also known to create a good atmosphere in the wedding by celebrating raucously, which is again an important marker for the success of the wedding.

However, even in the *valle*, not everyone is automatically a member of this festive union, and social as well as gender roles in this community are permanently contested. For example, a young, recently divorced woman who took part in the circle dance was criticized by other women who did not find it appropriate for her to engage in a happy *valle*, as she was seen as being 'returned' by her husband's family, her honor having been taken. Another young and still unmarried woman who was said to have (had) sexual relations with men was gradually excluded, as other girls quit dancing next to her as soon as she moved into the chain, not wanting even to speak with her.

Magjup music performance and the Valle Opojanes as ways to celebrate the grooms' fis and to create individual status and competition

Next to the *valle*, there is another important ritual which impacts community relations as well as social status, which is the music performance of *Magjup* players before the yard or within the yard of the inviting family. In front of the gate of the groom's house, on the street, the *Magjup* musicians play for the male members of the groom's family and the *mahalla*, who then sing, dance and scream jointly on the road—mainly without the groom, who is not supposed to celebrate too openly. They therewith perform and publicly exhibit the unity of the male relatives and the common patriline, and at the same time also upgrade the individual status of various male community members.

In fact, at these events, some of the men of the family beckon to the *Magjup* musicians to play for them individually, with the *Magjup* musicians then organizing a show for them. At the end of the show, the recipient publicly pays the musicians with as much money as seems appropriate to him, disregarding the fact that the musicians have already been paid for by the inviting family. The money is fixed on the head gear of the musician where it can be seen widely. While it starts with 5 Euro, often also high sums, such as 50 Euro, 100 Euro and in rare cases even several hundred Euro are given for a music show of several minutes.

It goes without saying that migrants often give the most money, creating status for themselves. Several have told me that the musicians, already known in the community as having played for various weddings in the year, knew who had money. They then approached these people with their music and played especially well for them. But locally based villagers also expected from their migrant relatives to pay for such a show, which kept migrants under pressure to finance the performances, 'buying' themselves into the community, instead of just belonging to it unquestioned. I also heard of migrants who paid *Magjup* musicians for continued performances, therewith fostering the community event.

However, the practice of paying for individual music shows is not limited to migrants, but also includes those with only a local income, who go into debt in order to compete with others. At one festival, the groom's father, who was a school teacher and earned only a meager income of 300 Euro a month, gave 500 Euro to the musicians simply to show off before the others. In this way, large sums of money are somehow 'crushed' in only in a few minutes, only to increase the status of the inviting family and *fis*. However, this also shows just how fragmented the community is, increasing social differences. 'Sameness' cannot thus be practiced so easily, but actually erects new social boundaries.

Another important 'male' ritual of the wedding is the traditional *valle* by men of the *mahalla*, which is a highly elaborate group dance with difficult step combinations and rhythms. It takes place on the third day of the wedding, in a neighboring yard, without female spectators. However, only very few and mostly elderly men know how to dance it properly and take part in the performance, as most boys and younger men of the Opoja region no longer learn it.[61] Perhaps because this dance is not very popular among the local youth any longer and there are often only a limited number of younger viewers. However, unlike the local youth, I realized that various male migrants showed a considerable interest in the dance and partly even actively involved themselves in it.

---

61 Interestingly, the social anthropologist Janet Reineck learned the dance and also performed it at weddings in the late 1980s. She therewith changed her sex at least socially and switched into the social role of a 'respected stranger' who was incorporated into the group. That I was allowed to watch and film the dances was also a sign that I was seen as a 'respected stranger' to whom the local female roles did not apply.

In one of the dances I observed, a migrant with sun glasses, a tie and shining silver trousers cut above the small group of four other dancers headed by an elderly man who was a kind of teacher. He was much better dressed than the other dancers and was obviously very excited to dance. The dance-style of the migrant expressed the happiness of being at home, and was a mix of the traditional dance (which he did not know completely) and some individual elements. With this style he clearly differed from the other dancers, who danced with calmness and prudence, expressing more reverence in their movements, following the lead of the eldest man, who knew the dance best. The migrant however did not recognize the authority of the eldest. While partly following him, he then started his own version and sometimes even tried to convince others to follow him. His performance was observed by others with irritation, but by many younger spectators also with some delight. In the end, the migrant gave 100 Euro to the *Magjup* musicians, a much higher amount than the others, who gave 5 or 20 Euro or nothing at all. He therewith stressed his appreciation for the dance; while at the same time his individual superiority and lack of regard concerning age and skills.

The fetching and arrival of the bride as the climax of patriarchal kinship affirmation

The climax of the wedding, in which again the community is organized along gender and kinship relations, is the fetching of the bride on the third day of the wedding. For this, women and men of the *mahalla*, often more than 100 people, travel by car to the bride's family in the neighboring village in order to fetch the bride and take her to the groom's home—albeit without the groom, who remains at home and who up to this time has no special position in the wedding celebrations.

When entering the bride's village, men and women split in two groups, and only the women enter the yard of the bride's house, where they are welcomed by the women of the bride's family and *mahalla*. For this welcome ritual, the women of the bride's family line up in a chain leading to the bride, therewith also demarking a border between the women of two neighboring villages. Also at this occasion, the women who newly married into the bride's *mahalla* wear their white wedding dress, and those who married in most recently are supposed to stand closer to the bride. Walking through a chain of brides, who welcome the guests with *temena*, it would be easy to take the wrong one home, if the new bride would not be covered with a red scarf, which is only lifted by the mother in law or the eldest sister in law. Throughout the entire ritual the bride must affix her eyes to the ground, symbolizing respect and even devotion to the groom's family and sadness about leaving her own family, as has been done for decades, if not longer.

It is noteworthy that brides who have been girls in tight jeans or short miniskirts until recently, and who often have chosen their husband themselves, more or less comply with this behavior as soon as they themselves marry. They seem to completely transform from one day to the other, not just in appearance (from a teeny girl to a 'serious' bride taken from a fairy-tale), but also in their movements and gestures, which suddenly express devotion and severity. Even brides who have spent their last 10 years in migration and who joke regarding their knowledge of the rituals and do not like the whole procedure, are transformed at their wedding and become part of the local community.

The festivities in the bride's yard do not take long (only up to one hour), and the bride is then taken by her mother in law and placed in the car. Then the guests all drive to the groom's family again, where men wait for the bride's car in front of the house and women wait in the yard. Again, *Magjup* musicians start to play for the male members of the family who arrive back home—who then also individually pay for the performance.

When the bride's car approaches the house, a scantily clad teenage girl (who is supposed to be a virgin, as pre-marital sex remains taboo) of the groom's family is placed on the engine bonnet, and animates the group by waving a plastic rose, with the whole *mahalla* and many other villagers and relatives breaking out in screaming and singing. The *Magjup* musicians then play for the girl who is waving a red rose, with other women doing the same. This is accompanied by the rhythmical beats of the *Magjup* musicians, which accelerate.

Asking for the origin of the ritual with the girl, on the engine bonnet, which reminded me of Harley Davidson posters or car calendars with skimpily-dressed women on motorbikes or autos, I was strongly rebuffed by an elderly man in supposing this was a new trend. He told me that this is an adaptation of an old ritual, as a young girl of the groom's family was placed on the horse which carried the bride home. As the bride is nowadays not brought by horse any more, but by car, the girl is now placed on the car, which creates a different picture, but is supposed to have a similar meaning, as he told me.

Today, this scenery definitely creates a very exiting atmosphere especially among the young girls and boys, who wait for the lifting of the bride from the car, followed by the lifting of her red scarf on her head by the groom. This is the first time when the groom has a public role in the wedding, while up to this time he remains in the background.

Later, the groom and bride open the circle dance together with the groom's family. The dance is again highly ritualized, with slow, majestic moves, headed by the groom who swings the red scarf. The groom's father and other male members then rotate positions, so that various male members of the family and partly also the mother head the circle dance for some time and swing the scarf. This again symbolizes that the wedding is not only a union between two individuals, but a union with all members of the groom's family, who welcome the new bride to the family.

With the end of the dancing, most guests bid farewell and the groom leaves the yard as well, together with his male relatives and other young men of the *mahalla* in order to prepare himself for the wedding night. The bride is taken into the living room, where she is awaited by the girls of the *mahalla* and other women of the house.

The girls of the *mahalla* then sing songs for her, to which she must stand and listen, while directing her eyes to the floor and not speaking visibly (see also Reineck 1991: 95). As those sung earlier, these songs too are not particularly supporting of the bride, but rather praise the strength and sexual qualities of the groom and the superiority of his family as well as his whole village, while downgrading the bride's family and her village of origin. They also stress the sadness of the bride's departure from her family and blame the bride's mother for abandoning her daughter. However, in most cases I observed, neither the girls nor the bride seemed to be particularly disturbed by this; they appear well used to this habit (as they took part in various weddings over the year) and did not feel personally offended by the subordinate role which the songs foresaw for the bride. Instead, they said that they would tease each other with this, and girls were often very excited about the singing. One bride however also cried when listening to these rather nasty songs—which she herself sung very emphatically for another bride, before she herself was married.

Wedding games as subordination to marriage life and to the patrilineal kinship

The importance and dominance of the patriline and the subordinate role of the in-marrying wife are also expressed in various wedding games—the most important of which are the bread making and bread breaking ritual. The night of the first wedding day ends with the preparation of dough for the wedding bread by two unmarried youngsters of the *mahalla*—a girl and a boy. When they start to prepare the dough, other young people of the *mahalla* shout at them and throw eggs or spill beer on them, symbolizing the hardships of marriage, which the couple will witness. Neither of them is allowed to shout out or to complain, as this would be a bad sign for the fortune of the marriage; they must accept the rules of the family and the *rrethe* (social circle). While one could suppose that the young people would rebel against this game, it is celebrated with lots of enthusiasm and fun, and is a special challenge for the two young people involved.

On the morning after the wedding night, the newly married couple publicly breaks the bread, in which both spouses grasp the bread on one side each and then break it. The one who gets the bigger piece wins for his/her village. The girls and boys from the *mahalla* watching it of course all support the groom, shouting the name of their village, as if the groom's victory would be a victory of the village over the bride's village. It goes without saying that the groom wins. In this way, the subordination of the bride is not only put as a matter between the spouses, or between the groom's and the bride's family, but as a matter between the groom's and the bride's village. As with the songs the girls of the *mahalla* sing during the wedding, these rituals are seen as fun, relics of old times, which are not taken seriously or personally. At the same time they still impact gender relations and age roles, as they are 're-traditionalized' within these rituals.

As I could observe at various weddings, these songs and wedding games were performed regardless of whether the bride or groom had lived for many years abroad, or had both resided in the area. It was the local community, the *mahalla*, which directed the program, and in case the bride or groom was insecure about his/her role, he or she would be taught how to behave and perform, as they were always surrounded by some supporting family and community members.

In fact, migrants marrying at home often did not know the rituals very well. One migrant told me for example that he was too young to be interested in weddings when he left in 1992, and as he had not been home often in the 1990s, his own wedding in 2001 was in fact the first one he consciously celebrated—therewith being a newcomer to the rituals and performances. However, as the wedding was largely organized by his family and his relatives and he was more of an observer with few obligations himself, he simply 'participated' in it. One other migrant who married at home told me that he had to ask a lot in order to find out about his own role and the organization of the wedding.

Migrants were at the same time sometimes supporters of these rituals which were largely initiated within the *mahalla*. A migrant who had married at home told me for example that he found it important to invite the whole *mahalla* in order to see each other and to know who belonged to his kin. Other migrants who were guests at the wedding said that they enjoy the celebration of weddings so much, as this is the time they can open their heart and sing and dance and celebrate, which is impossible for them abroad.

WEDDING HALLS AS PLACES OF ALTERNATIVE COMMUNITY BUILDING

Restaurant weddings as an addition or a substitute for weddings at home

Not all weddings today are solely celebrated at home, in the yard of the groom's house and in a neighboring yard. Instead, it becomes increasingly fashionable to celebrate in a wedding hall, which is often a newly built mirror-glassed 'palace' on the outskirts of a town, seating 300 to 1000 guests. While most villagers drive to town in order to celebrate there, there are also restaurant halls of a slightly lower standard at the edges of villages in the Opoja region. To celebrate these are more convenient, as the rather remote Opoja region is situated on a mountain plateau and villagers need at least a 40 minute drive to reach a hall in the town of Prizren in the plain. Additionally, it is also cheaper in a village hall. Generally, wedding parties in a restaurant, which began in this region only in 2005, became very trendy, and today, annually 70 weddings take place in the wedding hall in Zym, a village of the region, which seats 300 guests. Even more families celebrate their wedding in one of the halls in Prizren.

In towns like Prizren and Prishtina, but also in rural areas like Isniq, most weddings are more or less exclusively held in restaurant halls and not at home, and last only one day. In some regions such as Isniq, even the bride is often fetched from a restaurant, where she is celebrating with her kin before she leaves to the wedding party organized by her groom's family, which takes place in a different restaurant.[62] In other places, such as Prishtina, the wedding party of the bride may take place a few days before the wedding party which is organized by the groom's family, but as these are two separate parties, the families in question celebrate mainly only for one day. Most of them take place outside the house, so that the family is freed from most of its organizational responsibilities.

In the Opoja region, there is generally not the choice between a wedding in a restaurant or at home, as until today, the wedding party moves to the restaurant only after the bride is fetched from her home and has arrived in the groom's home, normally between 5.00 and 6.00 p.m. In this way, the restaurant wedding supplements the wedding celebrated at home, as the banquet in the restaurant begins in the evening, at 7.00 or 8.00 p.m. The wedding often still lasts three days, as it is entails the exchange and exhibition of gifts, which is celebrated on both sides. As the style of a restaurant wedding is quite different from that at home, it is striking that these two types of weddings

---

62 This is also described by Pichler (2009b) for Albanians from Veleshta in Macedonia.

are celebrated in one family, by more or less the same group of people, which stresses the simultaneity of quite ambivalent developments in the region and in Kosovo itself. While the wedding celebrations at home recreate 'patriarchal' gender, generational and community roles, the restaurant weddings are largely free from this and leave space to alternative gender and social positions. The two wedding styles still form a common whole, a bricolage of two juxtaposed components.

Furthermore, there are already many voices who criticize the long duration of the weddings in the Opoja region, because it is costly and also exhausting for the host family. As weddings in restaurants become increasingly fashionable, it is likely that in the future the restaurant celebration will not only become more prevalent, but will replace the traditional wedding at home, as this is already done in other regions. In the following, I want to describe the main characteristics of the restaurant celebrations. I want to explore in which way weddings in halls are bound to the continuing migration of families, and in which way(s) gender and community relations are defined differently at such weddings.

The costs of restaurant weddings and their effects on the guest list

Beginning from the important aspect of wedding costs, it can be said that the costs of a celebration in a restaurant are considerable, as a stronger focus is laid on the consumption of food, and the catering is more expensive than at home as there are less helping hands from the community. In most places, guests are served various kinds of meat in the turn of the evening. The restaurant celebration of a migrant family originating from Opoja, who celebrated in Prizren and who had invited 400 guests, cost 6,000 Euro, while another family, the groom of which was the only member abroad, spent 3,000 Euro (a bargain) for a wedding festival in a village restaurant with 300 people held in Autumn, the 'off season' for wedding celebrations. It goes without saying that these costs must be added to the costs for the many gifts to the bride as well as some household renovation, which is the standard for a local wedding. Families with an average local salary of 250–350 Euros a month in Kosovo therefore cannot afford to celebrate in a restaurant.

Of course, the upper level of costs for celebrating in a restaurant is open, as I have also heard of 9,000 Euro being spent for 450 guests in a restaurant in Isniq, and 13,000 Euro for a restaurant wedding with 150 people in Prishtina. At the same time, in the Opoja region it is still not expected that the guests will contribute to the wedding by bringing expensive gifts or money. Only in the urbanized social circles in Pristina, where weddings are celebrated in posh restaurants, are gifts expected of the guests and often taking the form of envelopes with money.

As the costs for restaurant weddings are calculated per person, the invitation of guests follows stricter guidelines. While in weddings celebrated in the yard of the house, invitation cards are directed to the whole household, which leaves the decision to the members of the household regarding joint participation or delegates, invitation cards for restaurant weddings most often include two members of a household who are perceived as most closely related (in kinship terms) to the inviting family. This cuts through the meaning of weddings as an affair of the whole *mahalla* (and until the mid of the 1990s even the whole village[63]). Particularly among young people, this also finds support. Blerta, a young woman from the village who studies in Prishtina, said for example that she does not want to invite so many relatives she does not even know, but only those who are meaningful to her. Others in her age group however, are desirous of a large wedding, stressing the importance of inviting the entire kin, knowing who belongs to one's kin, as belonging is created by face to face relations, and weddings are the most important events for this.

The inclusion of the bride's kin and the decreasing meaning of the groom's kin

Also the composition of the guest list has changed. While at weddings in the groom's yard, close relatives of the bride are not present and the bride is therefore on her own, without the support of her family, there is an important change when it comes to weddings in a restaurant, in which the closer relatives of the bride are invited, too. In fact, while the wedding party in the restaurant is mostly organized and paid for by the groom and brings together his kin as well as acquaintances, it became normal to reserve one or two tables for the bride's family, meaning that the bride is able to bring 20-60 persons of her closest kin. In this way, relations to the bride's relatives, which had been established from the time of the engagement on, and which are supposed to be nurtured throughout life by cyclical visits, are already acknowledged at the wedding.

This is also expressed in the descriptions of a young woman, who told me that at the wedding of her brother, who lived abroad but married at home, 60 seats had been reserved for the relatives of her mother, and another 60 seats had been reserved for the relatives of the bride. However, from the paternal kin, 280 people were invited, therewith expressing the continuing importance of the male blood line and kin. Furthermore, even good friends and colleagues from work were invited, stressing the increasing importance of non kin alliances.

In town, these changes are even more visible and rules have been partly shifted. In weddings in Prishtina, it occurs that the bride and groom have the same amount of guests, or the bride has even more, and that bride and groom share the costs, or that the bride assumes more of the costs. Still, these weddings are rather exceptional, even in towns.

The meaning and functions of the male kin in such restaurant celebrations however shifted enormously in the Opoja region. While in the wedding at home, the members of the groom's kin are essential for the functioning of the celebrations, as they have to offer their space and many of them must work to make the festival possible, the celebration in the restaurant is less bound to family and community support, as the food and drinks are served by waiters who are employed by the restaurant and paid by the groom's family. In this way, the wedding is less built on communal solidarity, and more on money.

At the same time, particularly young people stress that the festivals in restaurants are more fun than those at home, not least because the inviting family can also enjoy

---

63 In fact, the invitation of the mahalla is also a rather new habit and already a limitation, as before the war, until 1996 or so, the whole village was invited. When one family started to change owing to exorbitant costs, all families followed.

the celebration. As Donna, a 20 year old girl who was studying in Pristina said, a wedding at home is a huge hardship for the family, and all members are completely drained from working for it, while in the restaurant, they are guest themselves and can actually enjoy the celebration.

However, even in the Opoja region, most restaurant celebrations are preceded by long enduring preparations and festivals at home, at the conclusion of which family members remain tired when they finally do arrive in the restaurant, with various middle aged and elderly people remarking that they are happy when the celebrations come to an end soon after the arrival of the bride at 6.00 p.m., after three days of celebrations, and that they do not feel inclined to add a restaurant celebration, which is in their view an unnecessary evil.

Middle aged and elderly people also appreciate weddings at home for another reason, as it is said that having served guests at home is a special honor for the house: the family gains status with it, and the more guests who come, the more status the family receives. Having a festival in a restaurant, which means in most cases not even in their native village, nor serving the food themselves, but leaving it to 'strangers' also does not carry the same byline of being hospitable and therewith is also less bound to status and honor.

Shifting focus from the groom's family to the bridal couple, new partnership relations and new rituals

The meaning of the *fis* (the groom's kin) and the focus on the wedding as a family affair are however not only undermined through organizational aspects of a wedding in a restaurant, but also because suddenly, the groom's family is no longer the centre of attention, but largely the couple itself. While in the 'traditional' wedding at home, the celebrations at last for days, without the active involvement of the bride and groom, in the restaurant celebrations, the focus is shifted towards the arrival of the couple with the guests celebrating the union of the two, as a romantic relation. For this, many new rituals have been introduced, which are often copied from Hollywood films and therefore have a 'Western' appearance.

Different from weddings held at home, I observed for example that the bride and groom were both smiling when jointly entering the hall, and that their arrival was accompanied by children who strew flowers, as is done in many western, Christian weddings when newly married couples exit the church. On two occasions, I also observed that the entrance of the couple was accompanied with pyrotechnics (in one case a burning heart was placed on the ground; in another the lettering 'just married'). Unlike weddings in the groom's yard, the bride and groom are then jointly seated at the centre of the banquet, overseeing the wedding party all evening while being served food like all others (however, this is largely not eaten).

In one restaurant wedding, the Imam even came to the table giving his blessing, which is very different from the weddings held in the groom's yard, in which the Imam arrives at the house of the groom on the evening of the wedding, when the bride is already in the bedroom, and speaks the blessing at the bedrooms' door, in front of the groom, his parents and two witnesses, but without the presence of the bride. Asking for the circumstances under which the Imam came to bless the couple in the restaurant, I heard that the family paid extra for this service. The religious ceremony was then followed by the exchange of rings—and therewith with similar staging to the wedding ritual in a church, in which the exchange of rings follows the espousal through the priest. The exchange of rings was also the climax in other restaurant weddings I heard of. While in one case, this was also followed by a kiss between the groom and the bride, this did not happen in other restaurant weddings in Opoja at that time, as open intimacies were still considered taboo in the region. However, noticing that this taboo has been broken already and that this did not provoke 'riots', but was largely positively received (especially amongst the young generation), it seems that boundaries are easy to change and challenge in respect to weddings in Opoja. At the same time, I also heard of some restaurant weddings in which the interaction between the bride and the groom was rather limited and the bride performance did not differ much from her role in weddings held in the groom's yard, meaning that she averted her gaze in order to show respect to the groom and his family.

In the wedding of Delina and Isuf as well as in other restaurant weddings, the bride and groom also did not only dance the traditional circle dance (*valle*), in which the bridal pair was lined up with the relatives of the groom and therewith incorporated in to the grooms' kin, but also danced as a couple. During the paired dance of Delina and Isuf, many young people, who surrounded the dancing couple, applauded with excitement. The dances then generally shifted from the traditional *valle* to a partner dance, which was enjoyed not only by the young generation, but also by the middle aged generation, as women could finally catch their husbands and dance with them. This is also related to the music, which is different from those in the private yards, as there is no *Magjup* orchestra which leads the music with their drums. Instead, the host family mostly relies on DJs who play some Albanian folk music, which goes of course also with *valle*, but partly also disco music, at least in the last moments of the party.

This brings me to an important point, the diminishing of the gender division in the wedding, as guests shared tables according to kinship relations, and couples were placed next to each other. This is considerably different from a wedding in a yard, in which space is gender divided, and in many cases, women come largely without husbands, but with other women of their family and also with closely related (paternal) kin.

At weddings in restaurants, guests are mainly invited as couples, and suddenly it can also pose a problem when women come without their husband. This was the case for Dana, a migrant woman whose spouse could not join her as he had to work abroad. Dana explained to me that she felt uneasy when she went alone to the wedding of a relative of her spouse. She added that a wedding without a man is nothing for a woman.

Along with the diminishing of gender division, the very organized way of dressing according to age and kinship also suddenly disappeared, as in the restaurant, the bride was the only one with a wedding dress, and there were no women present with a *dimia*. Instead, all women wear evening dresses, and the younger ones have mostly knee length or even shorter dresses (which was partly disapproved by the elderly generation).

An important catalyzer of social interaction is also the alcohol which is served at most weddings held in a restaurant[64]; men are offered beer and *raki* (a strong brandy), while women do not drink alcohol. With the rising level of alcohol consumption during the evening, the atmosphere is increasingly lax, and an increasing number of men who are normally rather withdrawn start to dance and sing hilariously. This also facilitates the interaction between girls and boys, making it obvious as to why the young generation members present stressed to me that they have much fun during such weddings—much more than in the weddings held at homes. The middle aged generation also worries for these same reasons however. They reported that the consumption of alcohol could pose a problem of respect and control as most of the men were not used to drinking, and it also poses a security threat for traffic, as numerous men drive home drunk after the wedding.

Most weddings last at least until midnight and end with the serving of the wedding cake, which is often a five tier sugar crème cake as known from Hollywood movies or western series', and which is ritually cut by the bride and groom together. It became common that the bride's relatives leave soon after, and that the groom's relatives stay on for another one or two hours.

The young people however also aspire to something else: quite a few of them started to dream of a honeymoon holiday after the restaurant wedding, during which they have the time to enjoy themselves as a couple, away from the family and freed from all obligations which begin for the bride the first day after her marriage. However, as I heard from colleagues in town, even in urban areas very few realize these honeymoon aspirations, and for most young couples in the Opoja region this remains a dream, not least out of financial deficits. But there are also family roles which especially the bride is supposed to follow, and expectations from her new in-laws which she must meet. This also puts pressure on brides to adhere to these roles, and to forgo their own needs. This is the case especially for migrants who later return to their residence abroad.

One young bride who had migrated to Germany in the age of 12 and who returned to the village in order to celebrate her wedding at which she married another migrant from Opoja, said for example that she desperately sought to go on honeymoon after her wedding, but as she is in the village only for two weeks, her parents in law as well as the entire extended family would expect her to stay and perform her duties as a newly married bride, which include cleaning the house and yard in the morning and dressing nicely in the afternoon in order to welcome the girls and women of the village who wish to see her. Finally, she coalesced, as she wanted to please her in-laws.

CONCLUSIONS

In examining the wedding practices described above, it becomes apparent that there are two styles of weddings. In the Opoja region, both exist alongside each other and create a sort of simultaneity of temporal inequalities or social disparities, which are based on differences and inequalities which appear in Kosovo itself as well as the imaginations of Kosovar migrants abroad. It even seems that people from the region,

---

64 Generally, weddings are not celebrated during Ramadan.

migrants and local alike, invest into the social performances in two different directions: In the weddings at home, villagers and migrants seem to professionalize the 'old customs' which are partly re-invented and which stress the unity of the *mahalla* and patriarchal gender relations. Nowadays, families also spend much on these traditions. On the other hand, migrants as well as locals alike professionalize the wedding in the restaurant with various new rituals and elements.

As families who can financially afford to celebrate both wedding forms, they invest into two directions, therewith making 'everything possible'. They actively cherish and respect the patri-local and partly newly invented marriage rituals of the village while at the same time seek to link up to the global 'norm' and integrate dominant western wedding styles. The celebration in a wedding hall is accompanied by ambivalent and contradicting gender and generational relations: while the wedding in the grooms' yard, gender and age roles are (still) clearly defined by patriarchal roles expressed in spatial and visual arrangements, gender and generational differences seem to play a subordinate role in the restaurant wedding. Both wedding forms have a strong effect on community building. They therewith complement the fragmentation of family solidarity, evidenced by the increasing globalization of Kosovo as well as the continuing migration of villagers.

In fact, migrants have a very special role in the wedding, as it is migrant money which enables the celebration of large weddings and therewith supports community building. When investing in these weddings, and especially in those of their sons who have spent a formative part (if not all) of their youth abroad, migrants seem to long for the ritual incorporation of their sons into the family and the recreation of the unity of the family which they themselves have undermined by moving their family abroad. They therewith do not only reestablish their own position, but also the community which has fragmented. With the allocation of large sums of money for the wedding as well as gifts to the bride, that funding is lost for other investments, such as in the realm of education.

At the same time, the influence of migrants is also limited, as particularly in weddings at home, the organization and performance of the wedding is largely in the hand of the family and *mahalla*. This is supported by the fact that migrants often have only limited knowledge regarding the course and traditions which accompany the wedding, while locals know much more and therewith take the lead. Yet, migrants are at the same time often very excited about the 'authenticity' of these rituals and performances, which they see as an expression of their roots and culture to which they often relate themselves actively, as a way of creating belonging and identity. It is for this reason that migrants are often among those who create the best atmosphere at the wedding and who seem to enjoy it most. The wedding gives them the possibility to merge into a common body with those who stayed at home. In this way, weddings can be a means for community building which is paid for by migrants and orchestrated by the *mahalla* and family at home, and which is appreciated by both sides.

REFERENCES

Aarburg, Hans-Peter von and Gretler, Sarah Barbara. 2008. *Kosova-Schweiz. Die albanische Arbeit- und Asylmigration zwischen Kosovo und der Schweiz (1984-2000).* (= Freiburger Sozialanthropologische Studien, Bd. 18), Berlin: Lit.

Appadurai, Arjun. 2004. "The capacity to aspire: Culture and the terms of recognition," in *Culture and public action: A cross disciplinary dialog in development policy*, edited by Vijayendra Rao and Michael Walton (Stanford CA: Stanford University Press), 59–84.

Appadurai, Arjun. 2005. *Modernity at Large. Cultural Dimensions of Globalization.* London: University of Minnesota Press.

Carling, Jørgen. 2008. "The human dynamics of migrant trans-nationalism," *Ethnic and Racial Studies* Vol. 31 (8), 1452-1477.

Dahinden, Janine. 2005. "Contesting transnationalism? Lessons from the study of Albanian migration networks from former Yugoslavia," *Global Networks* 5, issue 2, 191-208.

European Stability Initiative (ESI). 2006. *Cutting the lifeline. Migration, family and the future of Kosovo.* Berlin, Istanbul, accessable at www.esiweb.org.

Erdei, Ildiko. 2011. "Migrants of the Future – Serbian Youth between Imaginary and Real Migration," in *Migrants in, from and to Southeastern Europe. Ways and Strategies of Migrating* (= Ethnologia Balkanica 14), edited by Klaus Roth and Jutta Lauth Baccas (Berlin: Lit), 109-128.

Fitze, Urs (ed.). 2007. *Young people in Kosovo: their situations, needs, and the prospects for youth policy development,* accessed July 2013, http://www.kullerat.net/resurse/youthPeopleKosovo.pdf.

Glick Schiller, Nina, Linda Basch and Christina Blanc-Szanton. 1997. "Transnationalismus: Ein neuer analytischer Rahmen zum Verständnis von Migration," in *Transnationale Staatsbürgerschaft* edited by Heinz Kleger (Frankfurt am Main, N.Y: Campus), 81-107.

Havolli, Sokol. 2009. *Determinants of Remittances. The Case of Kosovo.* Prishtina. Central Bank of the Republic of Kosovo (Working Paper 3).

Korovilas, James. 2009. *The economics of remittances: Microeconomic perspectives and evidence from Kosovo* (Manuscript).

Kaser, Karl. 1992. *Hirten, Kämpfer, Stammeshelden. Ursprünge und Gegenwart des balkanischen Patriarchats.* Vienna. Cologne, Weimar: Böhlau.

Kaser, Karl, 1995: *Familie und Verwandtschaft auf dem Balkan. Analyse einer untergehenden Kultur*. Vienna, Cologne, Weimar: Böhlau.

Kaser, Karl. 2000. *Macht und Erbe. Männerherrschaft, Besitz und Familie im östlichen Europa 1500-1900*. Vienna, Cologne, Weimar: Böhlau.

Kaser, Karl. 2008. *Patriarchy after patriarchy. Gender Relations in Turkey and in the Balkans, 1500-2000*. Vienna, Berlin: Lit.

Leutloff-Grandits, Carolin. 2010a. *Establishing Social Security through Family Bonds: The logic of giving and receiving among Kosovars across transnational spaces*. COST Working Paper, Action IS0803.

Leutloff-Grandits, Carolin. 2010b. "Kinship in Kosovo in European Perspective," in *Joint Research and Technology Development, Projects 2007-2010* (Multidimensional Project for the Implementation of an Institutionalised Partnership between Austria and Kosovo in the Field of Higher Education, Research and Innovation). Prishtina, 199-218.

Levitt, Peggy and Glick Schiller, Nina. 2004. "Conceptualizing Simultaneity: A Transnational Social field Perspective on Society," *International Migration Review* Vol. 38 (3), 1002-1039.

Luci, Nita. 2005. "Transitions and traditions: Redefining Kinship, Nation and Gender in Kosova," *Anthropological Journal on European Cultures* 14, 143-169.

Nieswand, Boris. 2011. *Theorising Transnational Migration: The Status Paradox of Migration* (= Routledge Research in Transnationalism). Routledge: Chapman & Hal.

Pichler, Robert. 2009a. "Migration, architecture and the imagination of home(land). An Albanian-Macedonian case study," in *Transnational societies, trans-territorial politics. Migrations in the (Post)-Yugoslav Region, 19th-21st Century*, edited by Ulf Brunnbauer (München: Oldenbourg), 213-236.

Pichler, Robert. 2009b. "Migration, Ritual and Ethnic Conflict. A Study of Wedding Ceremonies of Albanian Trans-Migrants from the Republic of Macedonia," *Ethnologia Balkanica* 13 (2009), 211-230.

Reineck, Janet. 1991. *The past as refuge. Gender, migration, and ideology among the Kosova Albanians* (University of California, Berkeley, PhD-thesis).

Rrapi, Gjergj. 2003. *Die albanische Grossfamilie im Kosovo*. Vienna, Cologne, Weimar: Böhlau.

Schmitt, Oliver Jens. 2008. *Kosovo. Eine kurze Geschichte einer zentralbalkanischen Landschaft*. Wien: Böhlau.

Schwandner-Sievers, Stephanie. 2001. "The Enactment of 'Tradition': Albanian Constructions of Identity, Violence and Power in Times of Crisis," in *Anthropology of Violence and Conflict* edited by Bettina E. Schmidt and Ingo Schroeder (London: Routledge), 97-120.

Turner, Victor. 2005. *Das Ritual: Struktur und Anti-Struktur.* Frankfurt a.M.: Campus.

Vertovec, Steven. 2004. "Cheap calls: the social glue of migrant trans-nationalism," *Global Networks* 4 (2), 219–224.

Wolf, Eric. 1999. *Envisioning Power. Ideologies of Dominance and Crisis*. Berkeley: University of California Press.

PART FOUR

WOMEN'S MOVEMENT AND THE IMPLEMENTATION OF GENDER QUOTAS IN TRANSITION

DELINA FICO

IS THERE A WOMEN'S MOVEMENT IN ALBANIA?

WOMEN'S RIGHTS ACTIVISTS

Quite often frustrated journalists, human rights activists, women, foreign diplomats or experts, and Albanian public officials will say that there is no women's movement in Albania. They mean that they do not hear loud enough the voice of women and girls, as well as that of women's rights activists in protesting against the violation of women's rights or against policies that perpetuate women's marginalization or/and discrimination in the country. In this article, I try to explore this claim and weigh in on whether they are right or wrong to make this statement. I will look at the development of women's activism in Albania, mainly in the shape of women's non-governmental organizations and their activities over the last twenty years and discuss their role in advancing gender equality. Where do these organizations come from and what inspires their work? Do they constitute a women's movement? Is there a substantial issue here or are the differing perceptions regarding the role of women's groups in Albania simply an image issue?

I will explore this issue in three steps. I will first decide on a workable definition of social movements that I can use for the purpose of this article. I will then look at the development of women's activism over the last twenty years in Albania and identify features that might or might not characterize it as a social movement. Lastly, I will modestly try to respond to the question 'is there a women's movement in Albania' and identify avenues for further research on this issue. I will stop there, but the next interesting question is: If there is a women's movement in Albania, is it a feminist one?

SOCIAL MOVEMENTS

The concept of social movements is one of the most difficult to pin down in the vast academic literature on this issue that flourished in North America and Western Europe starting in the early 1960s on the heels of such activities: the civil rights movement, environmentalism, the peace movement, second wave feminism, the animal rights movement, etc. Social scientists write about 'new social movements' to discern them from the social movements of the early to mid-1900s that were largely workers' movements fighting to change the power structures in the system of production. There are few themes in the literature on social movements that one should take into consideration while navigating towards a feasible definition of the 'new' social movements. First, the 'new' social movements differ fundamentally from the previous movements as they no longer define themselves principally in relation to the system of production (Della Porta and Dianni, 10). The new social movements stem from non-class conflicts and are often concerned with reclamation of autonomous spaces rather than material gains. For example, the feminist movement aims to transform gender relations that are based on the existing patriarchal system across countries and class. Second, social movements are at least about more than getting engaged in public life or doing good. Citizens groups or organizations that engage, for example, in delivering social services, would not count as part of a social movement. Some authors characterize these groups' work, at their best, as 'consensus movements' and emphasize that, despite the fact that actors of these movements share solidarity and an interpretation of the world, their sustained collective action does not entail a conflictive element (Della Porta and Dianni 2006, 22-23). Third, social movements are not equal to associative life, meaning organizations. This theme sometimes reaches an extreme such as the stance that non-governmental organizations (NGOs) are neither movements, nor surrogates for them. NGOs are generally much less active than women's movements, for example, in political contestation and mobilization and more active in service delivery and issue-specific activities. Several authors go further to voice their fears that NGO-ization may undermine movement's transformational character (Basu 2010, 16).

These themes and other theoretical debates about the definition of social movements are compellingly summarized in the definition by Mario Dianni that states: "A social movement is a network of informal interactions between a plurality of individuals, groups, and/or organizations, engaged in political or cultural conflict on the basis of a shared collective identity" (Dianni 2000, 162). In further writings about the social movement concepts, Dianni and Donatella della Porta provide a more nuanced version of this definition when they write that "social movements are a distinct process, consisting of a mechanism through which actors engaged in collective action: are involved in conflicting relations with clearly identified opponents; are linked by dense informal networks; and share a distinct collective identity." (Della Porta and Dianni 2006, 20). Note here the three main elements of this definition: conflicting relations, dense informal networks, and collective identity. Following this line of thinking, women's movements are characterized by the "[...] conscious and collective revolt on behalf of women, defined as a general category with a set of problems and needs specific to themselves, which in turn are created by a socio-cultural system that categorically disadvantages them relative to men." (Chafetz et.al. 1986, 48) I will use these two definitions as a basis to probe women's activism and mobilization in Albania over the last 20 years for traces of a social movement.

A BRIEF HISTORY OF WOMEN'S ACTIVISM IN ALBANIA

1. The first steps (1990–1994)

The establishment of the first women's non-governmental organizations in Albania during 1991-1993 stemmed from the need and desire for women to be identified as a group with particular interests and needs in a broader political and social context. The all encompassing and rapid political, economic, and social transformations that took place in Albania starting in December 1990 created from the beginning a very polarized public sphere divided along one perceived focus: those who claimed to have suffered at the hands of the former totalitarian regime and those who were perceived as having benefited from this regime. This broad and deep division that took even from the beginning the shape of a very antagonistic political fight, left little space for the definition in the public realm of special interest of various social groups, whose identity could not be defined only along this drastic and hazy division line. Women were one of these groups. In the early 1990s, political action and debate about Albania's past, present, and future was completely void of a gender analysis. While benefiting from the increasing political freedoms and economic opportunities, women were at the same time losing jobs en masse; losing husbands, fathers, and brothers to migration, and unexpectedly were being exposed to high level threats to their lives and freedom, through trafficking for forced prostitution and increased crime rates. Furthermore, women started being depicted in the public debate and the media either as victims (of political oppression in the past, of poverty and sexual exploitation in the present) or only as sex objects (hence the abundance of pornographic films shown in the cinemas remaining in the capital, Tirana, for example). Women's emancipation that had been proclaimed and pursued by the totalitarian regime was often seen as another 'sin' of the past 45 years that needed to be erased. Women themselves had mixed feelings about their place in a recent past that, on one hand, had provided Albanian women and girls with increased opportunities for education, work, and participation in public life, but, on the other hand, had condemned them, in particular in the 1970s and 1980s, to restricted resources, as well as political and economic hardship, for themselves and their families. The double-burden of hard work at home in the context of increasingly diminished economic resources and the restriction of freedom in the public and private sphere had become a weight too heavy to bear, so women joined the chorus of the rest of the Albanian society that loudly and gladly threw everything of the past away. There was little attention paid to what various social groups of women and girls were losing in the process, as well as little acknowledgement about the fact that building a stable and fair future would benefit from a critical analysis of the recent past.

In this context, the establishment of women's non-governmental organizations (NGOs) opened up a new space for public debate and action where women as a social group could articulate their identity and could take collective action in line with their collective interests. This need led to the founding in 1991–1993 of the first women's groups, such as the Independent Forum of Albanian Women, the women's association *Refleksione*, the association *Useful to Albanian women*, and the *League of Anti-Communist Women* (later called the *League of Formerly Persecuted Women*). The first women's organizations were mainly led by college educated urban women based in Tirana and in a few other towns. From the start, women's organizations undertook actions that addressed the most pressing concerns and needs of larger groups of women, with little knowledge of the history and the context of a larger women's movement that had flourished in many parts of the world starting in the late 1960s or of the feminist ideology that had inspired this movement. In the early 1990s, women's NGOs helped distribute humanitarian aid to poor families, educated women and girls about reproductive health and rights, provided skills training that would help women integrate in the market economy, and raised awareness about violence against women that affected women of all ages and levels of education in cities, towns, and villages. A concern for women's human rights and their participation in political decision-making was put on the table during these years but efforts to advance a women's rights agenda at the political level begun in full force only in the mid-1990s.

2. Expansion and specialization (1995-1999)

The number of women's organizations grew rapidly after 1995 and they flourished in urban and rural areas. The need to be seen and heard—the need for agency—remained a strong motive behind the establishment of more women's groups in the following years. But this is not the whole story. A number of other factors affected the development of women's activism in Albania. Support, funding, and technical assistance by international governmental and non-governmental programs and organizations played a crucial role in enabling women's groups to expand and step up their activism. The growing number of women's NGOs, increased funding by foreign donors, and the expansion of their interaction with women's organizations and networks in the Balkans, as well as in Europe and North America, led to the enlargement of the circle of issues that they dealt with and to their specialization. For example, public awareness campaigns on violence against women were followed by the establishment in 1995 of the *Counseling Center for Women and Girls*, the first center of this kind in Albania. The first non-governmental centers of reproductive health, services to street children, and for disabled women followed.

In the second half of the 1990s, we saw the emergence of the need for larger and more effective cooperation among women's groups on issues of common interest. The informal network of women's organizations coordinated by the then-Women's Center in 1994-1997 brought together politically independent women's organizations, as well as women's forums of political parties, and gave birth to several shared strategic initiatives. One such initiative was the *Women's Legal Group* that worked to advocate for gender-sensitive laws, including a fair reproductive rights law. This group led to the establishment of the *Women's Bar Association*, as well as that of the *Women's Legal Aid Center* (currently the *Center for Civic Legal Initiatives*). During this time, women's organization became involved with sustainable sources of funding and became engaged in income-generating activities to support their activities, an effort that more or less failed in the long-term. Cooperation with government structures developed and led sometimes to coordinated successful efforts. But the first protests against government policies took place, as well. In 1995, a loose coalition of women's groups organized a protest before the Tirana municipal council to raise their voice against the neglect of the city's physical infrastructure and lack of policies to control air pollution. This was a pioneer effort by women's NGOs to organize and occupy public space on an issue of concern to all citizens, as the street protest had been so far only the domain of political parties or men-led organizations.

The experience in service delivery and in cooperating with other NGOs and state structures bore fruit in 1999 at the time when Kosovar Albanians were expelled from their homes in Kosova and flooded into Albania. Women's organizations served as mechanisms for distributing humanitarian aid; found shelter for women and girls, as well as for those with special needs; offered counseling to women, children, and families traumatized by the war, and encouraged and supported the establishment of Kosovar Albanian women's organizations. Many leading women's rights activists consider this moment as a catalyst that expanded considerably the Albanian women's NGOs capacity to attract more volunteers, mobilize more resources, become more visible in the public realm, and act as important partners of international agencies and programs that worked to address the Kosovar refugees' crisis:

3. Consolidation and larger engagement with the state (from 2000 on)

According to the NGO shadow report for CEDAW (June 2010) there are 110 registered NGOs that profess to work on women's or gender issues. 23% of them provide legal aid; 18% include in their mission women and family/children; 11% work on women's economic empowerment; 10% focus on cultural activities; 9% on information-sharing; 6% provide counseling and direct services; 6% of them work with women in the rural areas; 4% are women's branches or forums of political parties; while 2% work on women in decision-making, health, religion, education, media, employment, and trafficking. The largest and oldest organizations are headquartered in Tirana, but some have branches and/or implement projects in the regions outside the capital. Except for a handful of organizations, most employ 2-5 full-time members as well as a complement of volunteers, mainly female students or unemployed women looking for some experience in an office setting. Some of these organizations are still led by women who co-founded them 10 or even 18 years ago. Some service delivery in the regions with awareness raising, mobilization, and advocacy work mainly focused in Tirana. The main areas of women's activism remain addressing violence against women and women's political participation. But new areas of activism have emerged in the last ten years, such as women's economic empowerment, engendering the education system, as well as the monitoring of government policies and programs. Gender studies are taught at Tirana University and a few private academic institutions and some of the women's organizations focus on research, although not exclusively. The specialization of women's organizations and the need to affect social change led to the proliferation of networking among women's organizations. The network of women's groups *Millennium* focused for years on women's participation in political decision-making. Another loose network, the *Coalition to Increase Women's and Youth Participation in Decision-Making* focuses on the same issue. The *Network against Gender-based Violence and Trafficking*, on the other hand addresses violence against women by providing services to victims of violence and advocating for larger and sustainable engagement by public institutions in preventing and eradicating this violence. These coalitions mostly serve to advocate for changes in the legal framework and policies related to gender equality and sometime engage in protests against violations of women's rights or gender-based discrimination. They issue statements, call media conferences, write open letters to decision-makers, and hold vigils to condemn such instances, with street protests being rare. One could mention, for example, the annual March 8 street event organized by the association "Useful to Albanian Women" that seeks to remind the public about female victims of violence and sometimes lauds women's contributions to the community and country's progress.

The last decade has seen women's non-governmental organizations interact constantly with public institutions and in particular with institutions that work to advance gender equality. Women's NGOs have worked with the government to draft and pass laws, as well as national strategies and platforms on gender equality and domestic violence. As a result, Albania has made major steps towards completing the legal framework regarding the protection of women's rights. The law "On Gender Equality in Society" that entered into effect in 2008, the law "On Measures against Violence in the Family" that entered into effect in early 2007, and the Anti-discrimination law "On Protection from Discrimination" that entered into effect in 2010 all provide a solid regulatory framework for preventing violence against women and gender-based discrimination, punishing the perpetrators, and providing services to victims. It is important to note that the law "On Measures against Family Violence" was drafted by civil society groups and presented to the Parliament in 2006 as a citizens' initiative after it received more than 20,000 signatures in its support. This is the only successful initiative of this kind in Albania since 1992. The law "On Protection from Discrimination" was also drafted by civil society organizations and passed with strong support by these organizations.

IS THIS A WOMEN'S MOVEMENT?

As noted at the beginning of this article, the main themes that define a social movement are conflictive relations, dense informal networks, and collective identity. It should be highlighted first and foremost that a large number of women's NGOs in Albania pertain to the service delivery community and, as such, 'exclude' themselves from the definition of social movement, in the sense which we use the term. For the remainder, it is fair to say that women's activism in Albania is based on a shared collective identity as women that are discriminated are done so based on their gender. But this shared collective identity is mainly focused on two main pillars: that of violence against women based on their gender and the lack of adequate representation in political institutions that decide on their lives and that of their families. There is little understanding of the deep-seated gender inequalities that stem from a patriarchal system that regards women primarily as caretakers and without representation and the need to address, at the source, these inequalities at all levels. For example, in public discussion about increased levels of violence against women, some women's rights activists rightly point to factors that exacerbate this violence, such as poverty, major deficiencies in the rule of law, and low levels of education, but fail to highlight the root of gender-based violence, which is a hierarchical power system that defines women only in relation to men and not as autonomous human beings with unalienable rights and that uses violence to maintain men's dominance on and control of women. This is reflected also in the rejection or neglect of a feminist discourse while discussing the agenda for women's activism in Albania. As has been noted repeatedly in discussions about Albanian women's NGOs, there are no organizations that openly define themselves as feminist. There are only few women's rights activists and even fewer members of the academia who do not shy from the feminist label.

Exploring the reasons for the rejection or fear of an openly feminist stance by Albanian women's rights activists would require a separate article. We will touch briefly upon two of them here however. First, except for few intellectual women who engaged in social work or contributed to publications in the 1930s, there is nearly no tradition of feminist thought or a movement in Albania, differently, for example, from countries of ex-Yugoslavia, where feminist studies and activism developed under the influence of the second wave of feminism in Western Europe and North America. Second, under the dictatorship, the family served often as the only place where men and women could take refuge from the pressures and control of an overwhelming and threatening state. This fostered a strong unity between men and women in the context of the family and did not encourage or allow for much dissent along gender lines. This approach was carried over after 1990 and was reflected also in the persistent effort by most of the women's rights activists to emphasize that women's groups in Albania do not work against men. Owing to a lack of adequate knowledge and stereotypes, feminism was and is often mistakenly understood as an ideology that positions women against men, so Albanian activists are not willing to be identified with an ideology that they feel does not represent their approach and their realities.

It is hard to define the relation between women's activism in Albania and its opponents—male co-workers or bosses that sexually harass women and girls in the workplace, non-responsive state institutions, perpetrators that exercise violence against women, political leaders that do not implement the gender-based quota in the electoral lists, etc.—as conflicting. With few exceptions, women's NGOs take a conciliatory approach to institutions and individuals who intentionally, or not, oppose or obstruct efforts to advance gender quality. To provide an example, the two major political parties failed to fulfill their obligations for a 30% gender-based quota on the electoral list for the June 28, 2010, local elections. One or two women's organizations pointed out publicly this failure, but took no steps to demand, for example, legal remedies for such a failure or a public apology by the parties, as well as a firm and official commitment that this will not happen in the next elections. The only obvious exceptions are the perpetrators of trafficking for forced prostitution and violence against women that find themselves unanimously condemned by women's rights activists and their supporters. And lastly, there is the lack of dense informal networks of women and men that continuously and over a long period of time debate about gender-based discrimination or marginalization, protest against gender inequalities, and contribute to public actions to redress such inequalities, including petitions, meetings with decision-makers, street protests, and community mobilizing events. As described above, with very few exceptions, women's organizations in Albania are still an affair of a limited number of people, mainly paid staff of small organizations and with limited numbers of members and volunteers. Sometime, one could see more than 150 women and men in the audience of a conference organized by a women's organization, but it is very difficult to discern their long-term sustained contribution to address the concerns that are being discussed at that conference. One encouraging sign was the petition in support for the draft law "On Measures against Violence in the Family" that was described above.

I am aware of the limited analysis offered in this article and I would not be bold enough to give a definite response to the question I raised at the beginning. But, I would like to point out those avenues which could be explored further to get to the bottom of the question as to whether there is a women's movement in Albania. First, we lack data and thorough analysis that document and will help to understand all forms of expression of women's activism in the country. Research on women's activism, levels of participation in activities that promote a gender equality agenda, and the scope of women's NGOs in the context of the civil society sector in Albania are still sporadic and rare. Second, we need to assess the full range of the impact that women's activism has had on advancing gender equality in the country in the last twenty years.

While it is easy to note outcomes in completing the legal framework and developing government mechanisms for advancing gender equality, as well as in pioneering services for women in need in the country, the impact of these outcomes on the everyday life and the political, economic, and social status of women and girls in the country needs to be investigated. Third, we need to fully explore the visible and invisible relation between feminist ideology and practice and women's activism in Albania.

REFERENCES

Albanian Coalition for the Preparation of Alternative Reports (ed.). 2010. *NGO Shadow Report on the Situation of Women and Girls in the Republic of Albania for the UN Committee for the Elimination of all Forms of Discrimination against Women (CEDAW)*. Tirana.

Basu, Amrita (ed.). 2010. *Women's Movement in the Global Era: The Power of Local Feminism*. Boulder: Westview Press.

Crossley, Nick. 2002. *Making Sense of Social Movements*. UK and USA: Open University Press.

Chafetz, Janet, Anthony Dworkin and Stephanie Swanson. 1986. *Female Revolt: Women's Movements in World and Historical Perspective*. Totowa, New Jersey: Rowman and Allanheld.

Della Porta, Donatella and Dianni, Mario. 2006. *Social Movements: An Introduction* (2nd edition). Oxford: Blackwell Publishing, Ltd.

Dianni, Mario. 2000. "The concept of social movement," in *Readings in Contemporary Sociology*, edited by Kate Nash (Oxford: Blackwell), 230-250.

Fico, Delina. 2008. "Një raport i parehatshëm – lëvizja e grave dhe feminizmi në Shqipëri [An uneasy relationship—women's movement and feminism in Albania]," *GAIA* 7.

Fico, Delina. 2001. "Women's non-governmental organizations and the development of a new political culture in Albania post 1990," in *90+10 - Women during the Post-Communist Transition Period* (proceedings of the national conference, Open Society Foundation for Albania, Tirana)

Fico, Delina. 1999. "Women's groups: Albanian case," in *Journal of Communist Studies and Transition Politics*, Vol.15/1, 30-40.

Kolins Givan, Rebecca, Sarah A. Soule and Kenneth M. Roberts, eds. 2010. *The Diffusion of Social Movements: Actors, Mechanisms, and Political Effects*. Cambridge: Cambridge University Press.

Opp, Karl-Dieter. 2009. *Theories of Political Protest and Social Movements*. London and New York: Routledge.

Ramet, Sabrina Petra (ed.). 1999. *Gender Politics in the Western Balkans*. University Park, PA: Pennsylvania State University Press.

Renne, Tanya (ed.). 1997. *Ana's Land - Sisterhood in Eastern Europe*. Boulder: Westview Press.

Interviews with: Valdet Sala, co-founder of women's association *Refleksione*;

Diana Çuli, founder and President of the *Independent Forum of Albanian Women*;

Sevim Arbana, founder and President of the association *Useful to Albanian Women*;

Vjollca Meçaj, former Executive Director of *Women's Legal Aid Center* (currently the *Center for Civic Legal Initiatives*);

Shpresa Banja, founder and President of *Women' Forum in Elbasan*.

EGLANTINA GJERMENI

IMPLEMENTATION OF GENDER QUOTA IN ALBANIA

INTRODUCTION

The equal participation of women and men in decision making is a cornerstone of democracy and social justice, and is strongly promoted at the international level. Gender balance in politics is one of the critical areas of concern of the Beijing Platform for Action (1995) and the Convention on the Elimination of all Forms of Discrimination against Women (CEDAW). This paper analyses the efforts and challenges to promote women's participation in decision-making processes in Albania with reference to laws promoting gender equality. Particular attention is paid to gender equality in the legislative process.

The history of women's struggle for equality in South-eastern Europe (SEE) provides a lesson in how fragile hard-fought rights for women are, and how easily women's social, cultural, economic, and political advances can be reversed. Statistics on the progress of women in SEE countries following the Second World War show that under communist regimes in which populations lost individual and, in many cases, human rights, women nevertheless gained political, cultural, and economic status within their political systems—a status that, paradoxically, has declined significantly in the turbulence of post-communist transition. Before the 1990s, literacy, education, employment, access to child and health care, de jure equality, the personal rights of women and even access to political power, were much better than in the majority of European countries with long democratic traditions. Post-communist transition however, has been accompanied by a revival of patriarchal power structures that, while never eradicated in the private sphere, were mitigated in the public sphere by communism's ideological underpinnings. After the collapse of the communist governments, oppressive stereotypes of women were reinforced and recycled. This resurgence of gender discrimination, accompanied by the devastating consequences of neoliberal shock therapy, brought a significant increase in cultural, political, and economic injustice for women (Lokar 2010). This backlash against women shows us that, especially at moments of historic change, women must organize to protect existing rights and advance women's causes in new social, political, and economic realities.

Across the Eastern European countries, the average number of women members of Parliament hovers at just above 15%, which is significantly below the critical mass of 30% that is considered necessary for women to influence political discourse in a meaningful way. The table below shows when and how laws requiring gender quotas in legislative bodies were implemented in the parliaments of the countries in the region.

Table 1: Enactment of Legal Quota in the Region and Its Progress over Time

Country	Legal Enacted	Quota WMPs % 1989	WMPs% 1995/6	WMPs% 2000	WMPs% 2005	WMPs% 2009
Bosnia and Herzegovina	1998	23	2.7	28.6	16.7	11.9
Kosovo	2000		5	27	30	30
Macedonia	2003	17	3.3	6.7	19.2	28.3
Serbia	2005	17	5.1	7.2	7.9	21.6
Slovenia	2005	26	13.3	7.8	12.2	13.3
Croatia	2008	17	7.9	20.9	21.7	20.9
Albania	2008	33.2	15	5.2	6.4	16.4

Referring to Table 1, Albania is performing at about the average level. In 1989, the percentage of women who were members of the parliament was 33.2%. The percentage declined considerably after 1989. In 2005, only 5.2% of the parliament members were women. The increase observed after the year 2005 follows the passage of the gender equality law (referenced above). Since 2005, the Speaker of the Parliament has been a woman. In 2009, the number of women who were members of parliament was 23 or 16.4%. There has been an increase in the women's representation in the parliament after 2005. However, much remains to be done.

HISTORICAL BACKGROUND

During the socialist regime, Albanian state policies, like those of other Eastern European countries, promoted women's participation in decision-making structures. This was due to the socialist ideology of equality between women and men. It is important to emphasize that this equality was propagandistic, and most of the time women did not have a real voice or power within the decision making structures. The percentage of women in parliament during this regime was relatively high. The highest representation of women in Parliament was 33%, in the year 1974. After 1990, the country began its transition, from a communist dictatorship to a free market democracy. The first democratic elections were in the year 1991, and the percentage of women in Parliament started to decrease, compared to the previous years, to 20%. The following table provides an overview of the representation of women in the Albanian Parliament from 1920-2009.

Table 2: Women participation in the Albanian Parliament over years

Year	Men No.	Men %	Women No.	Women %	Total
1920-1970	598	93.7	40	6.3	638
1970	192	72.7	72	27.3	264
1974	167	66.8	83	33.2	250
1982	174	69.6	76	30.4	250
1990	169	67.6	81	32.4	250
1991	199	79.6	51	20.4	250
1992	131	93.6	9	6.4	140
1996	119	85.0	21	15.0	140
1997	144	92.9	11	7.1	155
2001	132	94.3	9	5.7	141
2005	130	94	10	6	140
2009	117	84	23	16	140

Source: INSTAT, Women and men in Albania, 2010.

Albanian women were granted the right to vote in 1945. During the socialist regime (1945–1990) women's emancipation and participation in political, economic, and social life was one of the priorities of the government. Even though promoting women's participation of the public sphere was part of the communist propaganda agenda, which espoused egalitarianism, women in Albania benefited from it. However, despite the increased number of women holding public positions, women's decision-making power was substantially curbed by the social norms and customs of a highly patriarchal culture, in particular in their families, but also in their communities. In addition, the one-party state and the high degree of authoritarian control exercised by the dictator severely limited the decision making power of all citizens.

At the beginning of the transition period from the socialist dictatorship, women comprised 20.5% of the Assembly. Following the first free elections in 1991, women's representation in Albania's Assembly has dropped considerably, reaching its lowest level in 2001 with only 8 women MPs or 5.7% of the total number.

The pluralistic period should have created more opportunities for women's participation in all areas of life, including the decision-making structures and politics. Unfortunately, this was not the case. Transition has been a painful and long process with a negative impact on all citizens. Women in particular experienced negative consequences in both the private and public spheres. Under the communist regime, the state controlled most aspects of private as well as public life. Democracy promised individual freedom in the private sphere and greater representation in policy making. Unfortunately, it provided no safeguards against the brutal economic ravages of the public sphere. Albania is currently one of the poorest countries in Europe, characterized by high levels of corruption and a continuing attitude of authoritarian rule, which is still far from a functional democracy. The status of Albanian women today is strongly linked with and negatively impacted by these economic, political, and social conditions.

While women all over the world face obstacles to participation in decision-making structures—obstacles shared by Albanian women—Albanian women face additional obstacles specific to the history, mentality, economic and social development in Albania. According to Qirjaku and Dhimitri (2000), there are two primary categories of reasons that women have been 'left out' of Albanian politics. The first category includes factors related to the Albanian historical and cultural heritage. Throughout history, Albanian women did not have the proper opportunities to develop their personality as actors in the public arena, particularly as participants with rights equal to men in politics. The second category includes political, economic, and social factors. These factors are interlinked with each other and make this problem a complex issue. Other factors are related to the harshness of the political environment in Albania. The following issues are especially pertinent.

The strong patriarchal mentality that exists in the country posits politics as a 'man's profession' and reinforces strong negative stereotypes regarding women involved in politics.

In terms of social and cultural barriers, expectations that women serve as the primary caretaker of the family relegates women to spending their peak intellectual time confined to the care of home and family, being unable to engage in and contribute to the public sphere. In households, the main workload is still shouldered by women regardless of their participation in the public sphere. The research carried out by Plaku, Picari, Pino, Danaj, Gjermeni and Shtraza (2008), shows the presence of the mentality shared by men and women that taking care of home and children is an obligation that should be fulfilled by the woman. If the husband or partner wants to participate, this contribution is considered from both sides as 'help' and not as a fair division of work among two parties which voluntarily have chosen to build a future/family together. Girls and women share these beliefs regardless of educational level.

In this situation, a coordinated effort is required to intervene in the roots of the complex political, social, and economic conditions of women's exclusion from the decision making processes and to provide sustainable and long term results.

LEGAL AND POLICY FRAMEWORK REGARDING GENDER EQUALITY IN ALBANIA

In Albania, during the last 20 years of transition, civil society and in particular women's and human rights organizations have made many efforts to improve the legal framework on human rights (and women's rights as part of human rights). The contribution of civil society has been invaluable. Indeed, it is largely through their efforts that the Albanian government has ratified most important international conventions on human rights and women's rights and passed important legislation in the country. The country's laws are quite democratic and comparable with developed countries. For instance, Article 18 of the Albanian Constitution defines the equality of all citizens before the law and maintains that no one may be discriminated against for reasons such as gender, race, religion, ethnicity, language, political, religious, or philosophical convictions, economic, educational, or social status.

In addition to domestic laws, the Albanian government has signed numerous international conventions, including those encouraging equal treatment between the two sexes, such as the Convention for the Elimination of all forms of Discrimination against Women (CEDAW). CEDAW was ratified by Albania in 1993. Albania has also ratified conventions such as the European Convention on Human Rights, and for the Protection of Minorities. The CEDAW and the Beijing Platform for Action have provided detailed instructions on general issues regarding women and girls' rights and gender, thus serving as a guide for implementing the Millennium Goals. In addition, CEDAW encourages member countries to take into consideration the fulfillment of included obligations and to create structural mechanisms for offering equal opportunities for women and men.

While Albania's legal framework has room for improvement, what is more problematic is the existence of a gap between the 'de jure' and 'de facto' situation of women in Albania (Metani and Omari 2006) Albanian women do have legal rights, but most of the time they lack the environment to enjoy these rights, and the reality is different from what is written on paper.

In fact, the poor implementation of laws is one of the problems impeding Albania's progress towards EU membership. The country is behind on a series of issues, including the implementation of existing legislation. Implementation is a challenge for many of the new EU member countries, but Albania's challenges are particularly difficult in regard to a number of laws addressing gender equality. Among those laws addressing gender equality issues, we should mention:

(1) The Albanian Penal Code approved in 1995 (Law No. 7905) ensures the equality between the husband and wife in all fields of life, health, property, and dignity.
(2) The Labour Code approved in 2003 recognizes equal rights for work between men and women, for women's protection at the workplace, for paid holidays, and equal pay. This Code encourages and improves the situation of women and female jobseekers by materially compensating the employer.
(3) The Family Code approved in 2003 (Law No. 9062) provides for equal rights between the husband and the wife to freely choose marital engagements and

divorce, as well as their rights and obligations toward the family and the upbringing of children.
(4) Law No. 9970, issued on 24 July 2008 "On Gender Equality in Society" (LGES) further completed the legal framework regarding gender equality in education, employment and decision making.
(5) Law "On Protection against Discrimination" of 2010 established the Commissioner institution. This Commissioner carries out the functions of Ombudsman for issues of discrimination for any reason, including gender, but also gender identity, pregnancy, sexual orientation, family or marriage status, parental responsibility, which typically are closely related to the gender of a person.
(6) Unfortunately, as of this moment, there is a huge gap between the gender equality that these laws envision and women's experiences in practice.

GENDER EQUALITY LAW IN ALBANIA

The Albanian constitution has not provided any electoral quota for women's participation in decision-making structures but it does promote temporary measures regarding women's participation in public life. However, a new law holds promise for women and other discriminated social groups. Law Nr. 9904, (21.4.2008), revises Law Nr. 8417, (21.10.1998) "On procedures for reviewing the Constitution of the Albanian Republic." According to 9904, the Parliament would have 140 seats, elected through a proportional system. This changed the electoral system from a mixed proportional/majority system to a proportional one and increases the chances of a successful implementation of a gender quota. According to the experience of other countries, proportional representation systems are more favorable for women as well as for other discriminated social groups than plurality/majority systems.

Civil society organizations, international organizations and donors, and the forums of women in politics played an important role in launching the idea of the gender quota. In February 2006, the Children Human Rights Centre (CRCA) together with two major civil society actors (Independent Forum of Albanian Women and Albanian Centre for Population and Development) organized the largest gathering of women political groups, youth political groups and NGO's (women, young people and minorities), and 5 women members of the Parliament. The meeting concluded with the establishment of the Coalition for the Promotion of Women and Youth in Politics. Members of the Coalition are the political forums of women and youth, including minority organizations and NGO's in Albania. This was the largest Coalition in Albania. It had 87 members and sought to promote a proportional representation of women and youth in political life of Albania. During 2006, representatives of the Coalition started to lobby for the support of the Petition 'Quota 30' with the leaders of political parties in Albania. In April 2008, the Coalition for the Promotion of Women and Youth in Politics in cooperation with the Millennium Network campaigned together during a two-week period in a letter-signing campaign in support of approval by the Albanian Parliament for the draft-law "For Gender Equality in Albania". The draft met with strong resistance from smaller parties due to their potentially diminishing number of elected

MPs, which made it necessary for the civil society to lobby and campaign for its approval.

The Law "On Gender Equality in Society" was approved by the Albanian Parliament on 24 July 2008. The aim of this law is: a) to ensure effective protection against gender-based discrimination and against any form of conduct that encourages gender-related discrimination; b) to establish measures to guarantee equal opportunities for men and women in order to eliminate gender related discrimination in whatever form it may be manifested; c) to specify the responsibilities of the state authorities, both at a central and local level, for drafting and implementing normative acts and policies that support gender equality in society. The law includes new definitions on gender-related discrimination, in compliance with the definition of discrimination provided by CEDAW, gender mainstreaming, gender harassment and its prohibition, and equal gender representation. The law introduces special measures in the education system, employment, unpaid labor, and the collection of gender statistics. This law specifies that women should at a minimum comprise of 30% of all public-sector institutions at national and local levels.

The gender quota approved in the Gender Equality Law refers to the minimum representation of both sexes in all legislative and executive structures as well as in all other institutions. In this context, the Gender Equality Law considers political parties as the most important parties to ensure gender representation based on the quota system. The law permits the political parties to define the way and the measures needed to fulfill the conditions required by this law.

The gender quota is sanctioned at the Electoral Code and defines a special formula for the political parties for candidate ranking according to their gender. Article 67/5 specifies that "For each electoral zone, at least 30% of the multi-name list and/or one of the first three names on the multi-name list must be from each gender. Should they violate the provision of this article, political parties shall pay a fine of up to one tenth of the state funds received for the electoral campaign until the violation ceases" The role of political parties is critical in guaranteeing gender balance at the central and local government.

Evidence from other countries shows that the approval of the gender quota has a positive impact on women's representation in decision making (Anastasi and Olldashi, 2006), thus, it can be argued that the approval of the Gender Equality Law in Albania is a step toward achieving gender equality in Albania. However, as Mandro, Anastasi, Shkurti and Bozo indicate (2011), the implementation of this law faces several problems, and has its own limitations. The authors mention the fact that the established quota of 30% is lower than the 40% that other European countries strive for. Additionally, according to the Legal Code, the ranking order of the candidates does not necessarily ensure a gender quota even in the list of elected members of parliament, and the legal sanctions for political parties for not implementing the gender quota are very weak.

ISSUES IN IMPLEMENTING GENDER QUOTA LAW

Research from different countries shows that quotas are not only important in having women represented in politics, but also in encouraging women to be a part of the political process, thus bringing women's issues from a variety of different perspectives to the table. Certainly, this is one of the expected impacts that a gender quota would have. However, the effectiveness of the implementation of the gender quota in the future depends on the performance and activities of the women elected to Parliament.

The Albanian experience demonstrates that even though the gender quota is one of the most important electoral reforms, it faces strong resistance. The elections in Albania that followed the gender quota legislation indicate that the effective implementation of the gender quota lacks political commitment.

Referring to the results of the 2009 elections, 23 women were elected to the Parliament, compared to 10 in 2005. Women's representation increased from 7.1% in 2005 to 16.4% in 2009. The order that women candidates were placed on electoral lists influenced their success. While 27.8% of the Democratic Party candidates were women, they represent only 15% of their elected candidates (10 of 68). Women represented a slightly smaller share of the Socialist Party candidates, but their placement in higher-ranking positions resulted in women accounting for 20% of the SP's elected members of Parliament (13 of 65).

According to the report of OSCE/ODIHR, in the elections of 2009 women made progress but at levels lower than was expected. Referring to the report, "Women are generally underrepresented in Albanian politics but the issue of gender balance gained momentum in the run-up to these elections. The new gender quotas increased women's representation in Parliament, but weaknesses in the formulation of the legal provisions undermine their objective."

The effective implementation of quotas is also dependent on the sanctions for non-compliance. The experience of the 2009 elections showed that the most effective measure to ensure implementation of the gender quota was the Central Election Committee's refusal of the candidates list of political parties who did not respect the gender quota. This sanction was stronger compared to the sanction that required political parties to pay 30,000 lekë ($300).

Referring to the OSCE/ODIHR report for the local elections of 8 May 2011, there were only 14 women among the 872 mayoral candidates (1.6%). Six of the women candidates for mayor were elected. According to the media monitoring institution, women politicians received an average of 4.4% of the total news coverage on monitored TV broadcasts.

Over time, the participation of women in politics has become more acceptable in Albanian public opinion. According to a survey conducted prior to the 2009 elections, initiated and supported by UNIFEM now UN Women (Acer and Aset 2008), there is increased awareness in society about the participation of women in politics. Referring to the survey results, 73.4% of the interviewees think that it is necessary to increase the participation of women in public life. More women (46%) than men (36%) supported special measures such as quotas but substantial numbers of both women (35%) and men (46%) expressed resistance or uncertainty about them. As this survey shows, the public had a positive perception of women's participation in politics.

Despite modest recent gains, an analysis of historical, social and cultural factors reveals barriers to the participation of women in Albanian politics. These include patriarchal gender perceptions, as discussed earlier, such as the belief that the political arena is too aggressive for women, men in politics use rude language that is unsuitable for women, and politics is a dirty and corrupt business that is best left to men. Enduring structural issues also pose significant obstacles, such as the lack of time on the part of women due to their responsibilities for taking care of the home and the family, lack of political experience that is necessary to be an effective candidate, general social exclusion at the community level due to stereotypes and social norms, lack of financial and strategic support from political parties, and biased and unfair media coverage of female candidates and elected officials that focuses on their performance as wives and mothers (Acer and Aset 2008).

Some scholars argue that women who are involved in decision-making structures and in the highest levels of decision-making do not represent the actual trend of Albanian society. Fuga (Qendra për Popullsinë 2009) draws comparisons between Albanian women in politics and Albanian football players and argues that even though there are famous Albanian football players that are playing in different well-known clubs, they do not represent the real quality of the football championships in Albania. According to Fuga, the same holds true for women in politics. Albanian reality shows that the situation of women in Albania is not uniform throughout the country. There are significant gaps between women from urban and rural areas in levels of education, exposure to international norms, and socioeconomic position. In many rural areas, patriarchal attitudes and behaviors are deeply entrenched with few possibilities for offsetting them. Along with cultural differences between northern and southern regions, these factors combine to impact the level of women's participation in decision-making. This complex reality shows that gender equality is not a trend in Albanian society, but it is for sure a step forward on achieving gender equality de facto.

A recent study conducted on women's participation in decision making shows that women in Parliament face different expectations. Quota women reported that they have to meet high expectations because the public is more critical of them than of men who holding the same position in politics (Dragoti et.al. 2000). Media also is considered key in promoting and supporting elected women in order to increase their performance and become role models for other women. Civil society organizations are considered allies of women in decision-making structures in order to ensure partnership in addressing women's needs and interests in policy-making processes.

RECOMMENDATIONS AND ADDITIONAL MEASURES

Women's participation is not only an indicator of the democratization, but also can bring crucial changes regarding gender relations and gender stereotypes. Gender quota is a temporary mechanism that accelerates women's participation and representation in decision-making structures. The proportion of women in elected bodies may very well be increased by measures other than quotas, such as targets and recommendations, actions plans and capacity-building activities in individual parties. Quotas do not automatically result in equal representation of women and men in political decision-making. Several studies suggests that the introduction of quotas may fall short if they are not compatible with the electoral system in use and do not include rules about rank order and sanctions for non-compliance.

Gender quotas may increase women's political presence in quantitative terms, but other measures are needed to ensure that women have a voice and that they are considered as representatives of equal status with their male colleagues within the parties as well as within the elected assemblies. Women's roles in decision-making structures cannot be measured only through their numbers or percentages. It would have been much easier if only numbers would make possible the division of power. In order for women who are either elected or appointed to become a critical mass and influential actors, they need to make allies with women and men, and they need support from political parties, political forums, civil society, media, etc. The real problem of gender inequality is not only to add more women per se in different structures or processes, but how to design these processes to create the space and opportunities for them in order to contribute in a meaningful way.

Political parties need to review their programs from a gender perspective, ensuring that women's needs and interests are addressed. Because the standards and inner-workings of political parties and elected assemblies have been organized around the male model, they need to be changed. This can be achieved only by increasing women's presence. Political forums of women could serve as efficient means to create change. They can be promoted at the local and central level. Through them, women could be more active and have a more powerful voice in implementing a gender quota.

Increasing women's representation in political decision-making is linked to promoting better policies for the reconciliation of work and private life for both women and men. These efforts would encourage men to do more unpaid care work at home.

The presence of a strong women's movement is also an important factor in the promotion of women in politics. Women's organizations can mobilize the electorate and put pressure on the political parties or on governments to adopt special measures to enhance the political representation of women. Without an active pressure group, women's political representation might not increase as quickly as desired by women in politics.

REFERENCES

Albanian Center for Economic Research (ACET) and Albania Social Economic Think Tank (ASET), eds. 2008. *Public Perception of Women's Participation in Elections in Albania*. Tirana, http://www.aset-al.com/dokumente/unifem.pdf.

Aleanca Gjinore për Zhvillim. 2008. *GAIA* 8.

Anastasi, Aurela and Dhëmbo, Elona. 2009. *Barazia Gjinore Në Shoqëri. Paketë Trajnimi mbi Ligjin për Barazinë Gjinore në Shoqëri*. Tiranë: Botim i MPCSSH.

Anastasi, Aurela and Olldashi, Enklejda. 2006. "Sistemet e Kuotave Zgjedhore dhe Rëndësia e tyre për Arritjen e Barazisë Gjinore në Jetën Publike," *Studime Juridike* 1.

CRCA (ed.). 2009. *Raport mbi Përmbushjen e Rekomandimeve të Deklaratës së Debatit të 1-Rë Kombëtar për të Drejtat e Njeriut në Shqipëri* [Report on the fulfilment of recommendations of the declaration of the first national debate on human rights in Albania]. Tiranë.

Dahlerup, Drude. 2005. "Increasing Women's Political Representation: New Trends in Gender Quotas," in *International Idea, Women in Parliament: Beyond Numbers*. Stockholm: International IDEA.

Dahlerup, Drude (ed.). 2006. *Women, Quotas and Politics*. New York and London: Routledge.

Dahlerup, Drude and Freidenvall, Lenita. 2003. "Quotas as a 'Fast Track' to Equal Political Representation for Women," in *World Congress IPSA*. Durban.

Fico, Delina. 2007. "Legjislacioni dhe Politikat Gjinore: Sa Efektive Janë Ato? [Legislation and gender politics: How effective are they?]," in *Të Jesh Grua Në Shqipëri Pas Viteve 1990*. Tiranë: Botim i Qendrës Aleanca Gjinore për Zhvillim.

Fuga, Artan. 2009. "Gratë në Listat e Kandidatëve për Deputetë: Arritje apo Kurth? [Women in candidate lists for deputies: Achievement or trap?]," in *Politikanet e Reja-Manual Trajnimi*. Tiranë: Botim i Qendës Shqiptare për Popullsinë dhe Zhvillimin.

Gender Alliance for Development Centre (ed.). 2006. *Representation and the Quality of Democracy in Albania*. Tiranë.

Goetz, Anne Marie, and Shireen, Hassim, eds. 2003. *No Shortcuts to Power. African Women in Politics and Policy Making*. London/New York: Zed Books Ltd.

Government of Albania, Ministry of Labour, Social Affairs and Equal Opportunities (ed.). 2007. *National Strategy on Gender Equality and Domestic Violence (2007-2010)*. Tirana.

Government of the Republic of Albania (ed.). 2008. *The Electoral Code of the Republic of Albania*. Tirana.

Government of the Republic of Albania (ed.). 2008. *Gender Equality in Society, Law Number 9970*. Tirana.

Government of the Republic of Albania (ed.). 2010. *Third Periodic Report of the Government of Albania to the Committee on the Elimination of Discrimination against Women*. Tirana.

INSTAT. 2009. *Women and Men in Albania, 2008*. Tiranë.

Inter-Parliamentary Union (IPU), (ed.). 2008. *Women in National Parliaments: World Average Table Situation as of 31 May 2008*, http://www.ipu.org/wmn-e/world.htm.

Karam, Azza, and Lovenduski, Joni. 2005. "Women in Parliament: Making a Difference," in *Women in Parliament: Beyond Numbers*, edited by International Institute for Democracy and Electoral Assistance. Strömsborg, 187–213.

Lokar, Sonja. 2010. "Challenging Gender Stereotypes," in *Ministry of Labor National Conference*. Albania.

Mandro, Arta. 2008. "Survey on Current Activities Towards Implementation of UNSCR 1325," Tiranë: Austrian Development Cooperation.

Mandro, Arta, and Anastasi, Aurela. 2010. *Çështjet e Barazisë Gjinore në Standartet Ligjore dhe Jurisprudencën Kombëtare e Ndërkombëtare* [Issues of gender equality in legal standards and national and international law]. Tiranë: Shkolla e Magjistraturës.

Mandro, Arta, Aurela Anastasi, Emira Shkurti and Aurela Bozo. 2011. *Barazia Gjinore dhe Mosdiskriminimi*. Tiranë: Dajti.

Metani, Artur, and Omari, Sonila. 2006. *Drejt Rrugës për në BE: Monitorimi i Shanseve të Barabarta për Gratë dhe Burrat në Shqipëri*. Tiranë: Botim i Qendrës Aleanca Gjinore për Zhvillim.

Ministry of Labour, Social Affiars and Equal Opportunites (MoLSAEO), Directorate of Equal Opportunities. 2008. *The Albanian Woman and Gender Equality*. Tirana.

MPCSHB. 2010. *Vërejtje Përmbyllëse të Komitetit mbi Eliminimin e Diskriminimit ndaj Grave*. Tiranë.

OSCE/ODIHR. 2009. *Final Report of the OSCE/ODIHR Election Monitoring Mission*. Warsaw.

OSCE/ODIHR. 2011. *Final Report of the OSCE/ODIHR Election Monitoring Mission*. Warsaw.

Picari, Blerta. "Barazia Gjinore, Kusht për Integrimin Evropian." Tiranë: Botim i Qendrës Aleanca Gjinore për Zhvillim, 2008.

Plaku, Ani, Blerta Picari, Samira Pino, Sonila Danaj, Eglantina Gjermeni and Irena Shtraza. 2008. *The Division of the Private and Public Life in the Albanian Households - a Gender-Based Approach*. Tiranë: Gender Alliance for Development Center.

Qirjaku, Sonila and Dhimitri, Rolanda. 2000. "Civil Society and Women's Free Associative Movement," in *Study on the Written Contribution of Women's Movement in Albania 1990-1998* (Tiranë: Women's Center), 134-35.

Quota project, Global database of women. 2009. *Rrjeti i Grave Barazi në Vendimmarrje* [Growth of women equality in decision making]. Tiranë, accessed April 27, 2014, http://www.quotaproject.org/aboutQuotas.cfm.

Studies on South East Europe
edited by Univ.-Prof. Dr. Karl Kaser (Graz)

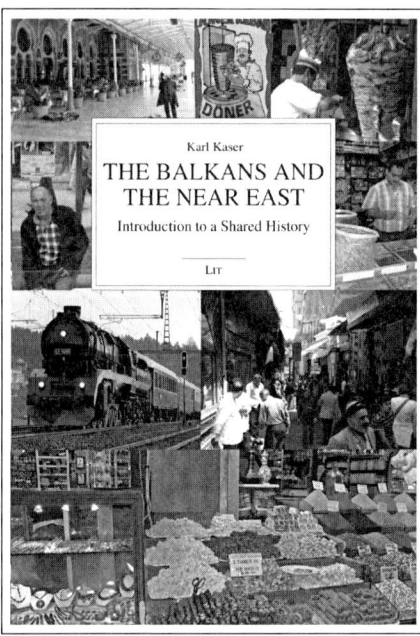

Karl Kaser
The Balkans And The Near East
Introduction To A Shared History
The Balkans and the Near East share millennia of a joint history, which stretches from the settling of the human being to the 20th century. The task split between the various scholarly disciplines into the fields of Balkan studies and Near (Middle) East studies has resulted in dividing a shared history into various sub-histories. The aim of the monograph is to reunite these isolated histories. Therefore, this monograph opens up completely new historical perspectives.
Bd. 12, 2011, 416 S., 29,90 €, br.,
ISBN 978-3-643-50190-5

Karl Kaser (Ed.)
Household and Family in the Balkans
Two Decades of Historical Family Research at University of Graz
On the occasion of the 20th anniversary of the foundation of the 'Balkan Family History Project' at the University of Graz in 1993, this volume unites the most outstanding essays of the project members that have appeared over the course of the previous two decades, scattered in various journals and books. They cover the interval from the 19th to the 21st century and reflect the current status of Balkan family research in historical, anthropological and demographical perspectives.
Bd. 13, 2012, 632 S., 79,90 €, br.,
ISBN 978-3-643-50406-7

LIT Verlag Berlin – Münster – Wien – Zürich – London
Auslieferung Deutschland / Österreich / Schweiz: siehe Impressumsseite